AF266706

Mystical
MOODS OF IRELAND
Enchanted Celtic Skies

Volume II
Second Edition

Praise for James A. Truett's work...

"Very very magical!" ~ **Susan Johnson**

"Oh James! I had tears in my eyes... viewing your treasures.... Thank you for sharing!" ~ **Susan Mitchum Pendergrass**

"Mind Boggling Beauty!!!" ~ **Joel Andrew Mentzos**

"Excellent scenery, & always eloquent commentary!" ~ **Patricia Finnerty**

"Absolutely breathtaking!" ~ **Graceen Hunsberger**

"I don't even know if you are aware of how beautiful and inspiring your lovely pictures and sayings mean to me and countless others. It makes my heart smile. Thank you." ~ **Judy Long**

"James, your photos heal the soul!" ~ **Lyn Gibbs**

"James, you are a beautiful rainbow in our cloud for sure." ~ **Sue Ann Stannert Rivera**

"I pray all the time to be in Ireland one day. Your pictures keep my dream alive." ~ **Jennifer Dudley Nelson**

Mystical
Moods of Ireland
Enchanted Celtic Skies

Volume II
Second Edition

James A. Truett

www.JamesTruettBooks.Com

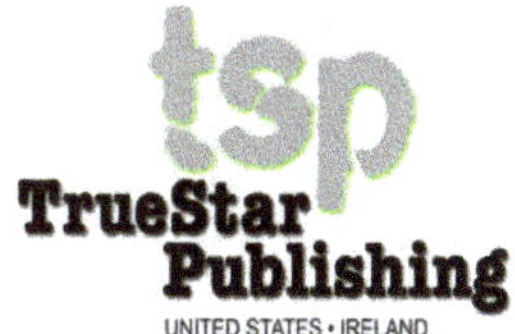

TrueStar Publishing
UNITED STATES · IRELAND

Copyright © 2016 by James A. Truett

All images & Text by James A. Truett, *www.JamesATruett.Com*

The moral rights of the author have been asserted.

All Rights Reserved. No part of this book may be reproduced, stored in a retrieval system, or transmitted, in any form or by any means without the prior written consent of the publisher, nor be otherwise circulated in any form of binding or cover other than that in which it is published and without a similar condition being imposed on the subsequent purchaser. Although the author and publisher have made every effort to ensure that the information in this book was correct at the time of publication, the author and publisher do not assume and hereby disclaim any liability to any party for any loss, damage, or disruption caused by errors or omissions, whether such errors or omissions result from negligence, accident, or any other cause.

Published by TrueStar Publishing
United States • Ireland
www.TrueStarPublishing.Com

Ordering Information:
All products in the Moods of Ireland series including books, calendars, posters, cards and prints are available at special quantity discounts for bulk purchases for sales promotions, premiums, fund raising, educational, corporate or institutional use. Specially customized books, calendars, posters, cards and prints can also be created to fit specific needs. For details, please e-mail the publisher at:
specialsales@truestarpublishing.com

ISBN: 978-1-948522-01-4

First Edition: September 2014
Second Edition: May 2016

10 9 8 7 6 5 4 3 2

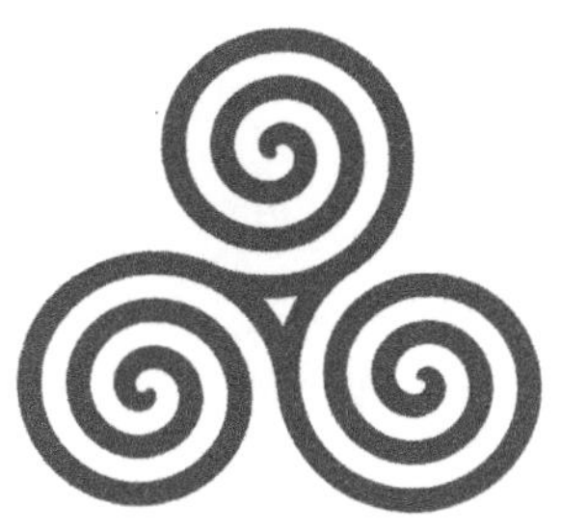

Dedication

For those who left,
Those who returned,
and for the Irish at Heart Worldwide.

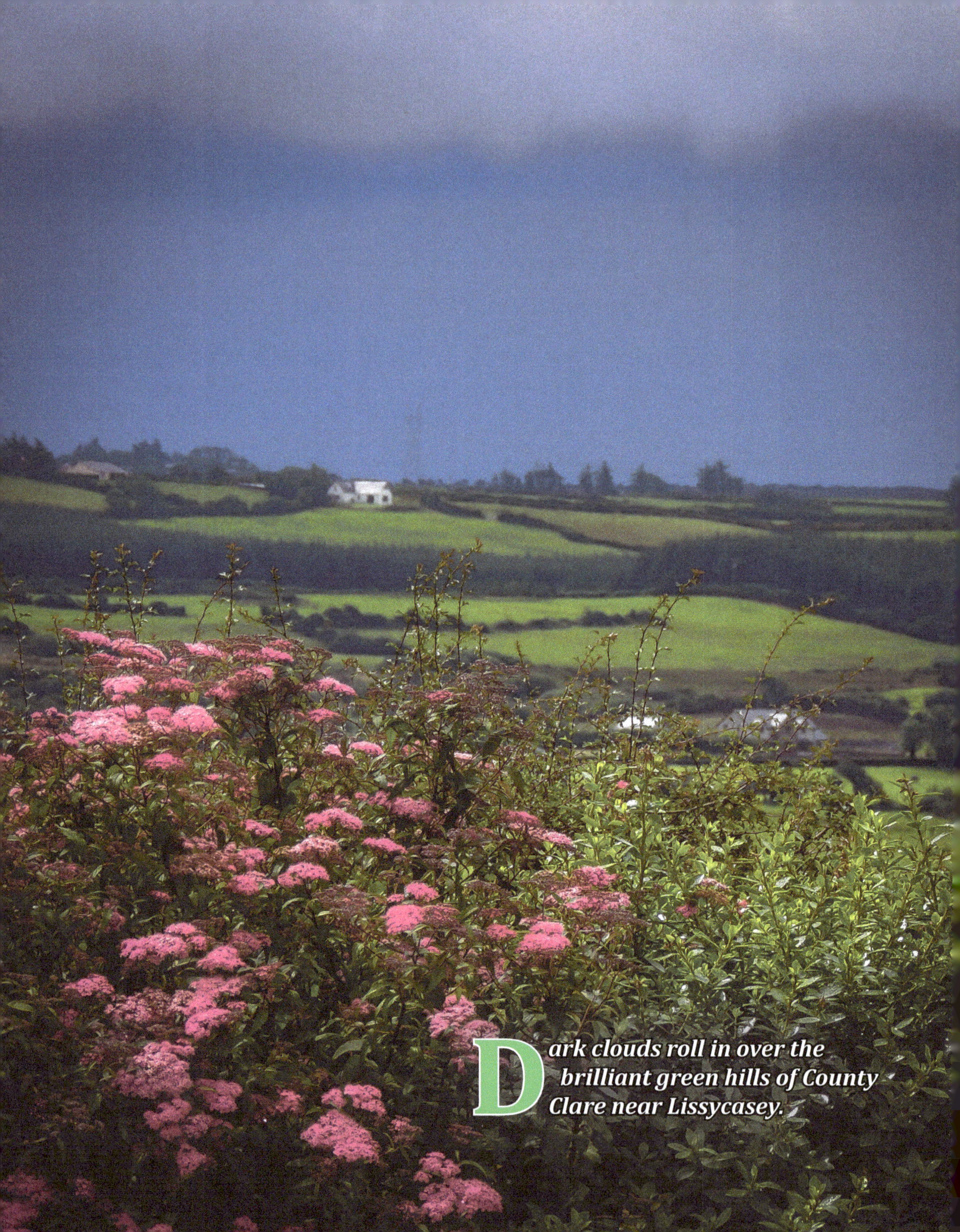

Dark clouds roll in over the brilliant green hills of County Clare near Lissycasey.

Introduction
Enchanted Celtic Skies

One could sit for hours, admiring the ever-changing skies over Ireland, seeing a different image, a different mood, every few minutes. The unique, swift-paced Irish weather produces spectacular displays year around.

Volume II of "*Mystical Moods of Ireland: Enchanted Celtic Skies*" covers some of the more intense expressions of the Irish skies:

- Sunbeams bursting through the local cloud cover.

- Rainbows painting arcs over the Irish countryside.

- Dark clouds announcing impending storms.

- Air traffic and jet trails over the Emerald Isle.

- Sunsets with their muted pastels and frequent splashes of brilliant color.

I hope you are able to experience at least in some small way the tremendous wonder, peace and awe-inspiring beauty I find in photographing and sharing the scenery of this amazing land.

Cead mile failte! *(pronounced: "kade meela fall-cheh")*
A Hundred-Thousand Welcomes!

James A. Truett
County Clare, Ireland

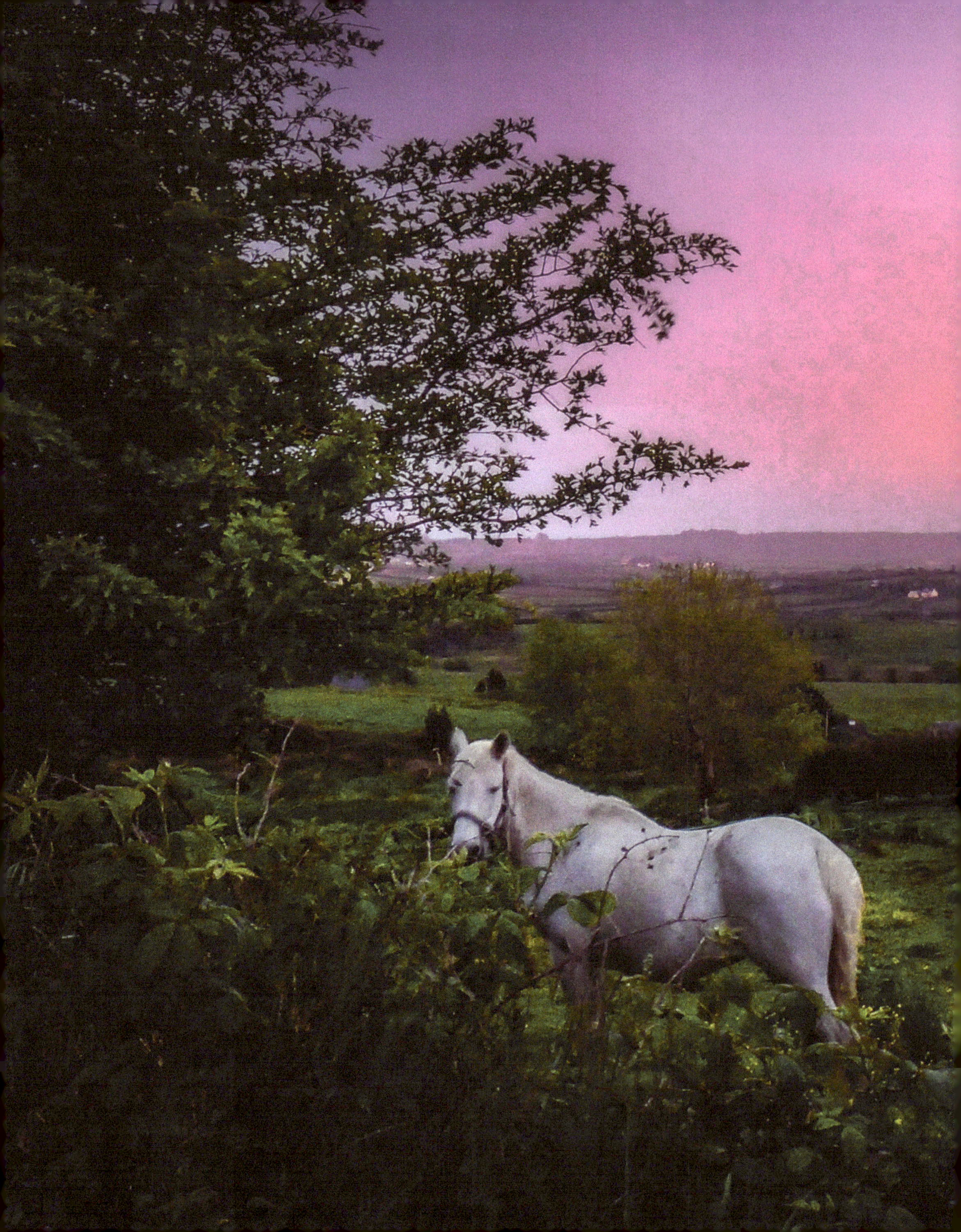

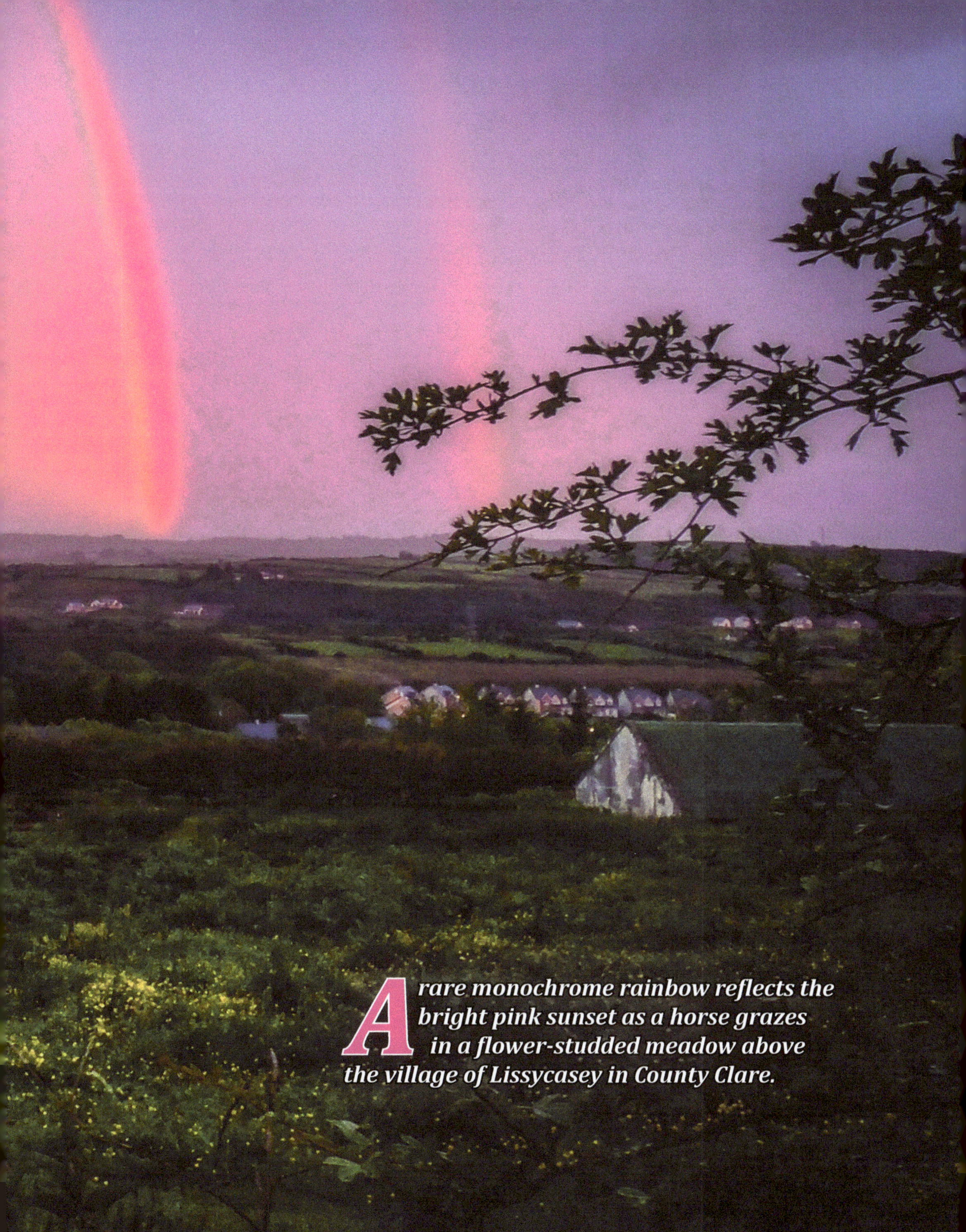

A rare monochrome rainbow reflects the bright pink sunset as a horse grazes in a flower-studded meadow above the village of Lissycasey in County Clare.

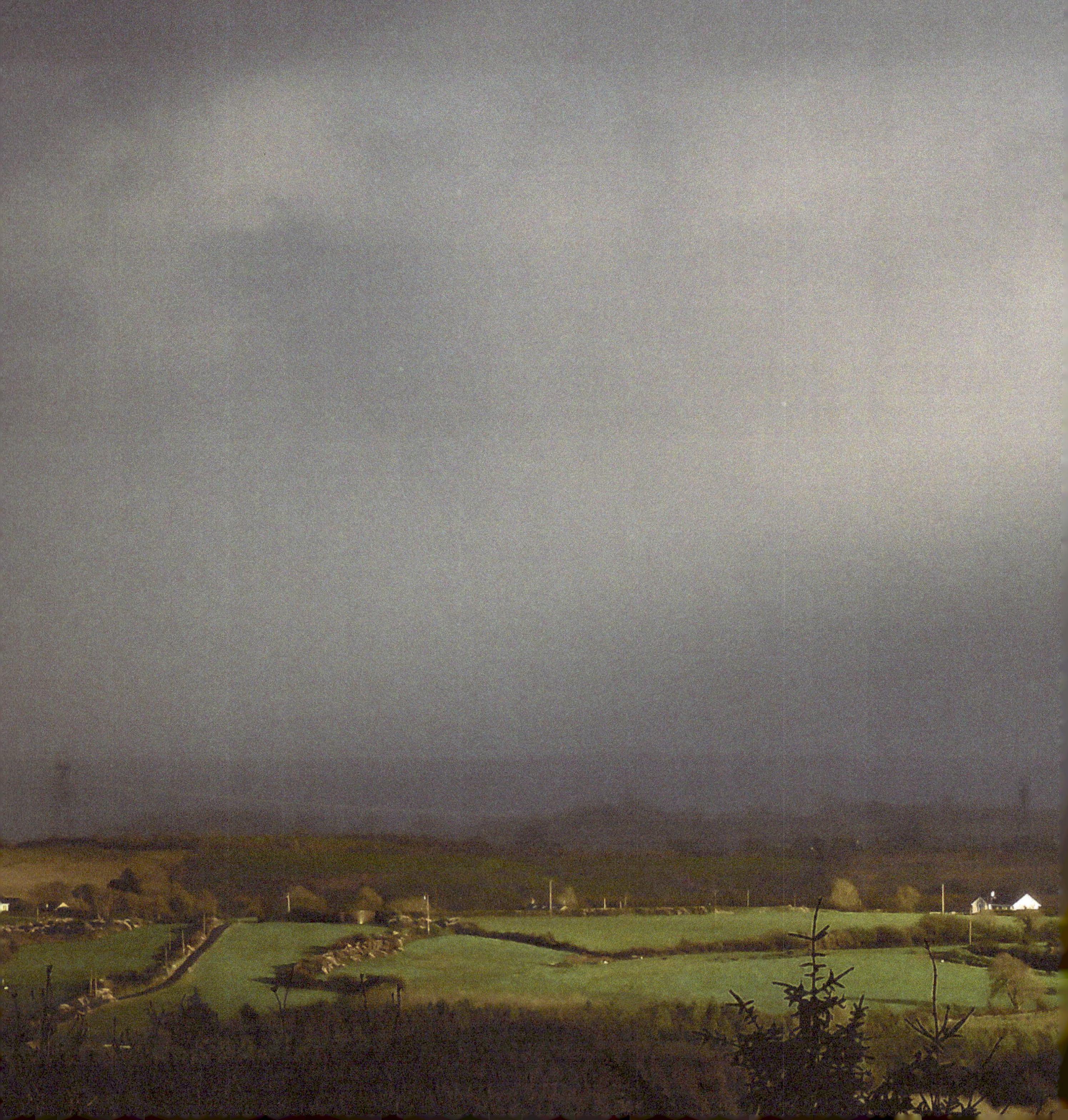
A sunbeam highlights a brilliant rainbow over the rolling hills between the villages of Lissycasey and Ballynacally in County Clare.

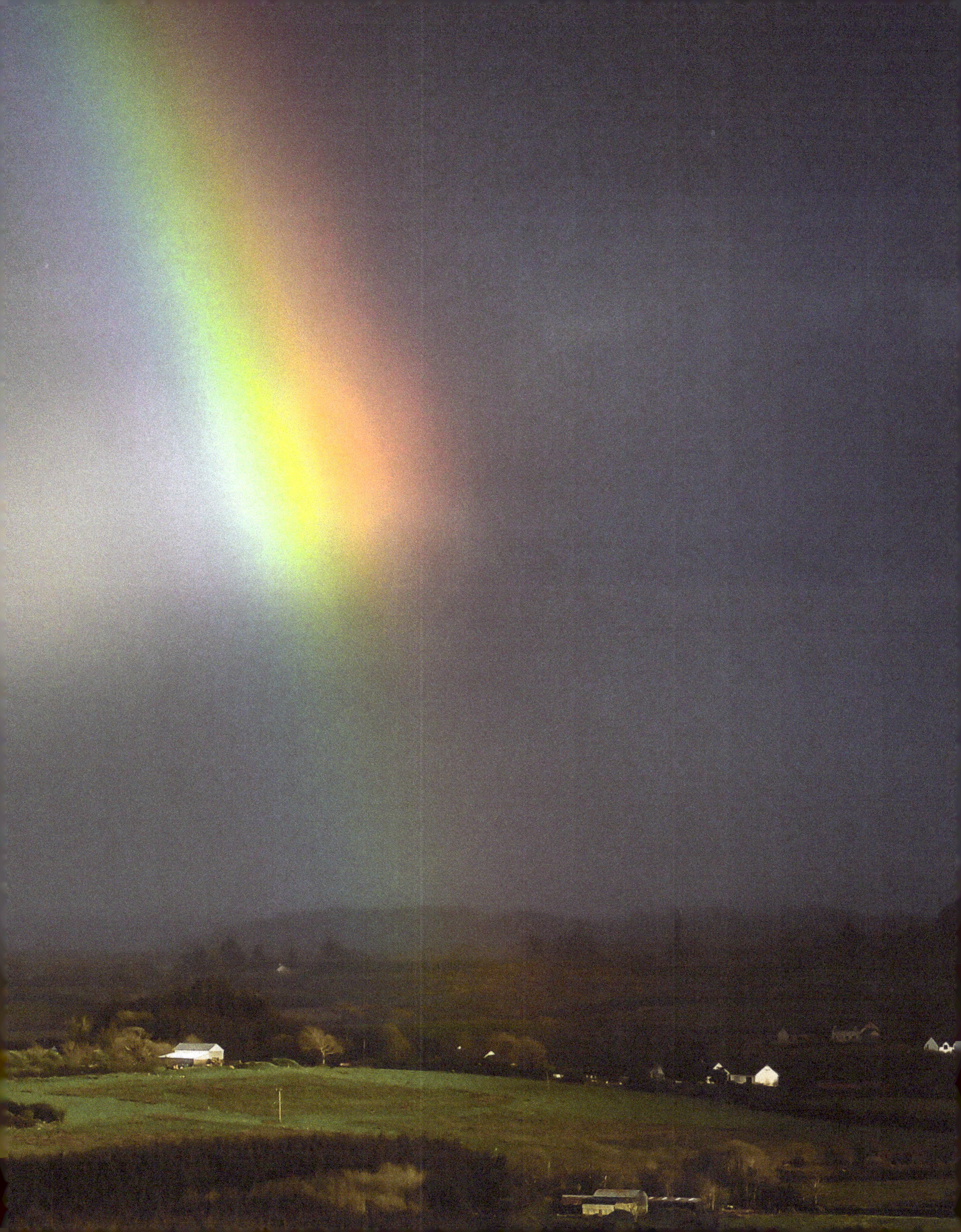

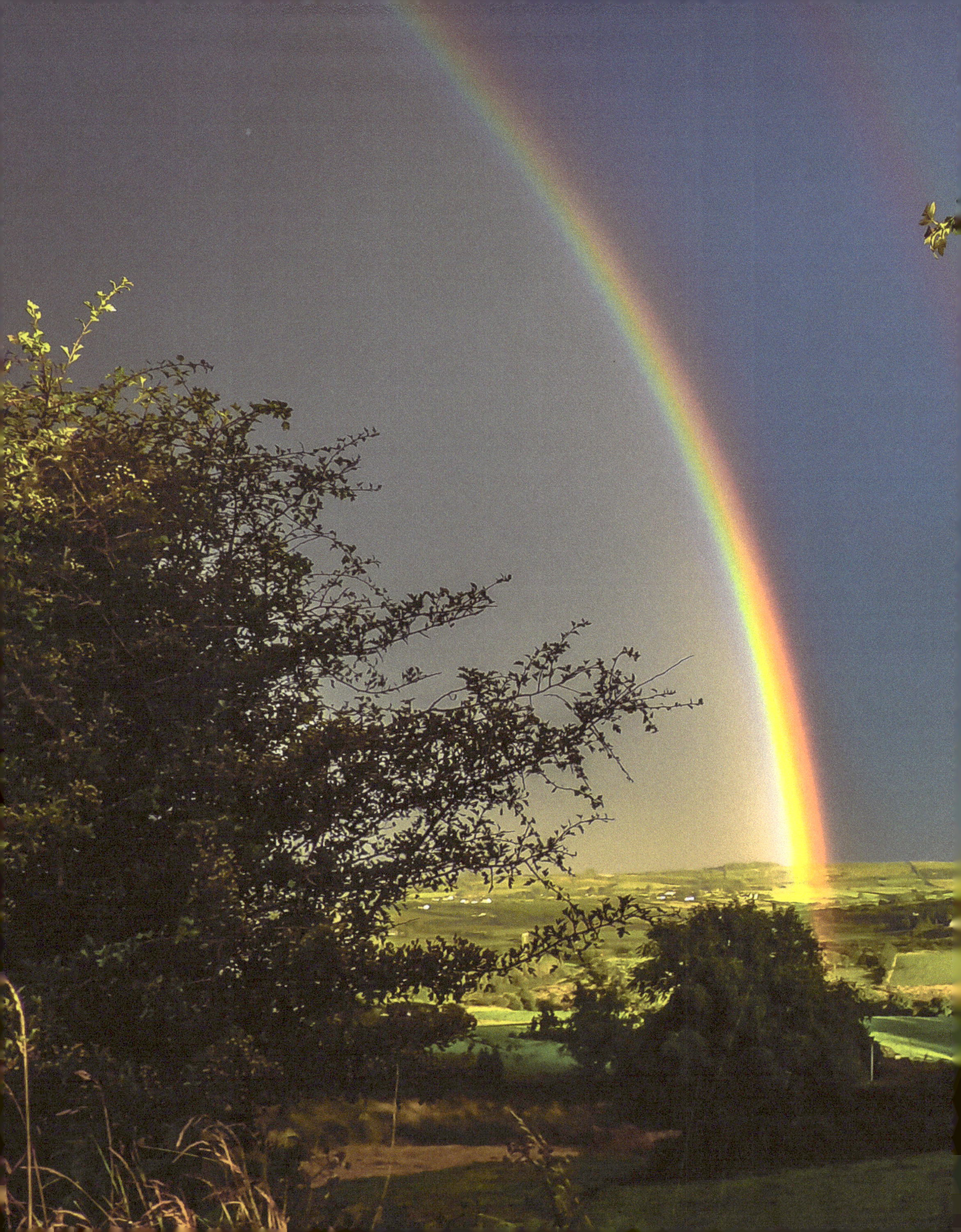

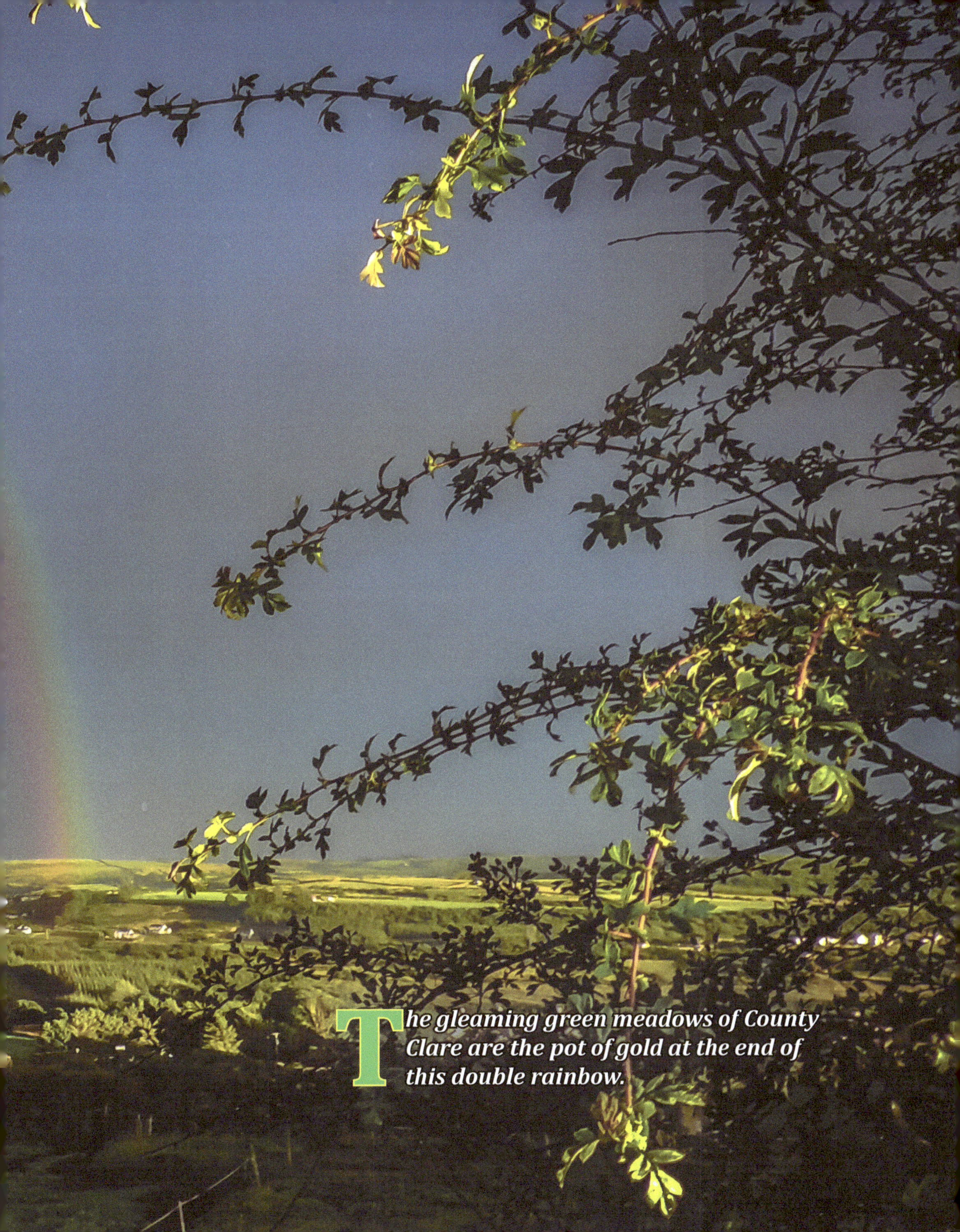

The gleaming green meadows of County Clare are the pot of gold at the end of this double rainbow.

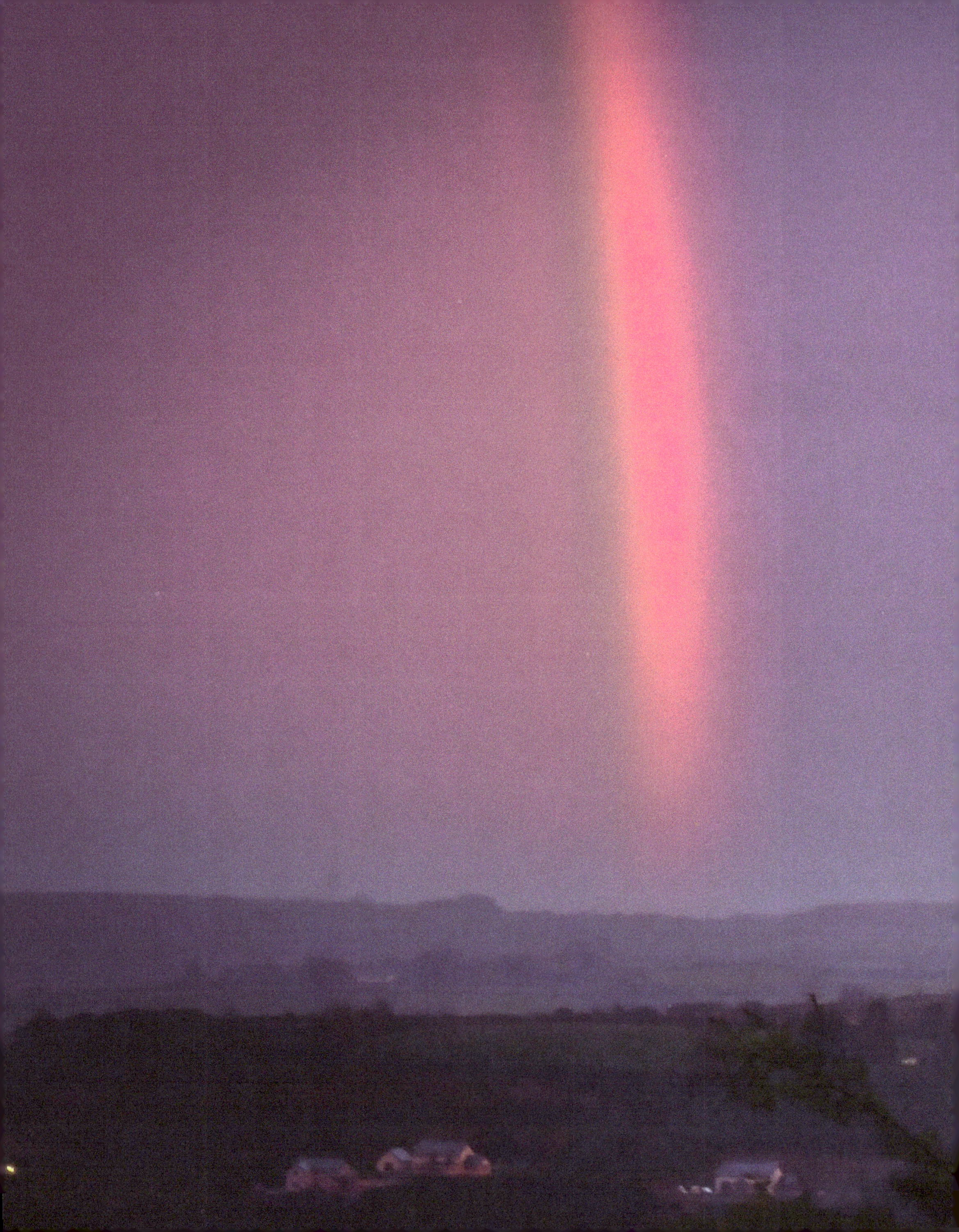

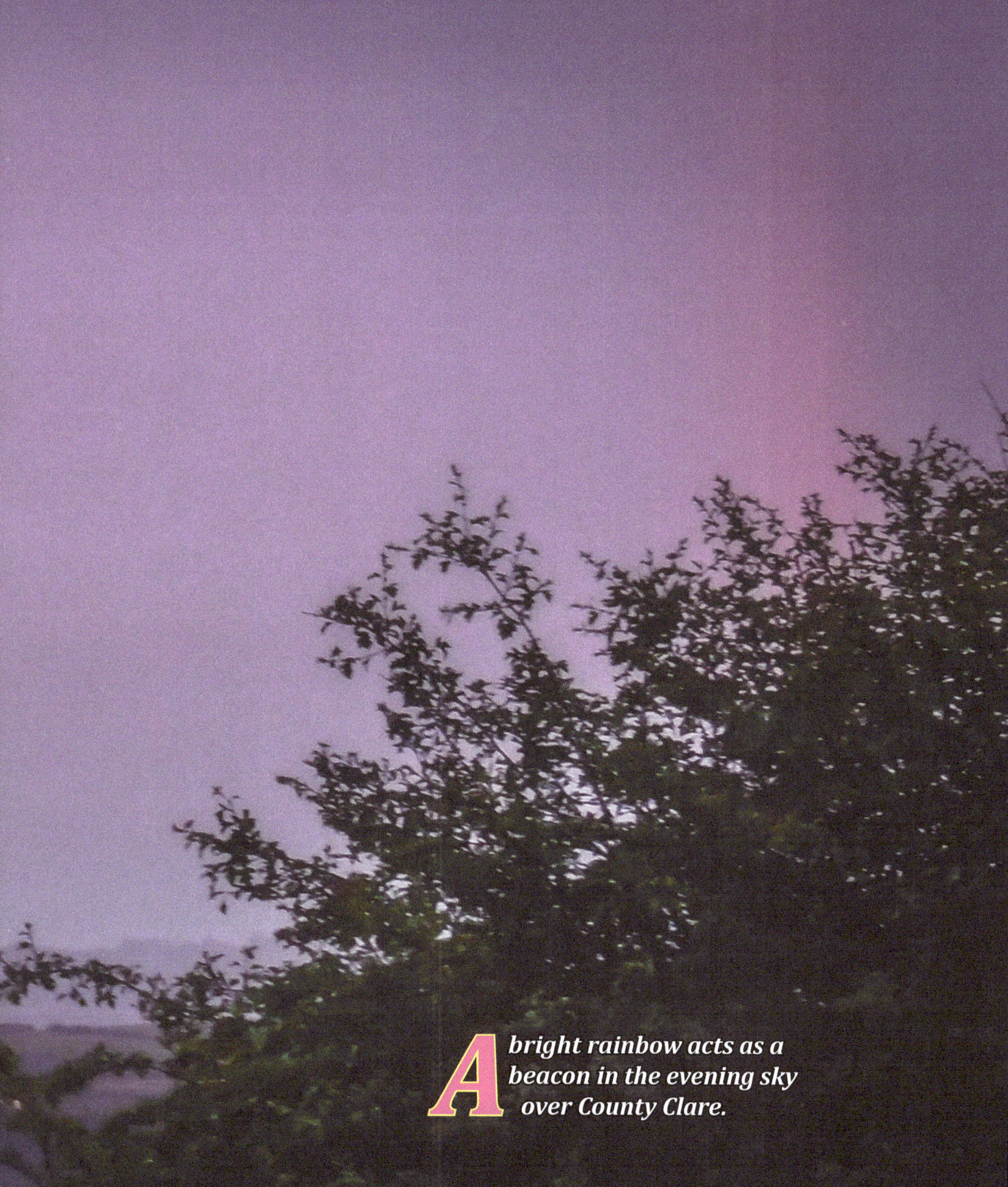

A bright rainbow acts as a
beacon in the evening sky
over County Clare.

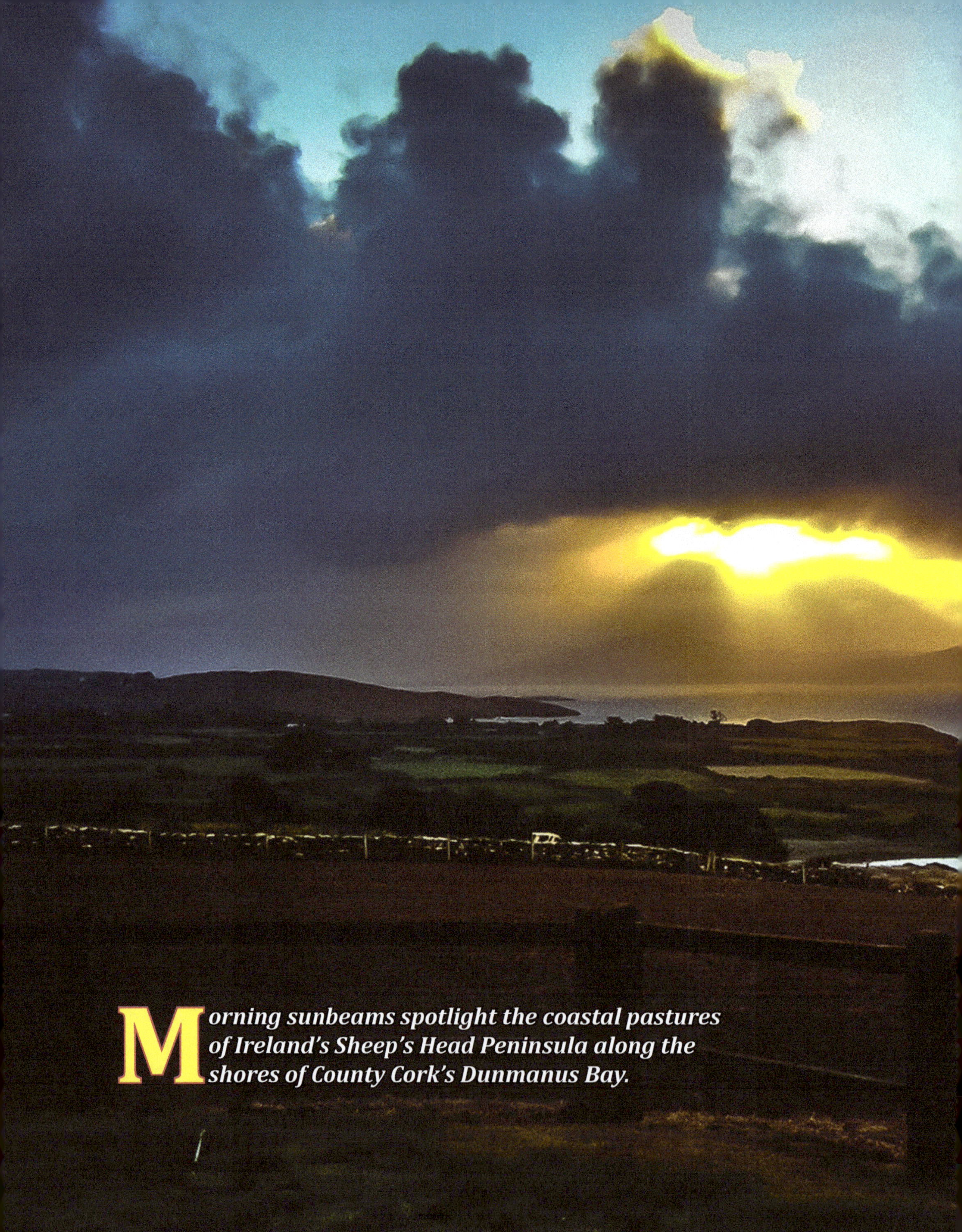

Morning sunbeams spotlight the coastal pastures of Ireland's Sheep's Head Peninsula along the shores of County Cork's Dunmanus Bay.

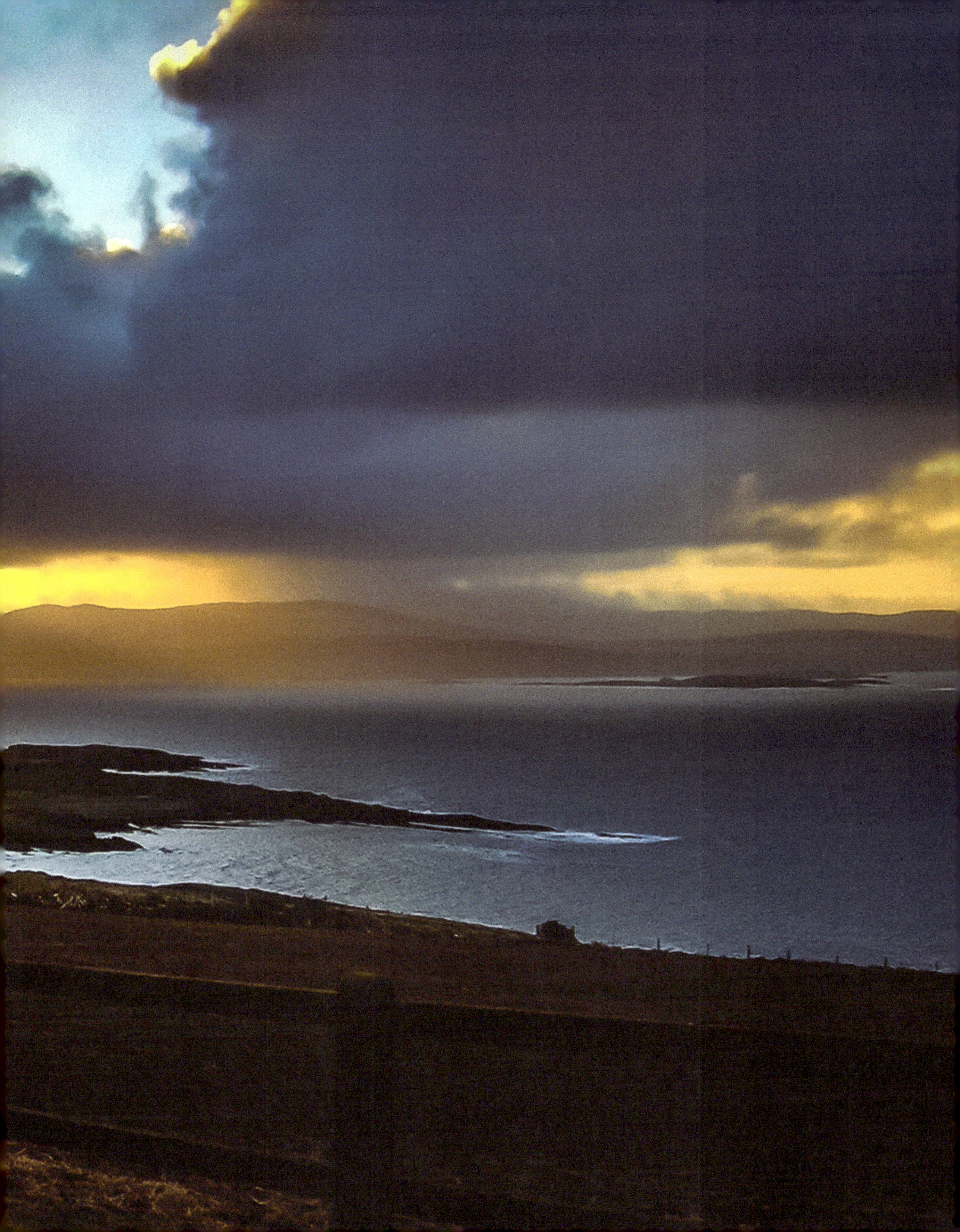

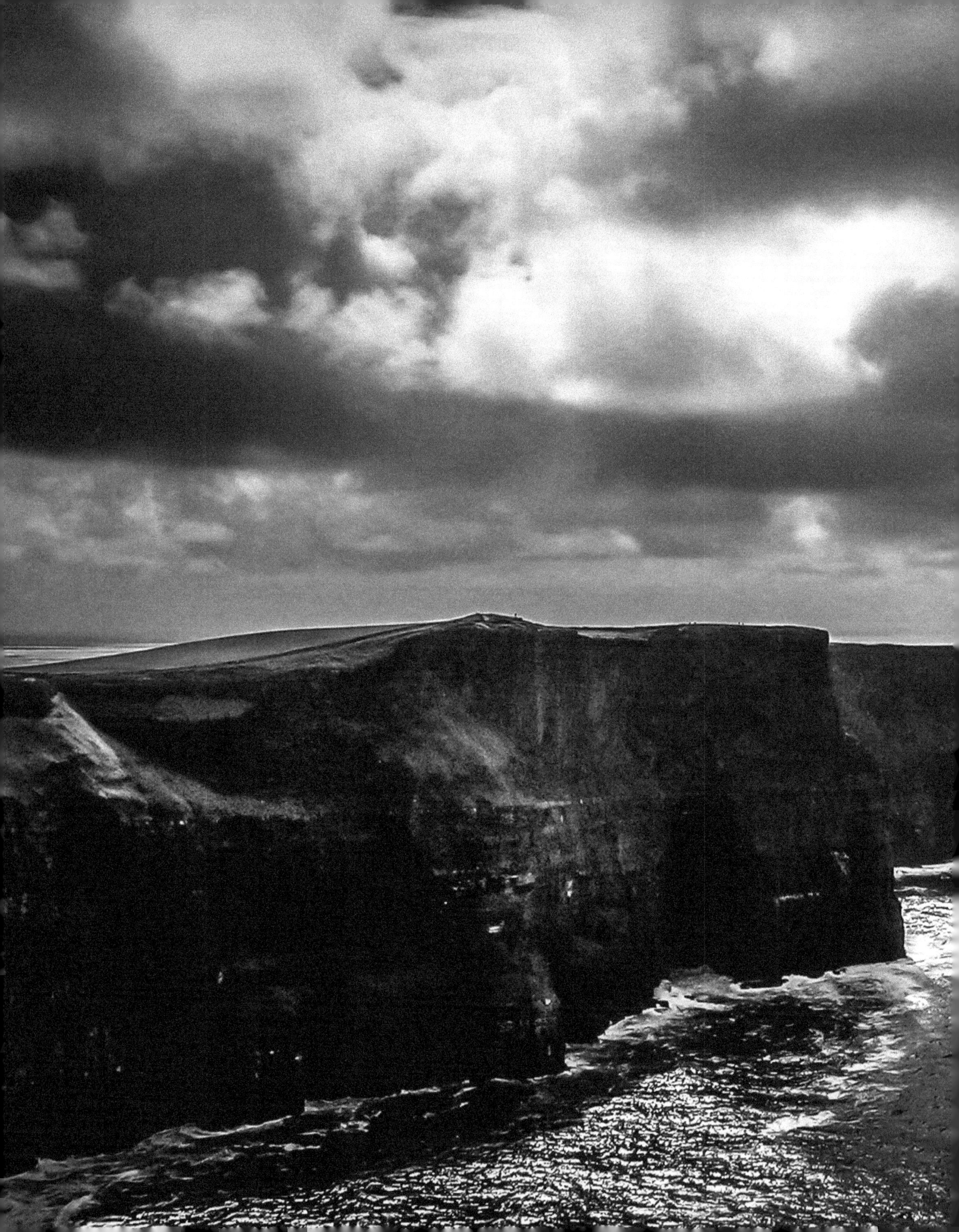

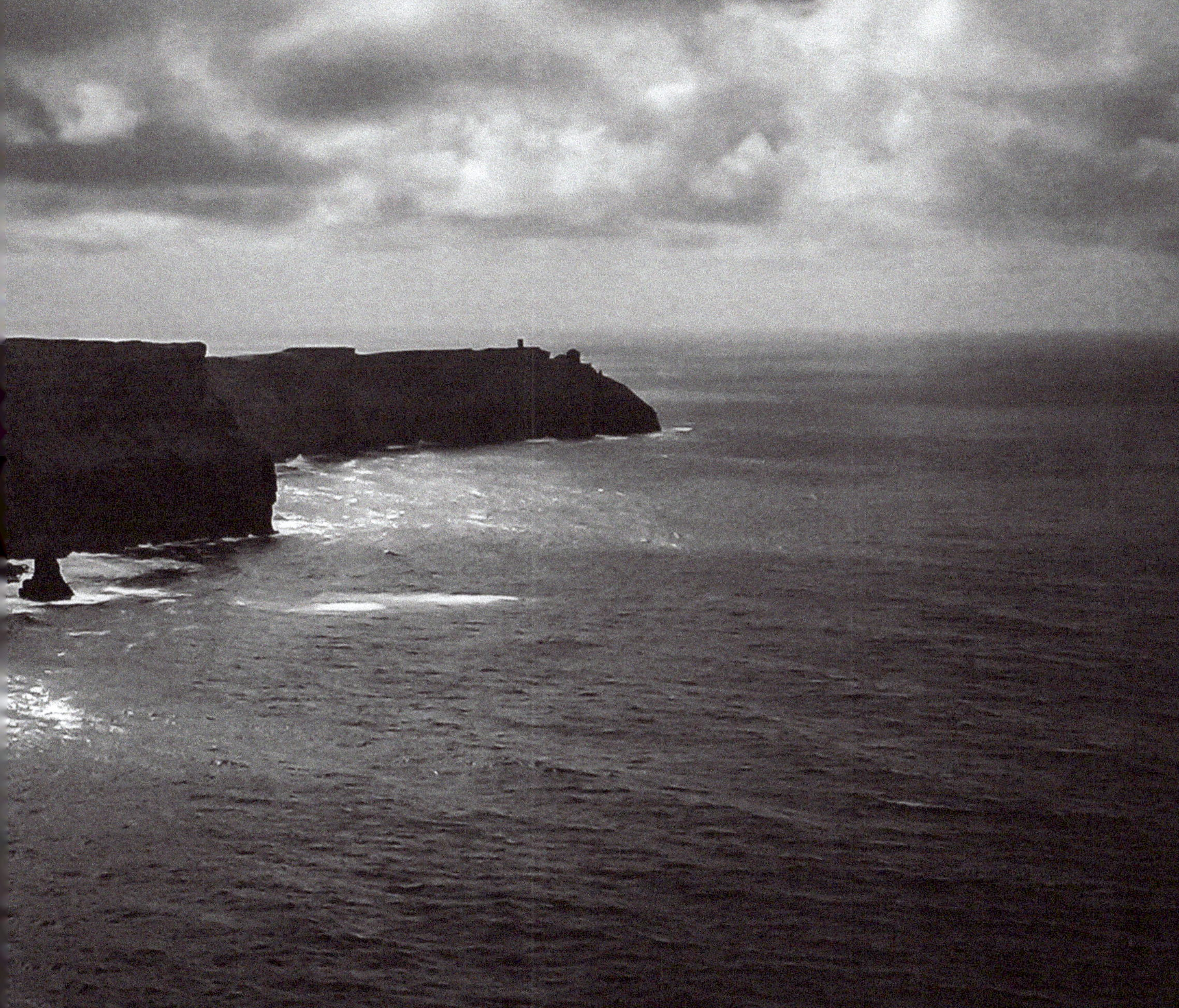

A foreboding dark sky hangs over Ireland's iconic Cliffs of Moher, the country's most-visited tourist attraction. The 8-kilometre stretch of cliffs along the Wild Atlantic Way in County Clare tower 214 meters (about 700 feet) over the crashing waves of the Atlantic Ocean.

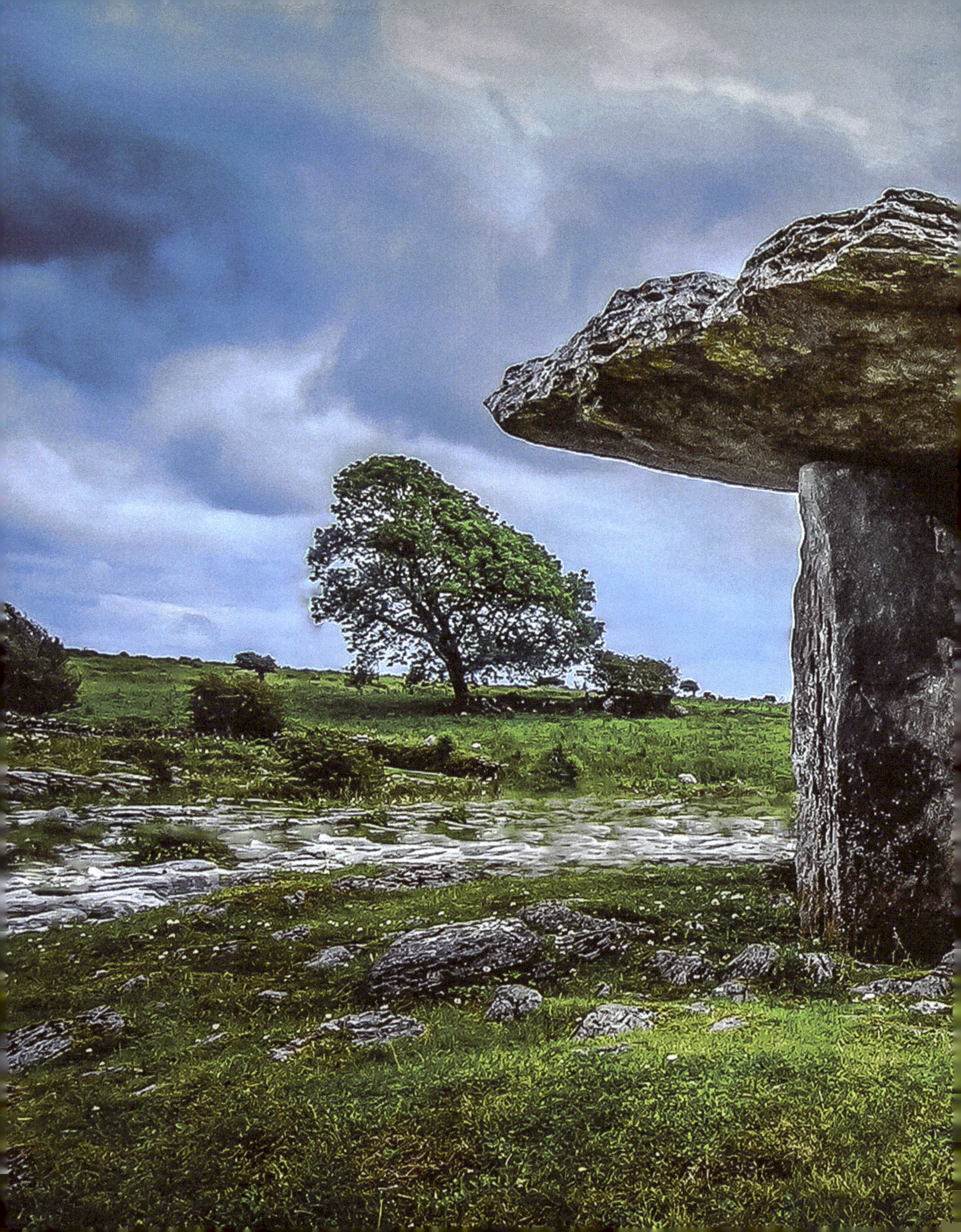

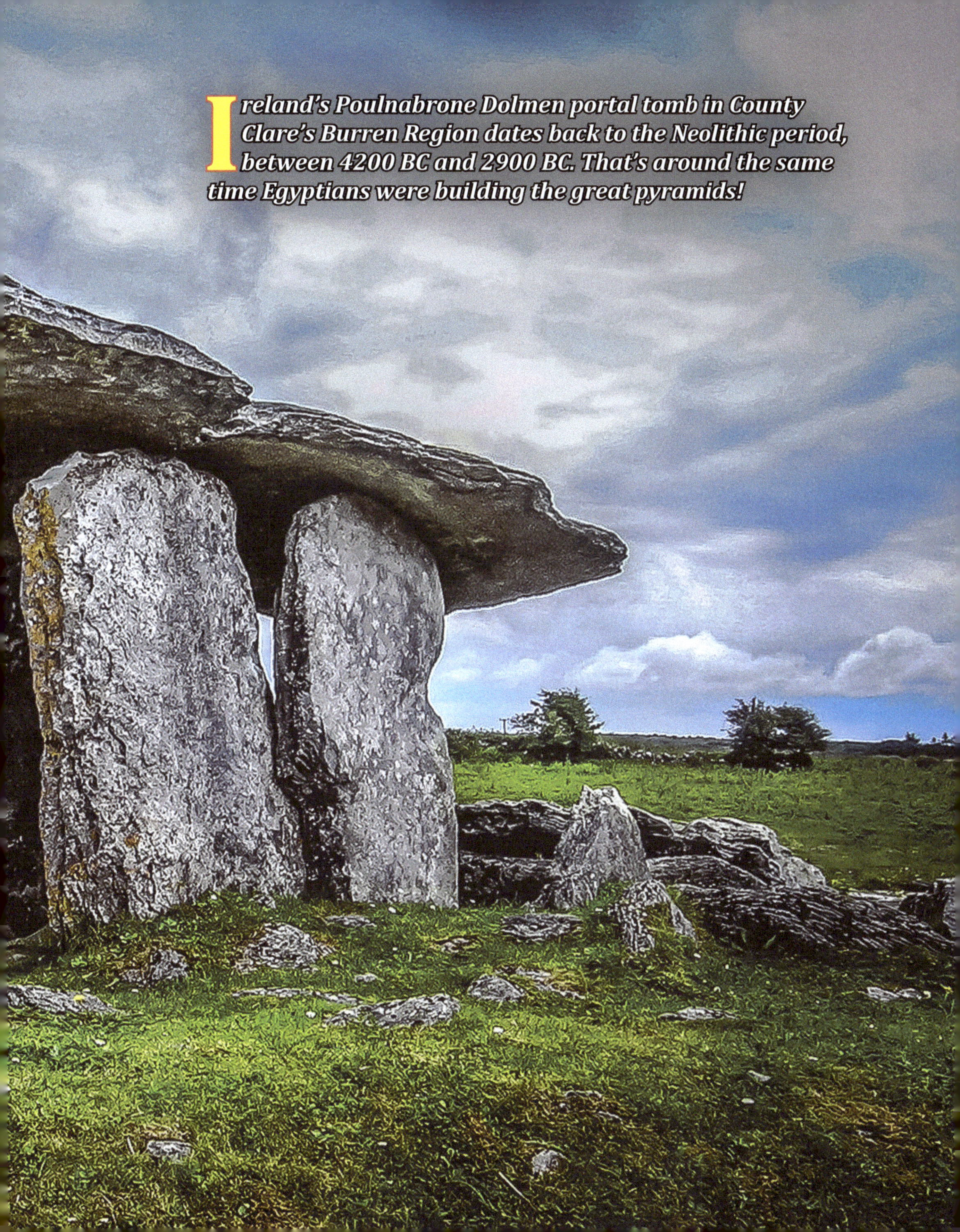
Ireland's Poulnabrone Dolmen portal tomb in County Clare's Burren Region dates back to the Neolithic period, between 4200 BC and 2900 BC. That's around the same time Egyptians were building the great pyramids!

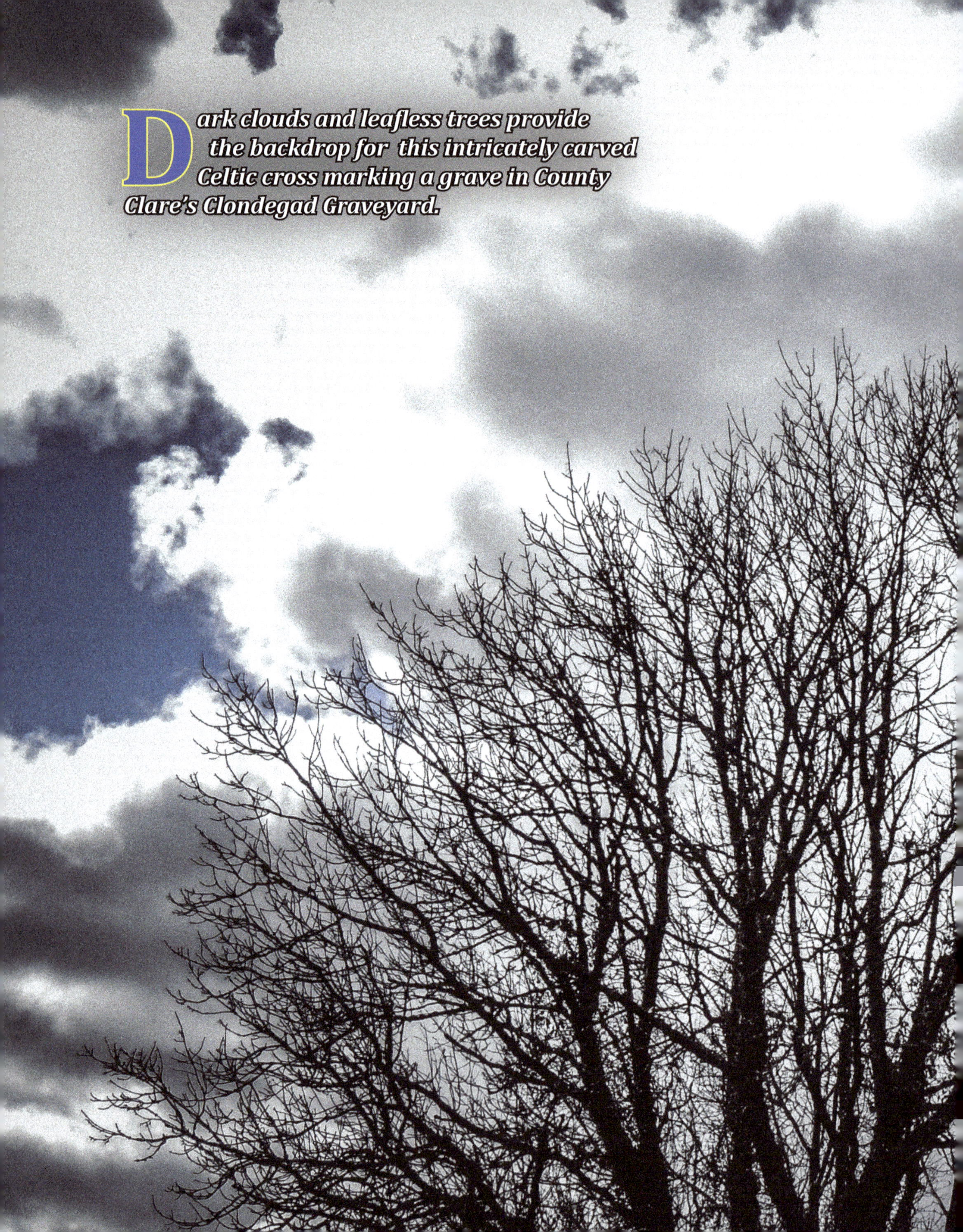

Dark clouds and leafless trees provide the backdrop for this intricately carved Celtic cross marking a grave in County Clare's Clondegad Graveyard.

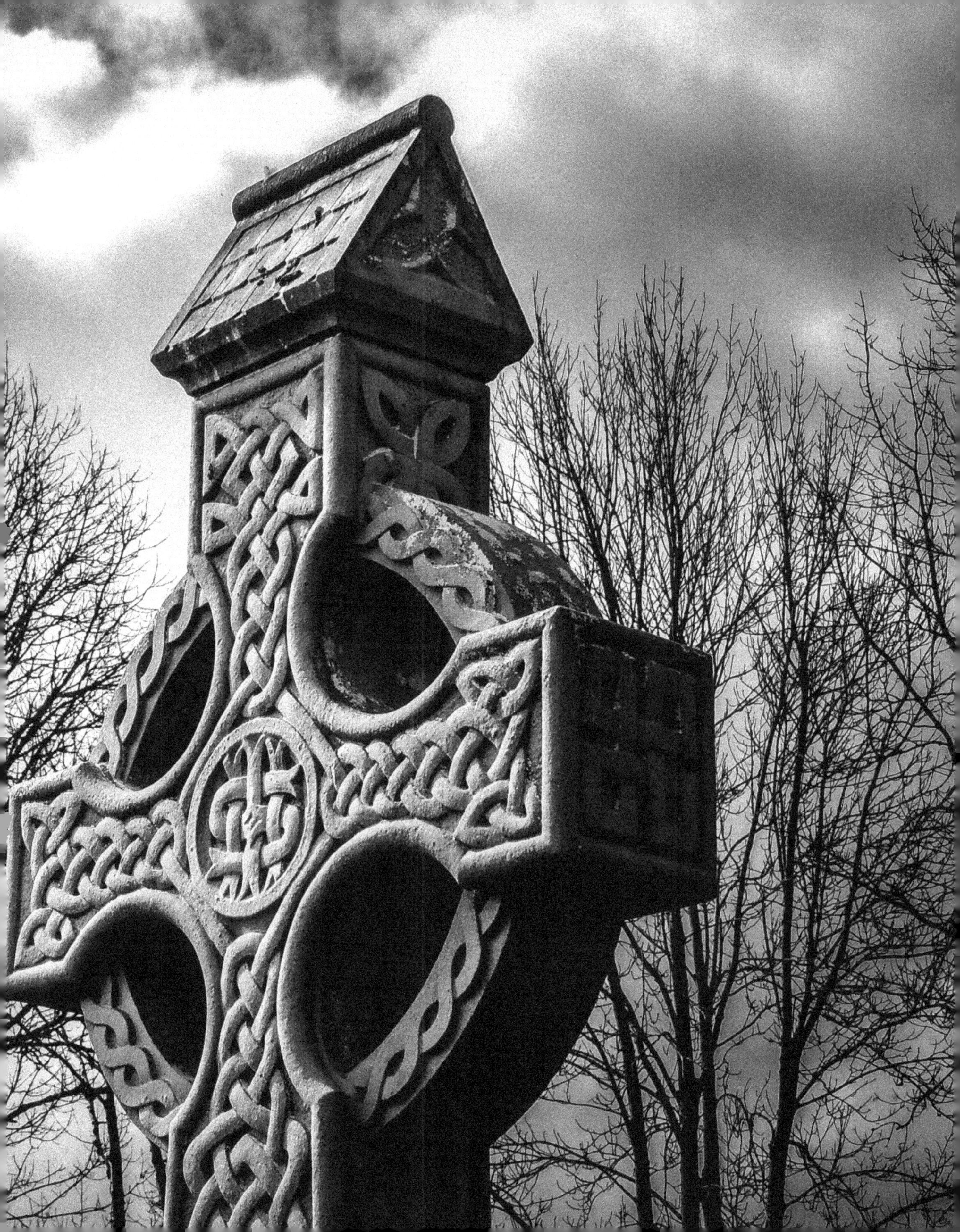

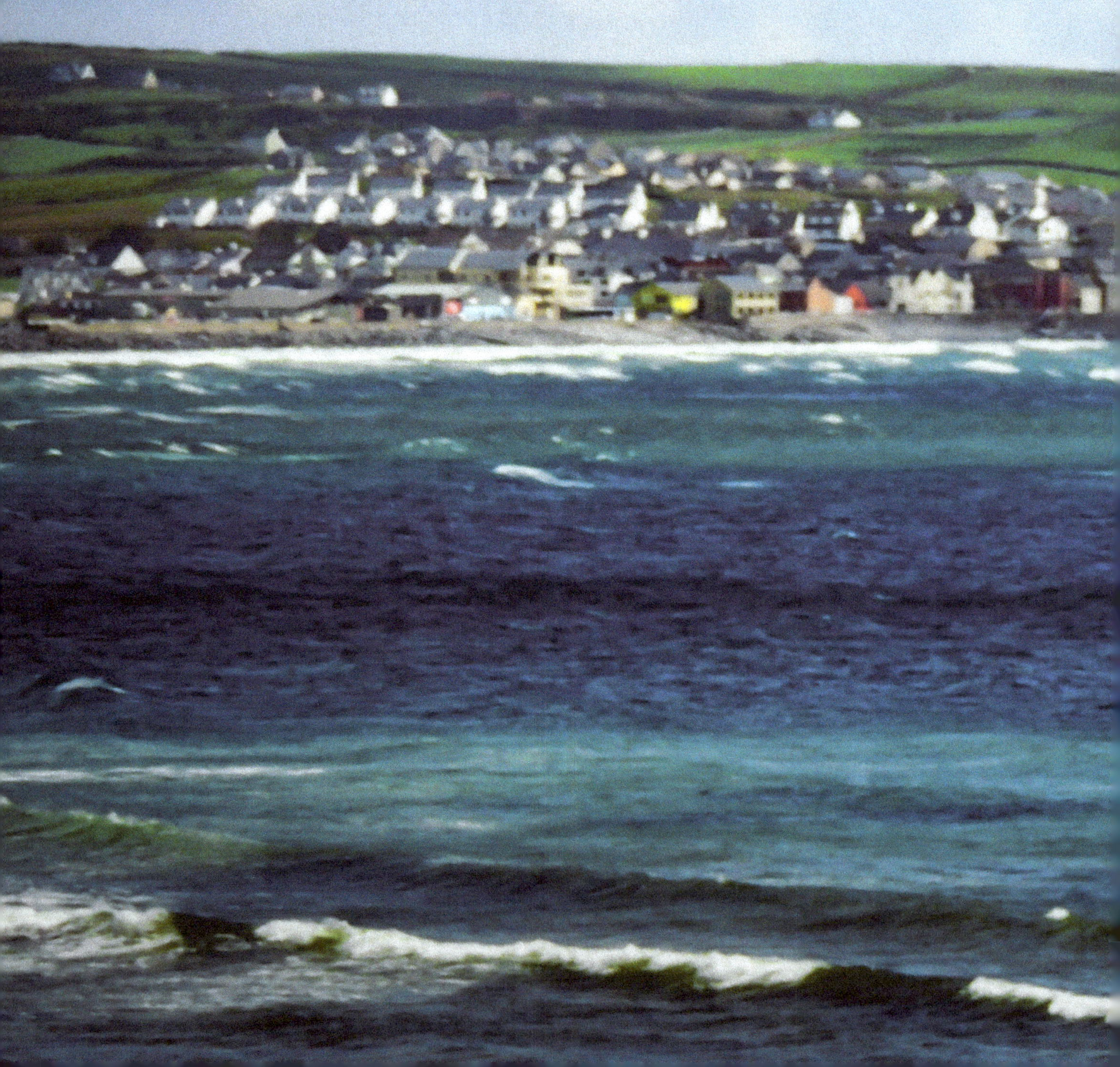A cross in the Kilmacreehy Cemetery near Liscannor appears to stand guard over the deep blue and aquamarine waters of County Clare's Liscannor Bay with the popular surfing village of Lahinch on the distant shore.

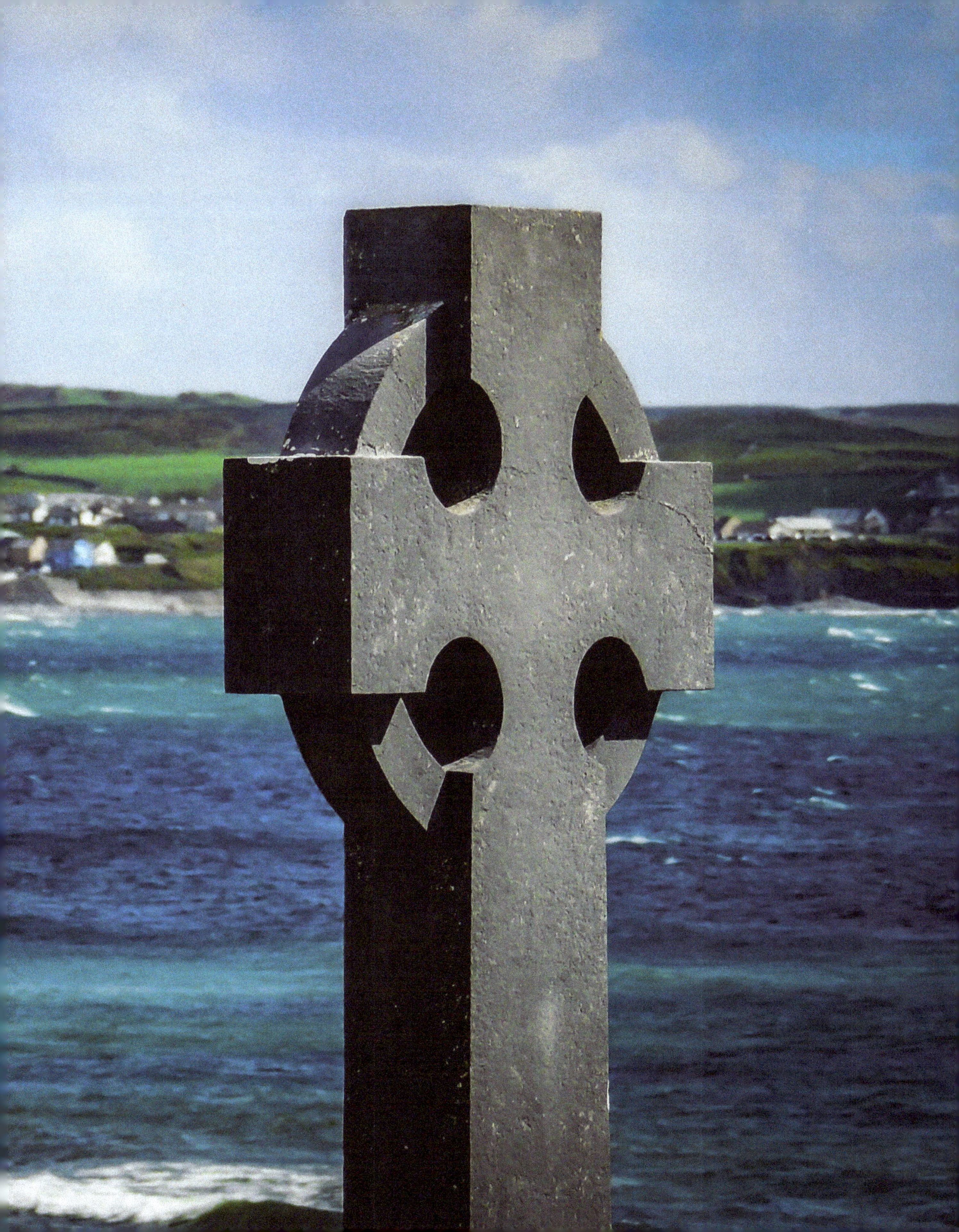

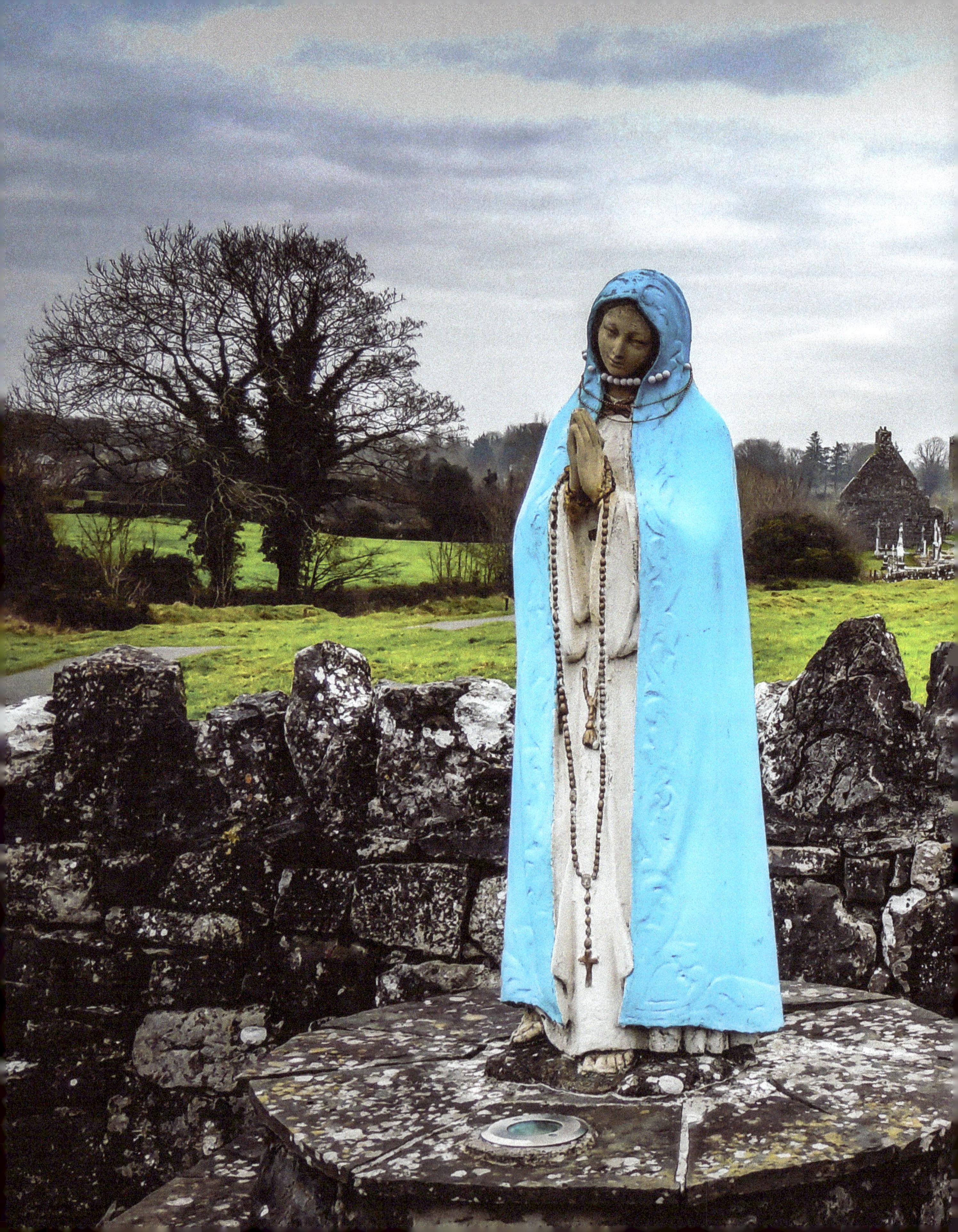

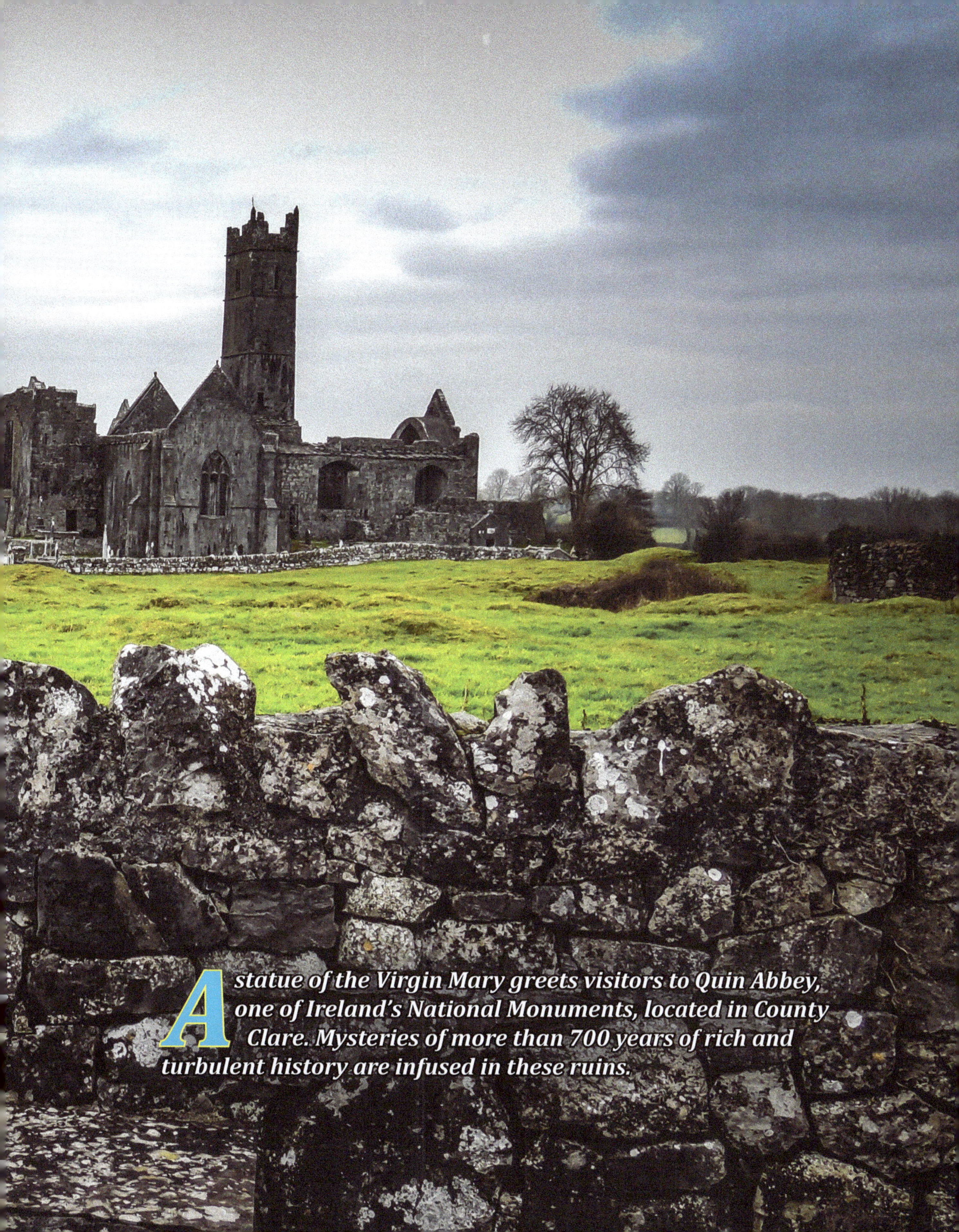

A statue of the Virgin Mary greets visitors to Quin Abbey, one of Ireland's National Monuments, located in County Clare. Mysteries of more than 700 years of rich and turbulent history are infused in these ruins.

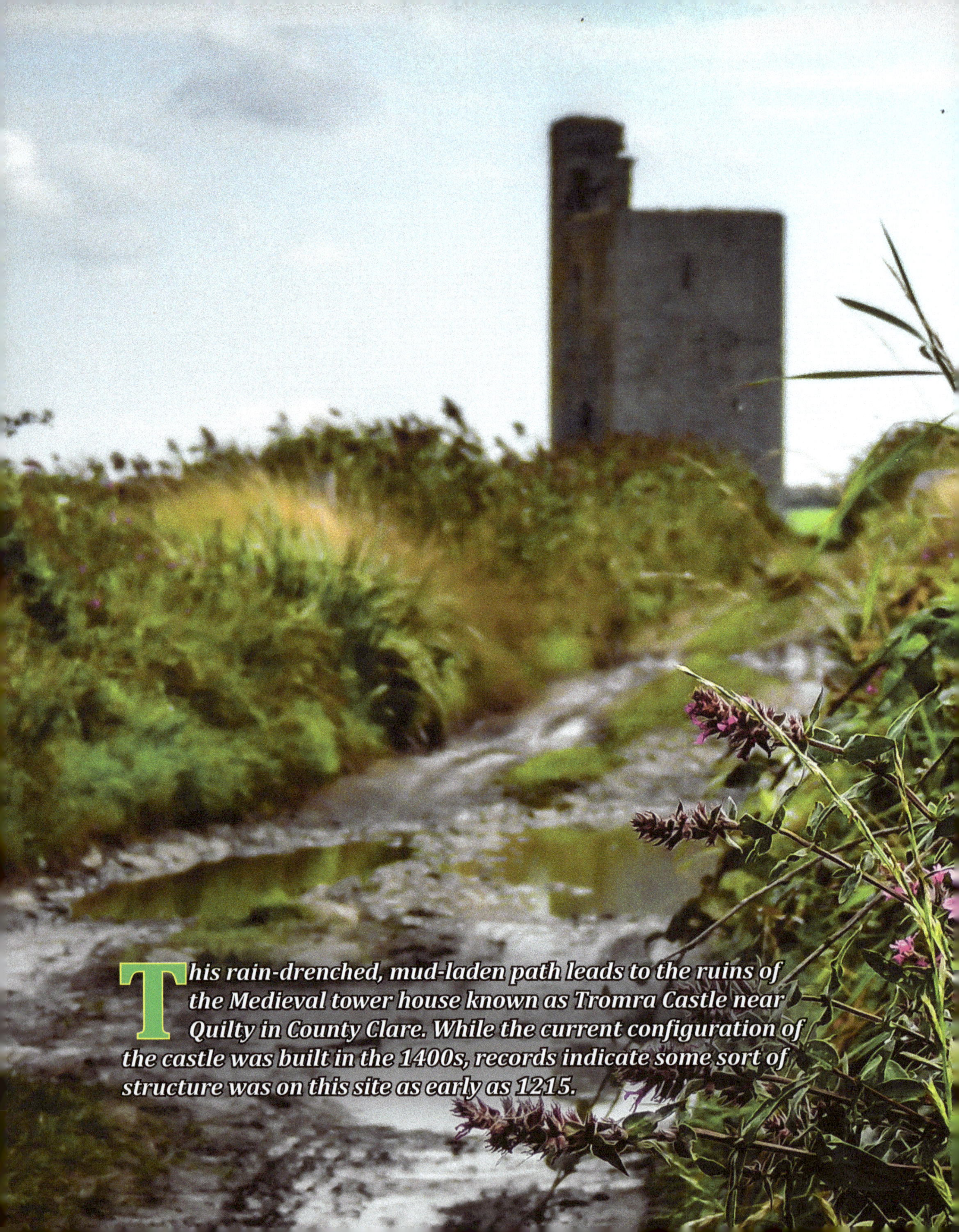

This rain-drenched, mud-laden path leads to the ruins of the Medieval tower house known as Tromra Castle near Quilty in County Clare. While the current configuration of the castle was built in the 1400s, records indicate some sort of structure was on this site as early as 1215.

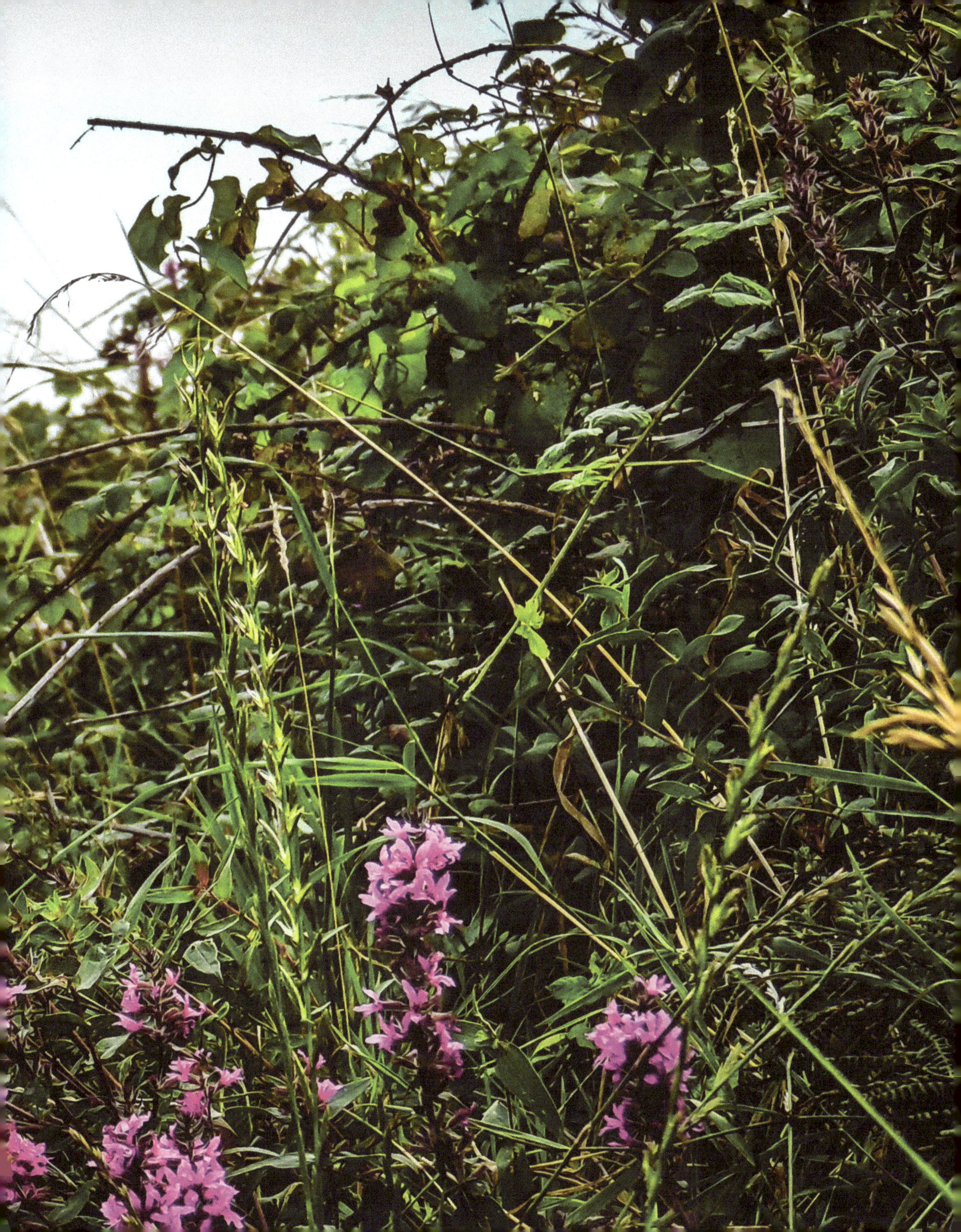

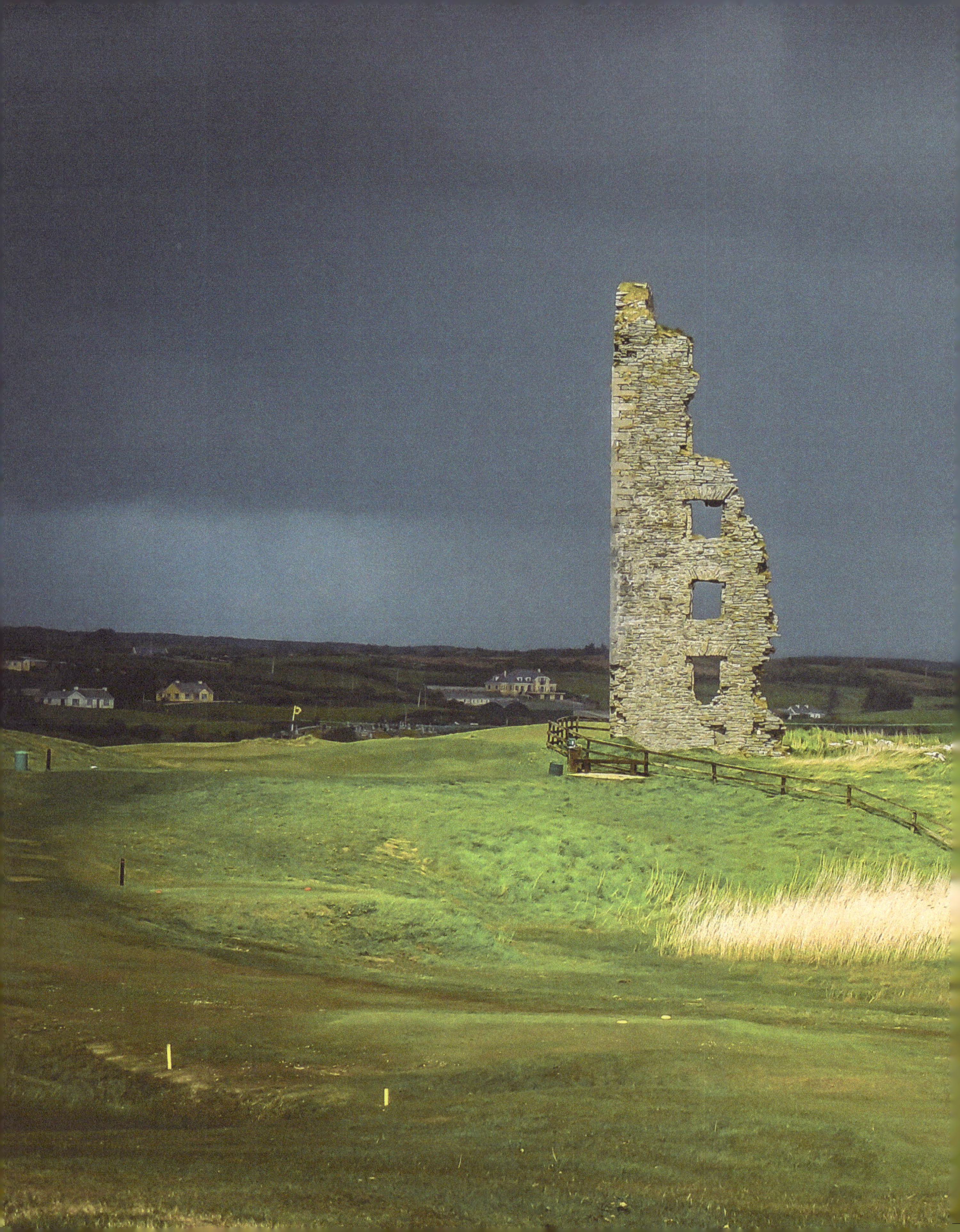

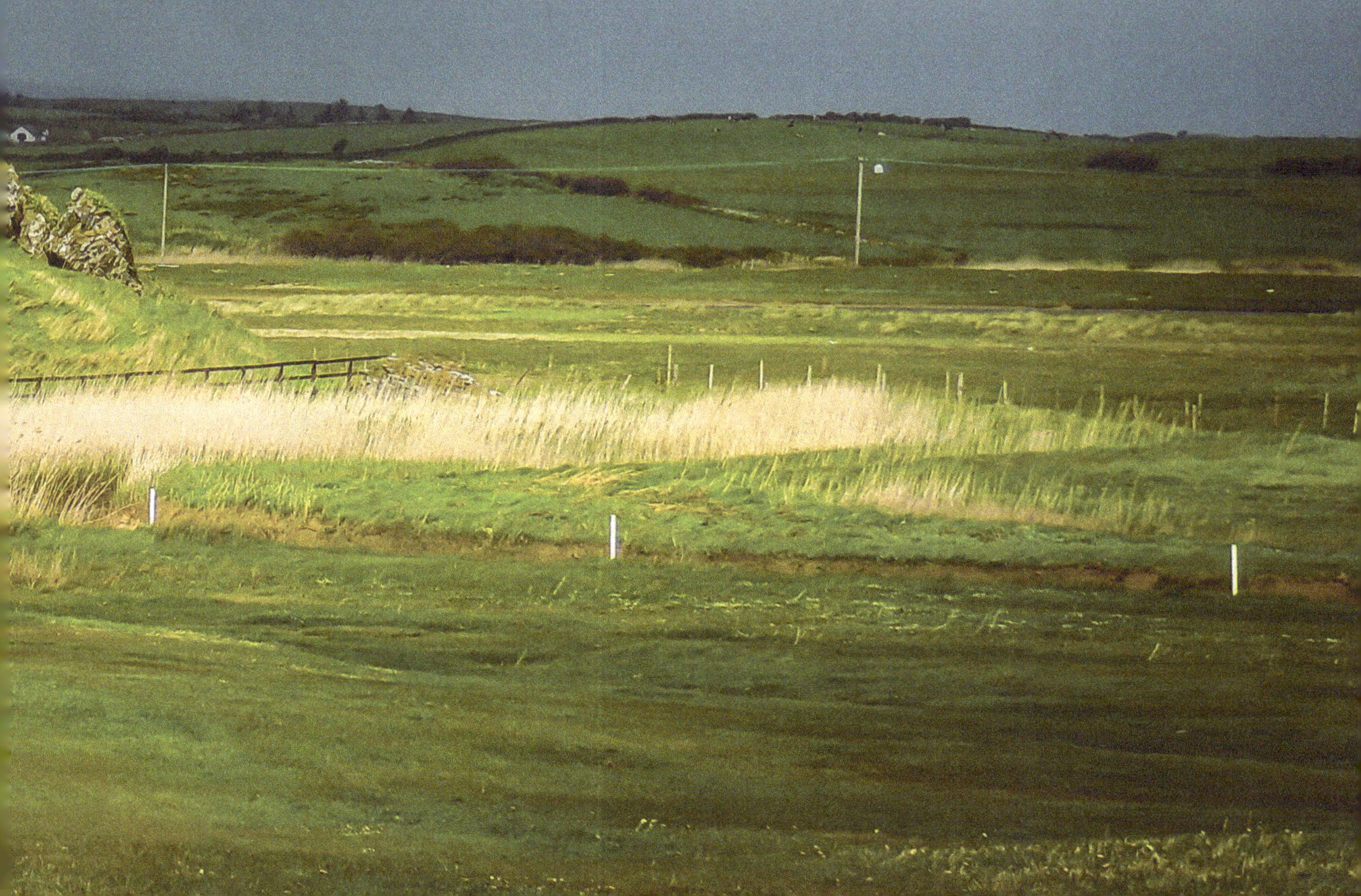

A menacing Spring sky provides the dark backdrop for ruins of this 14th Century castle, a landmark at the exclusive Lahinch Golf Club in County Clare. Built in 1306 by the O'Connor Clan, the castle became a stronghold of the O'Brien Clan by 1584.

During Cromwell's rampage to destroy castles in Connacht and Clare in 1654, Dough Castle survived, thanks to one of Cromwell's officers, a Col. Stubber. Unusually, the castle's ruined state has little to do with battles — it was built on sand at the confluence of the Inagh and Dealagh rivers and has collapsed several times during its existence.

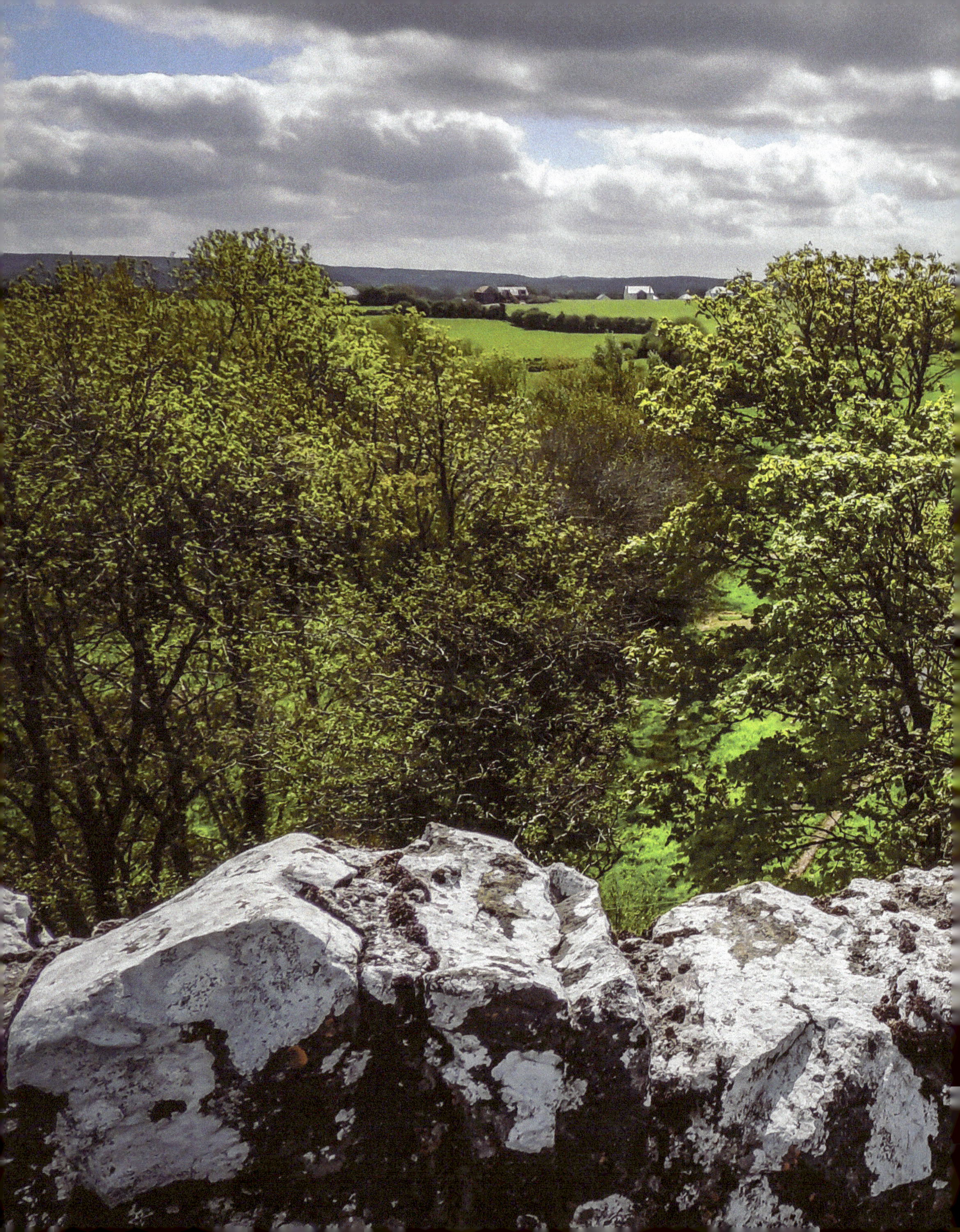

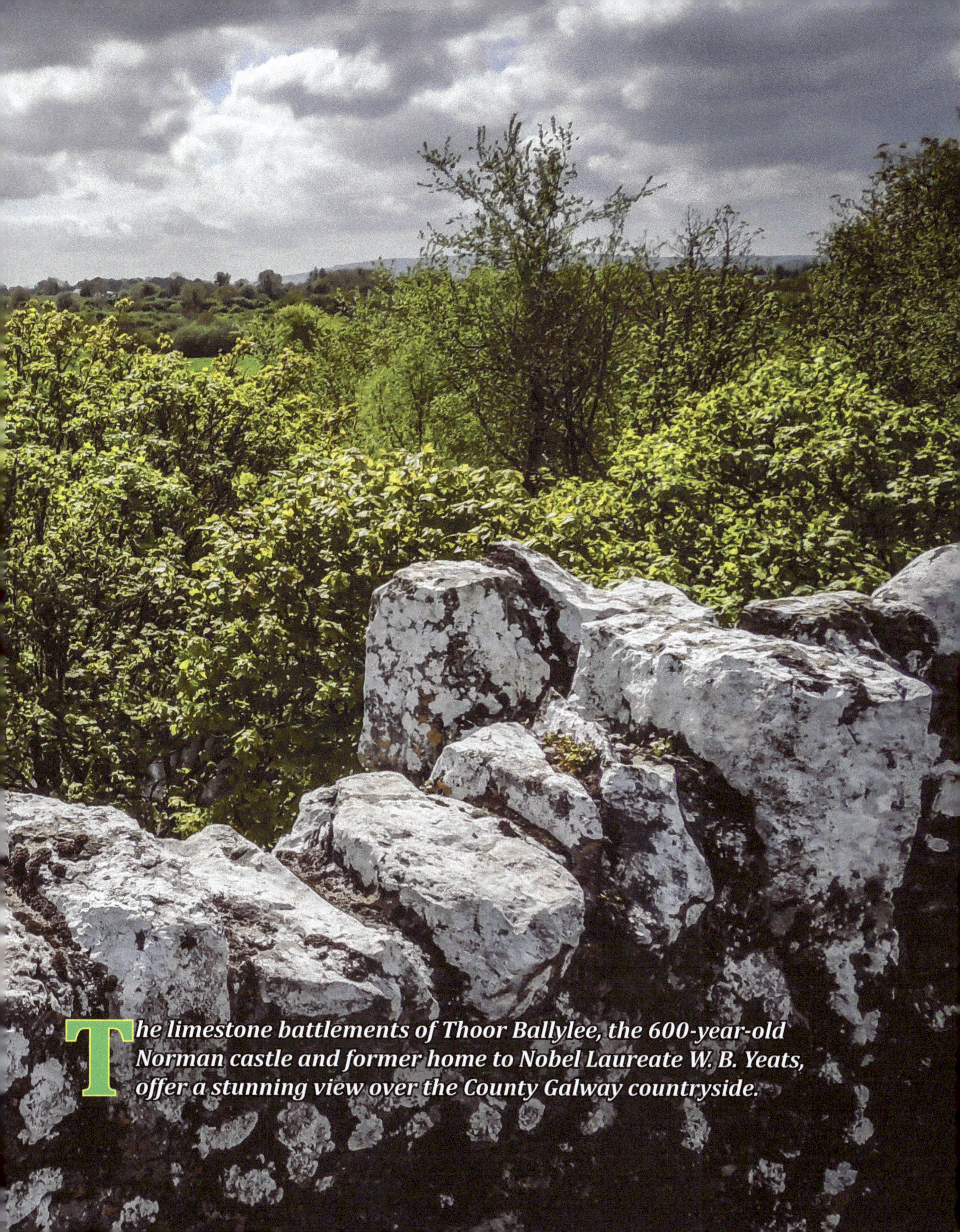

The limestone battlements of Thoor Ballylee, the 600-year-old Norman castle and former home to Nobel Laureate W. B. Yeats, offer a stunning view over the County Galway countryside.

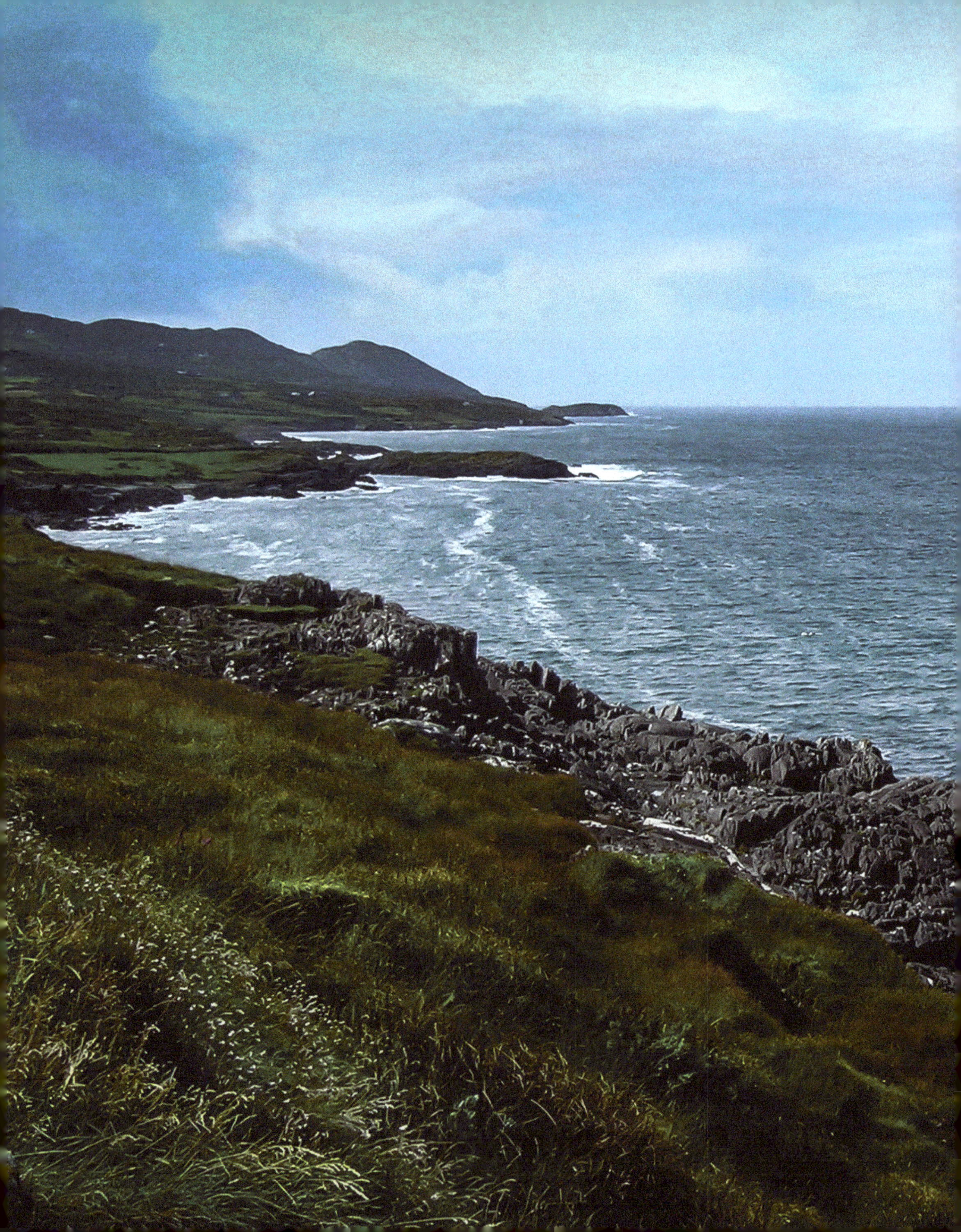

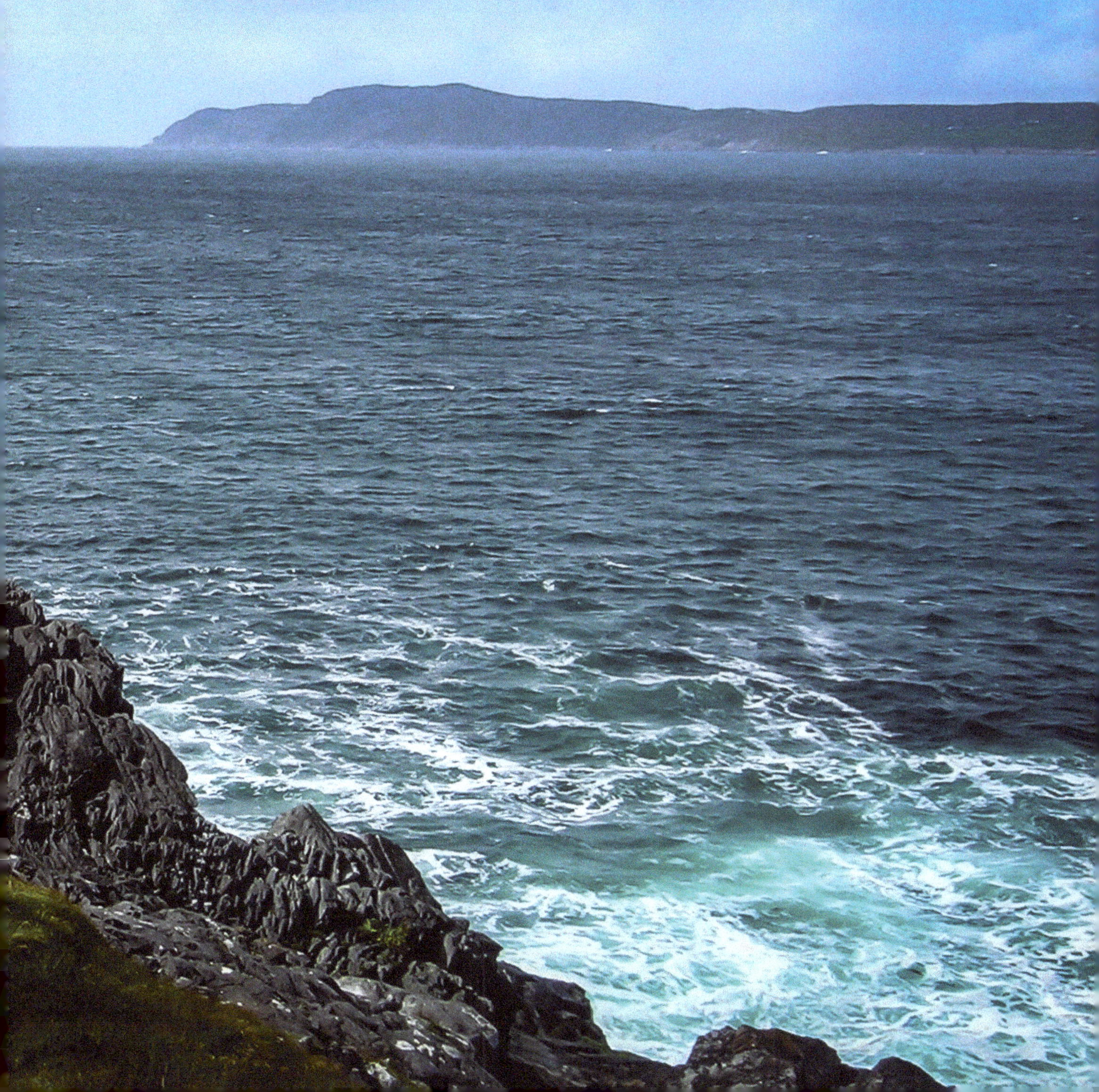
The rocky shores of County Cork's Mizen Peninsula exchange wavelets with the Sheep's Head Peninsula across the historic waters of Dunmanus Bay. This bay has played a significant role in the commercial development of Southwest Ireland.

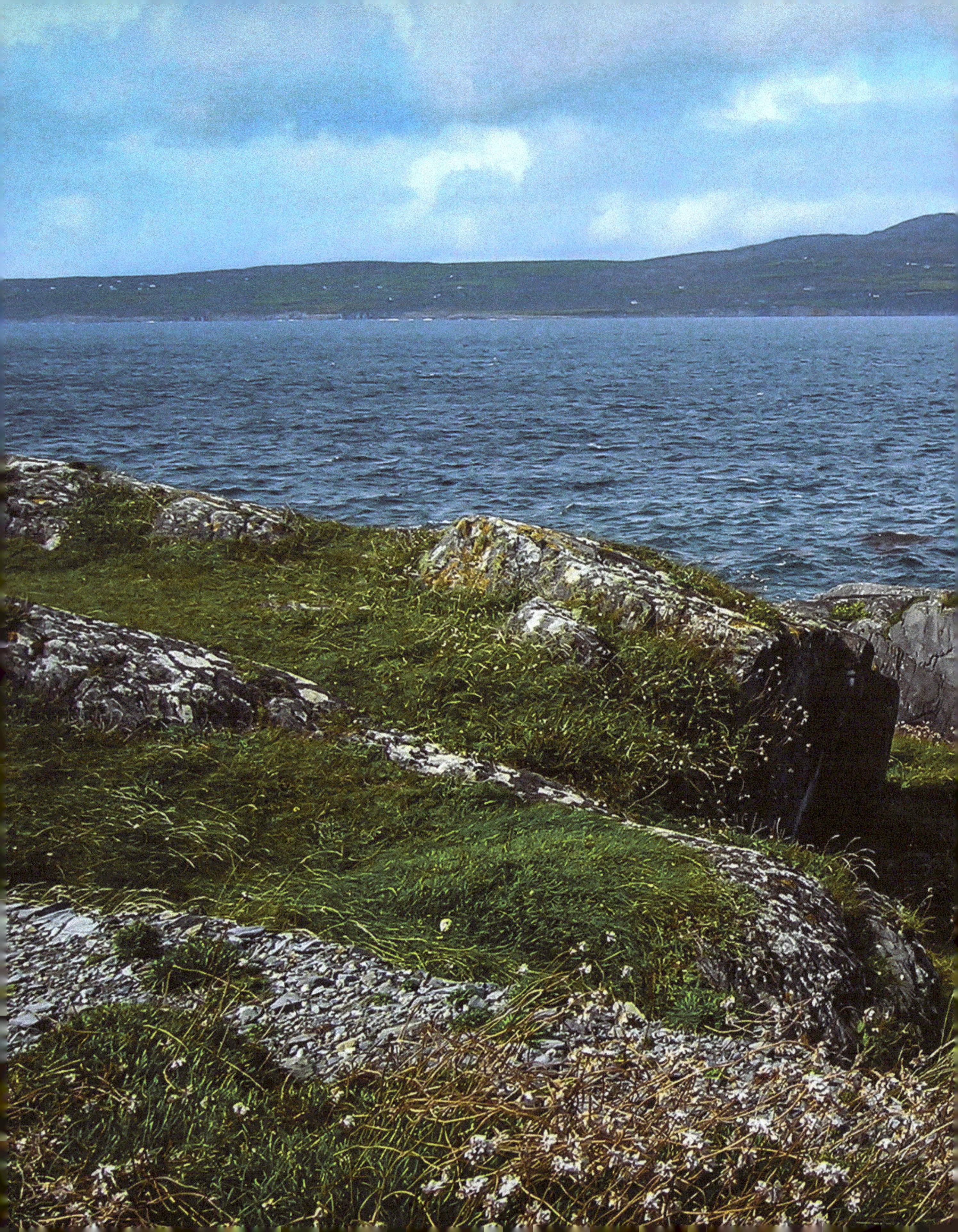

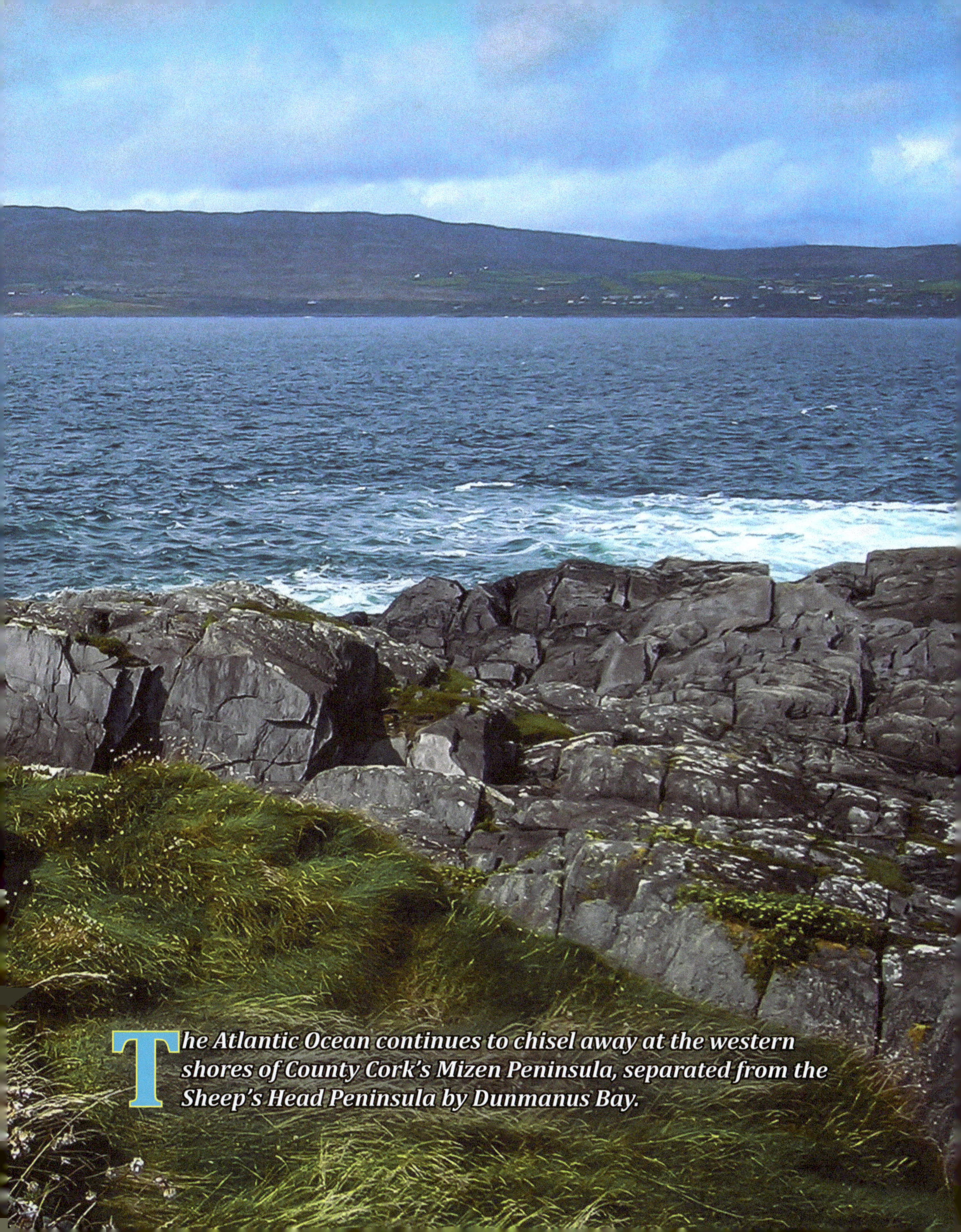

The Atlantic Ocean continues to chisel away at the western shores of County Cork's Mizen Peninsula, separated from the Sheep's Head Peninsula by Dunmanus Bay.

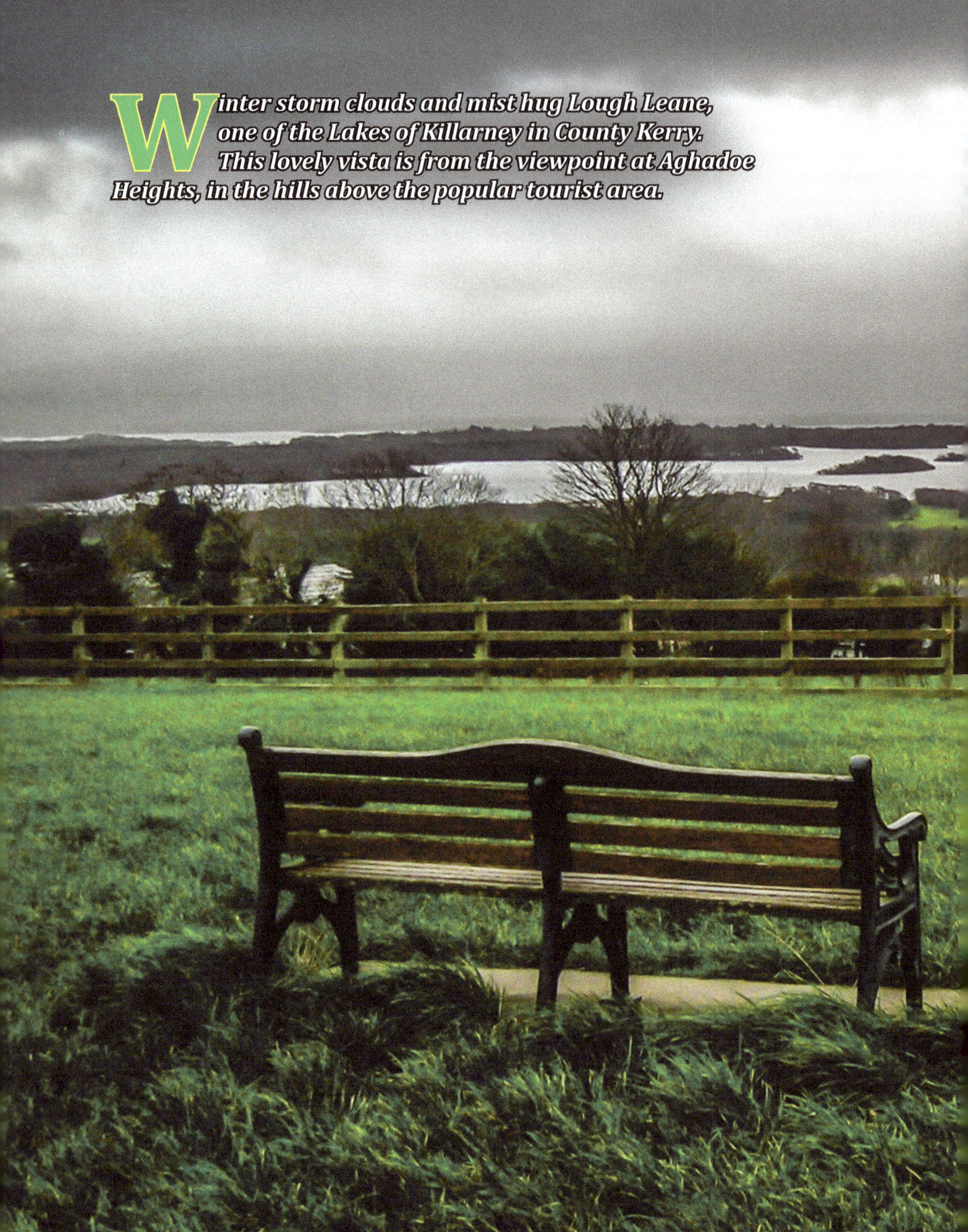

Winter storm clouds and mist hug Lough Leane,
one of the Lakes of Killarney in County Kerry.
This lovely vista is from the viewpoint at Aghadoe
Heights, in the hills above the popular tourist area.

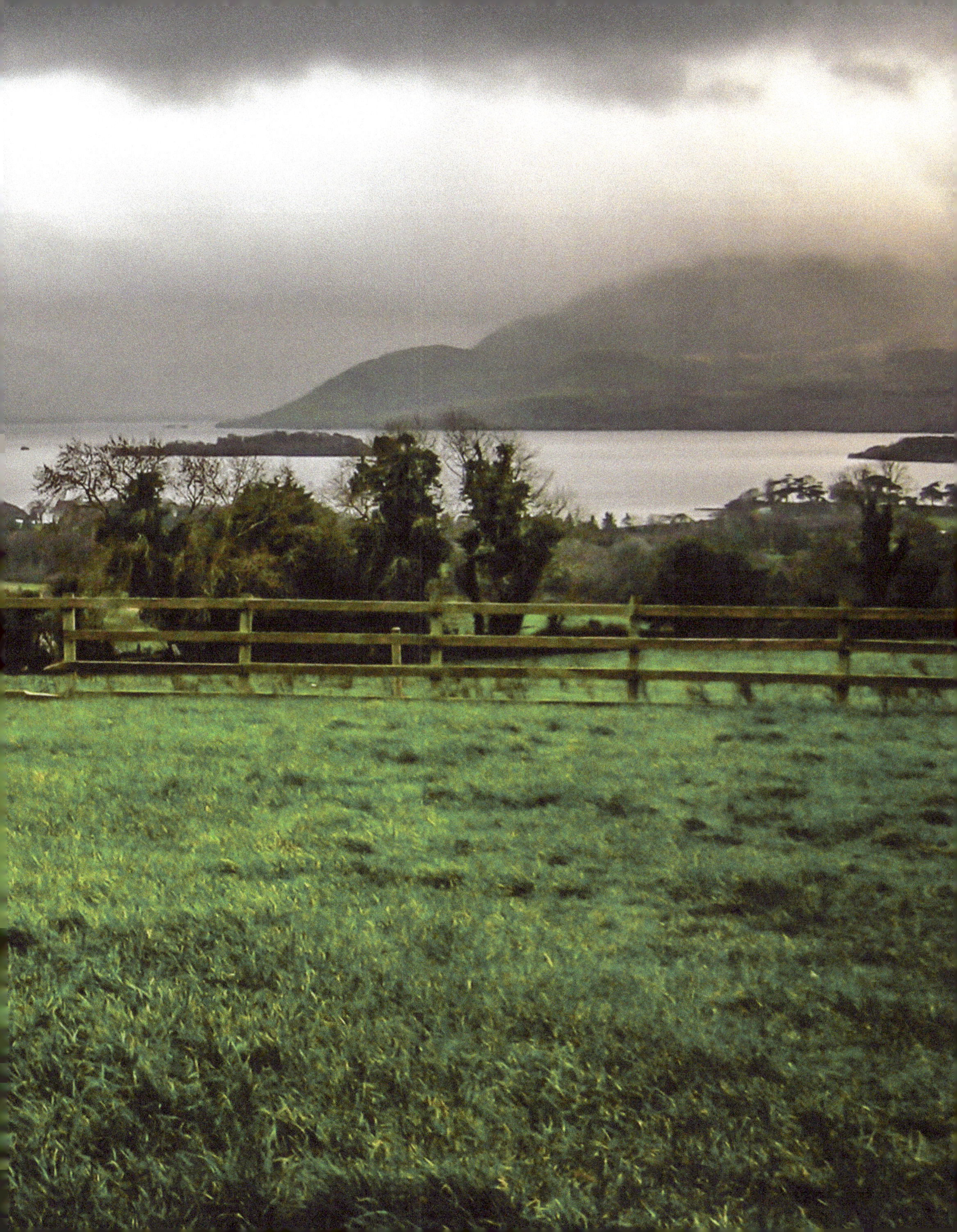

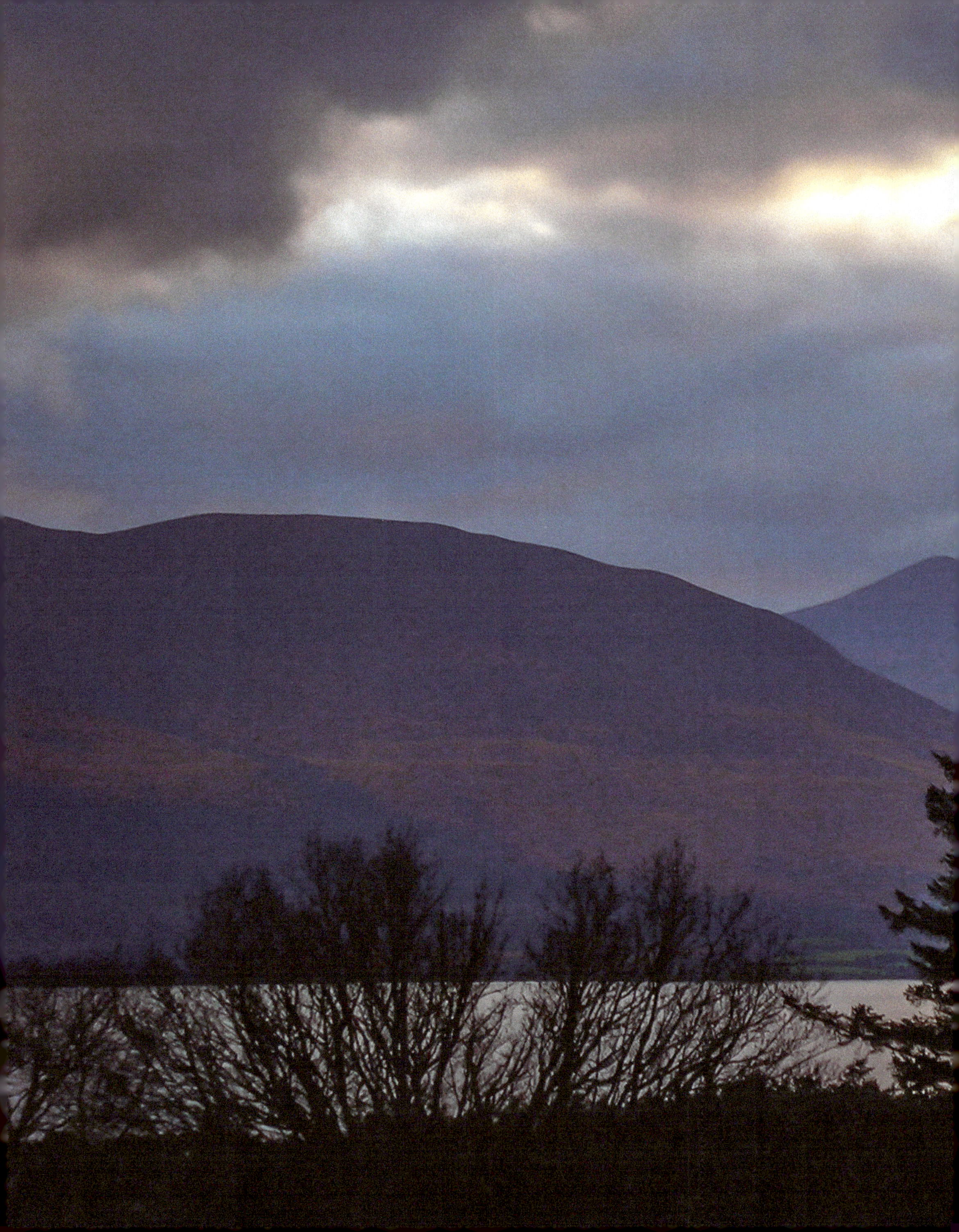

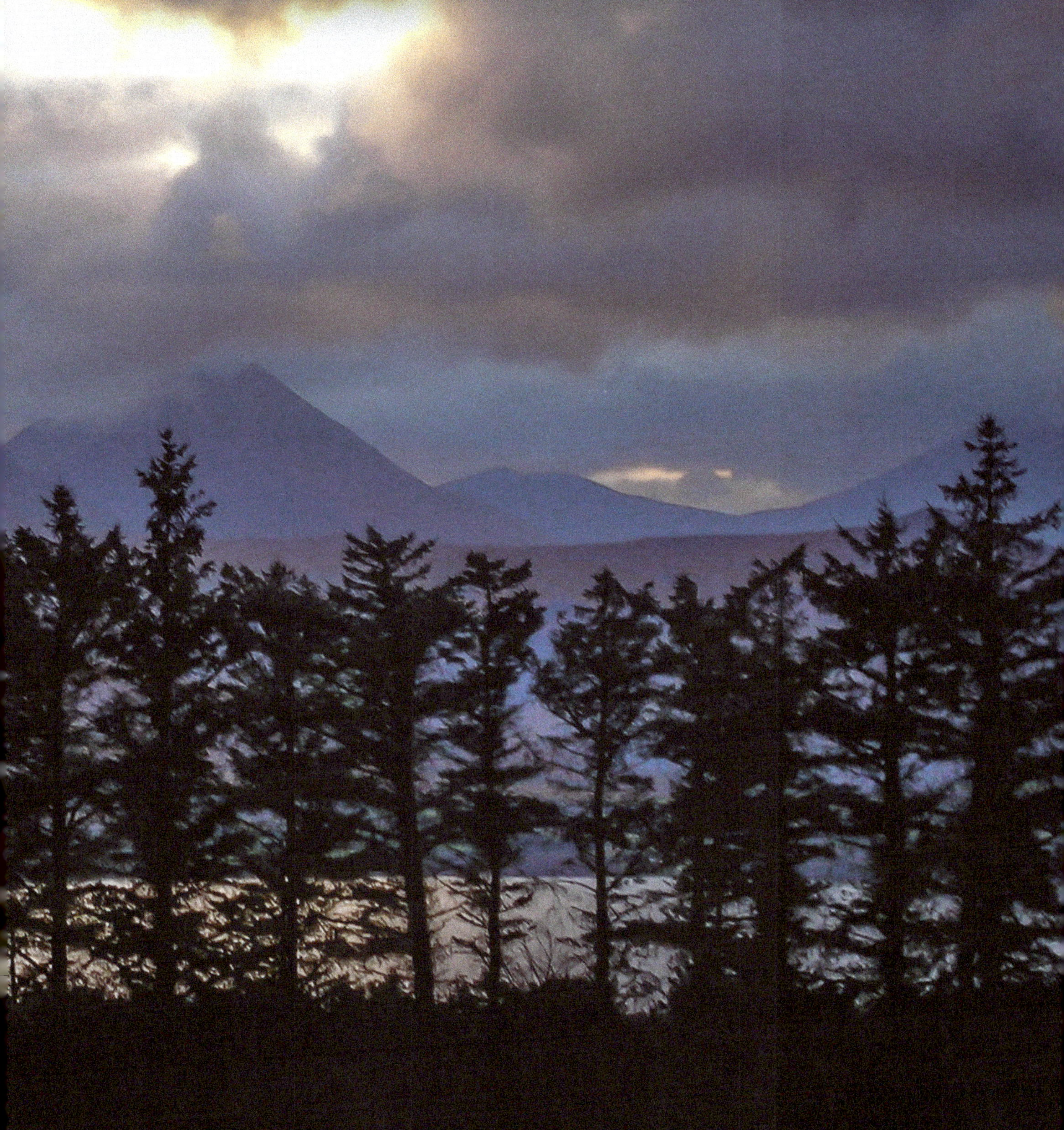

Dark clouds descend over Carrauntoohil, the highest peak in Ireland at 1,038 meters (3,406 ft.). It's the centerpiece of the Macgillycuddy's Reeks mountain range in County Kerry.

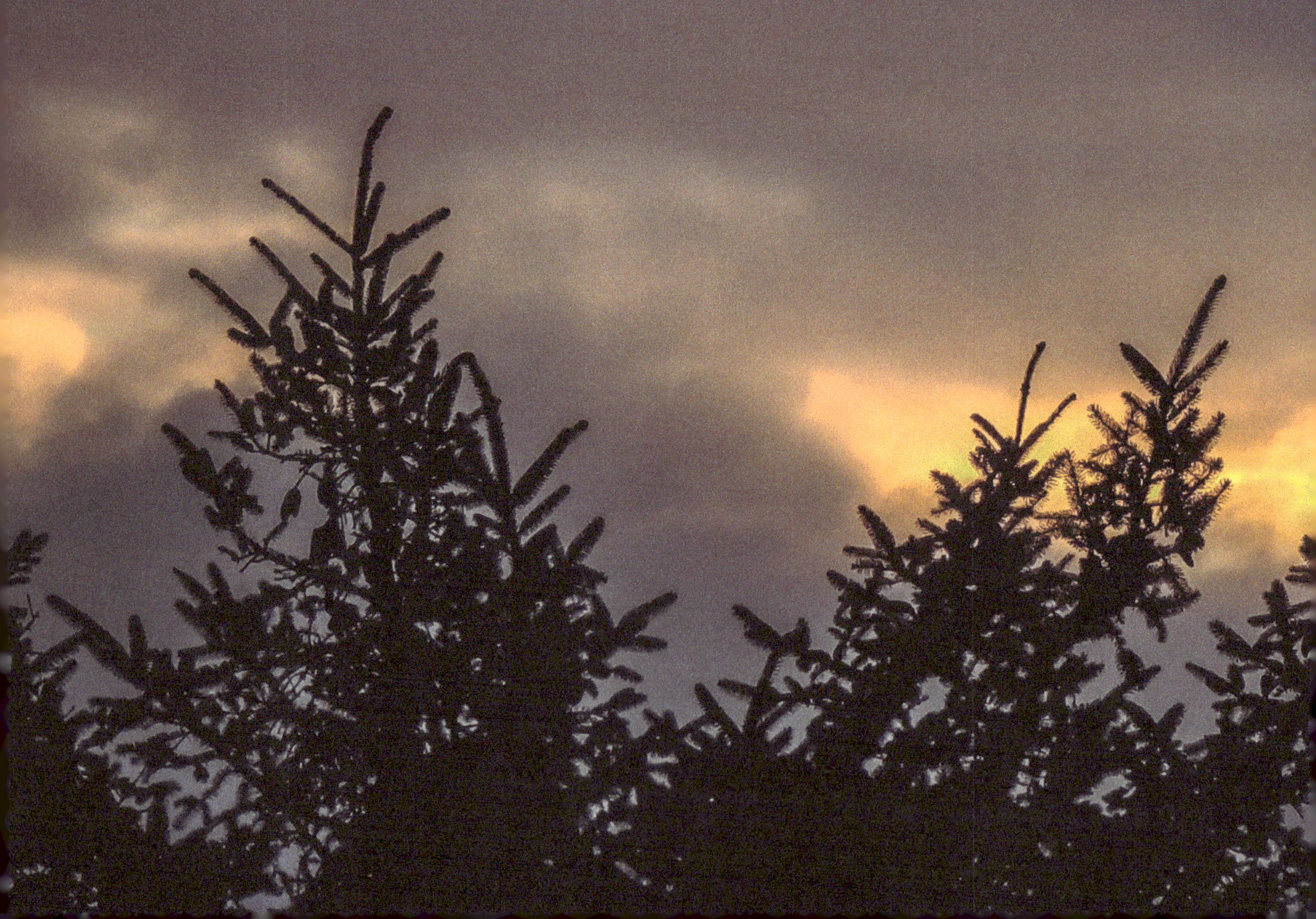

Rays of sun escape an
encroaching storm over
Western Ireland.

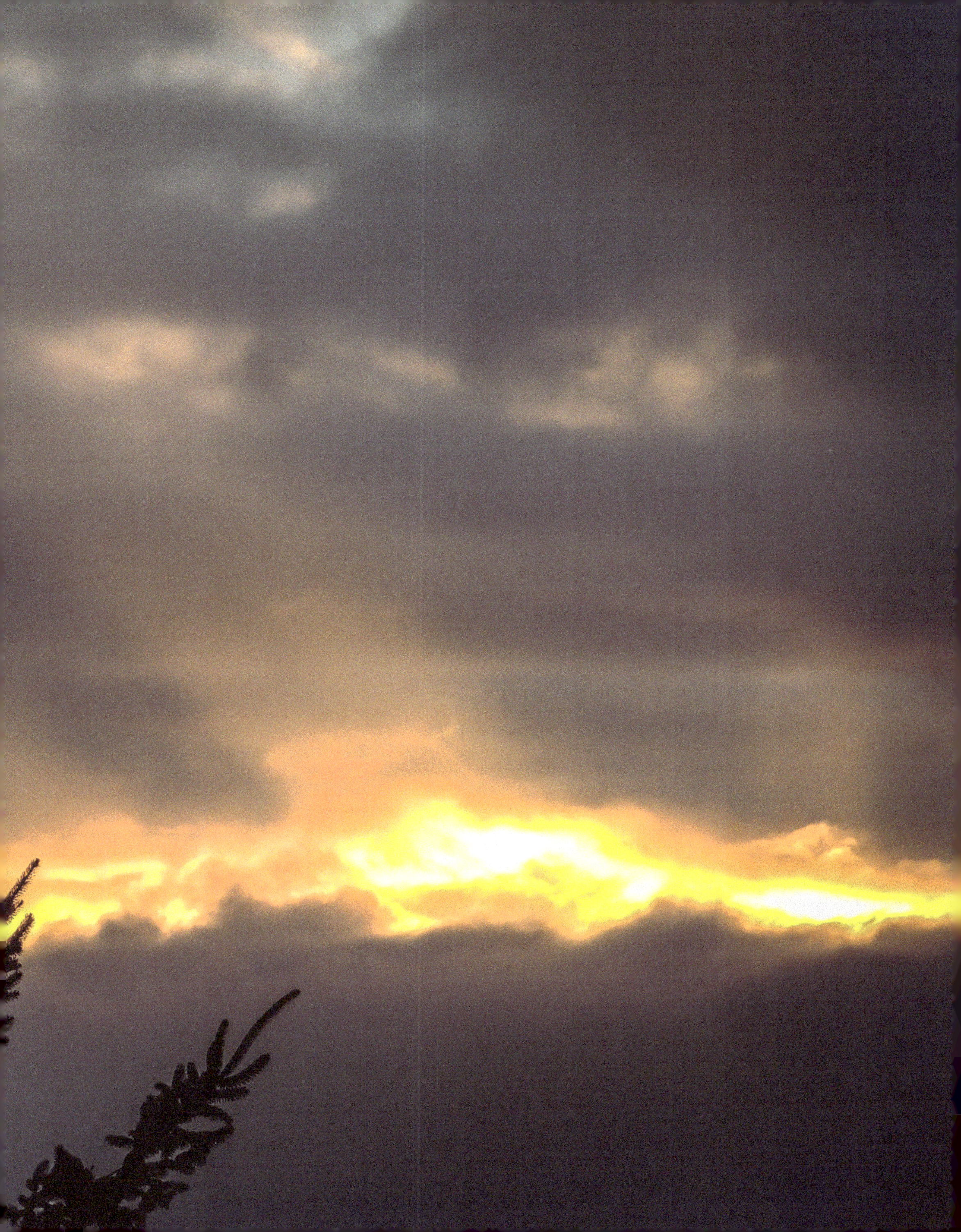

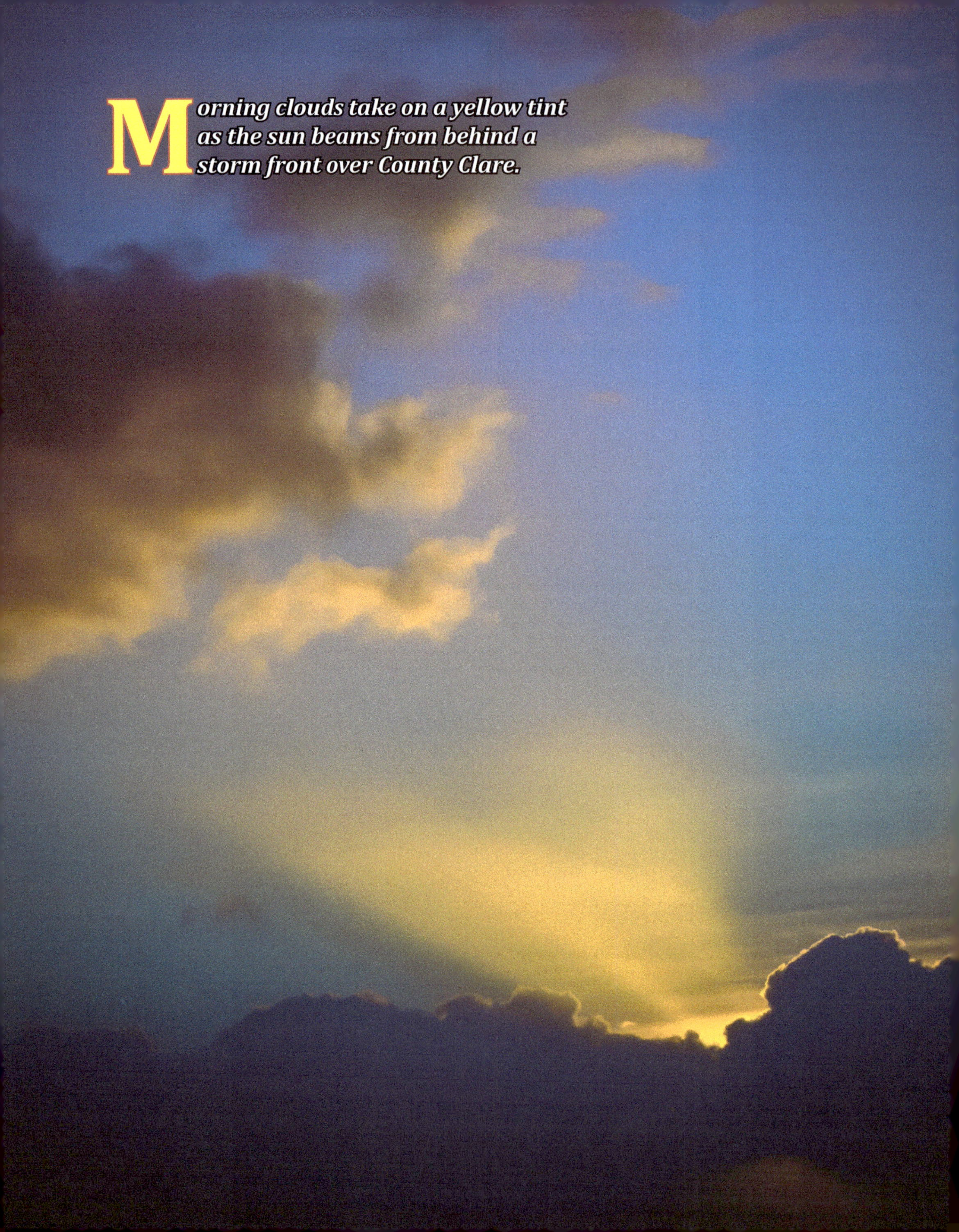

Morning clouds take on a yellow tint
as the sun beams from behind a
storm front over County Clare.

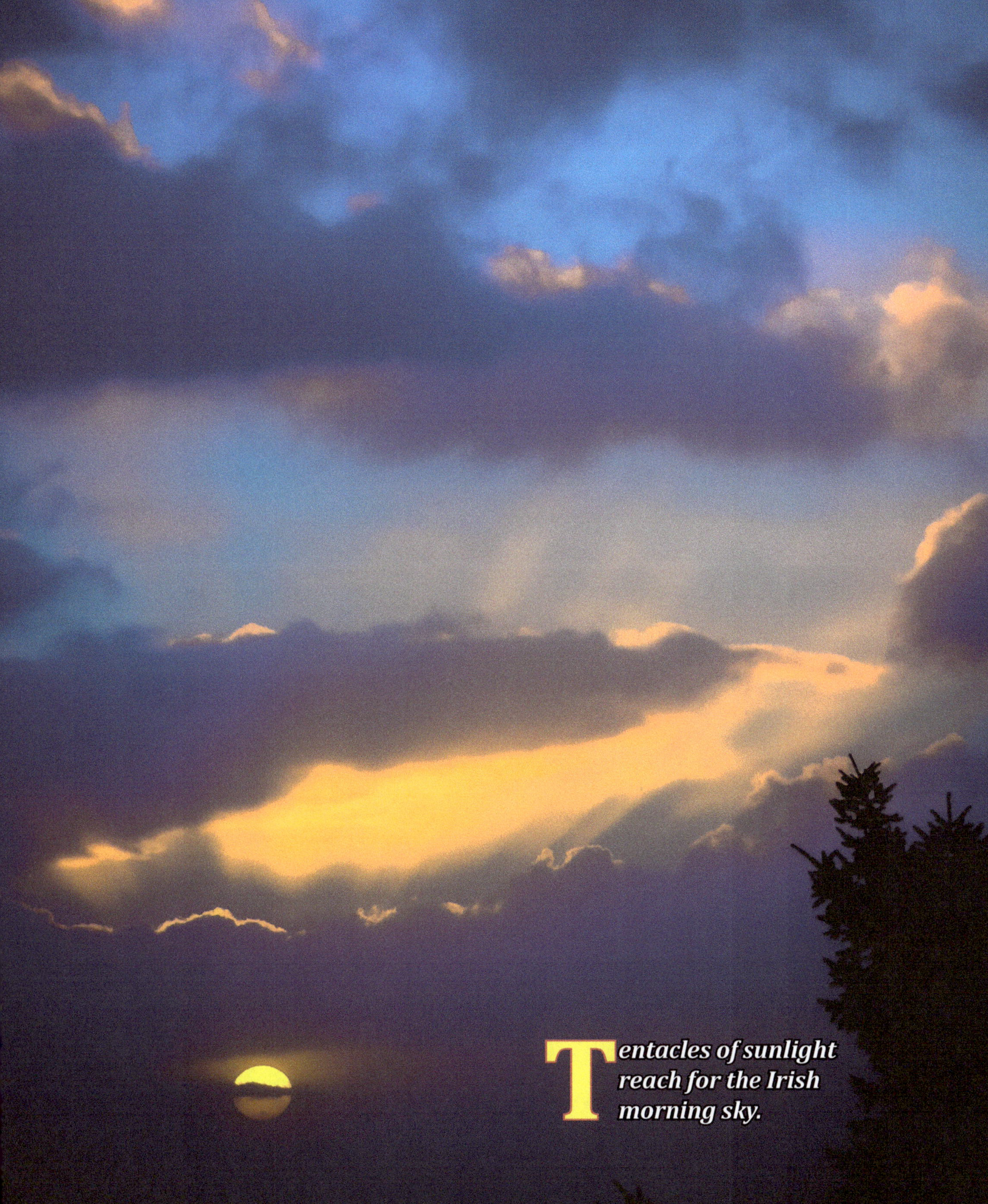
Tentacles of sunlight
reach for the Irish
morning sky.

White beams from the heavens
conquer the morning sky over
the County Clare countryside.

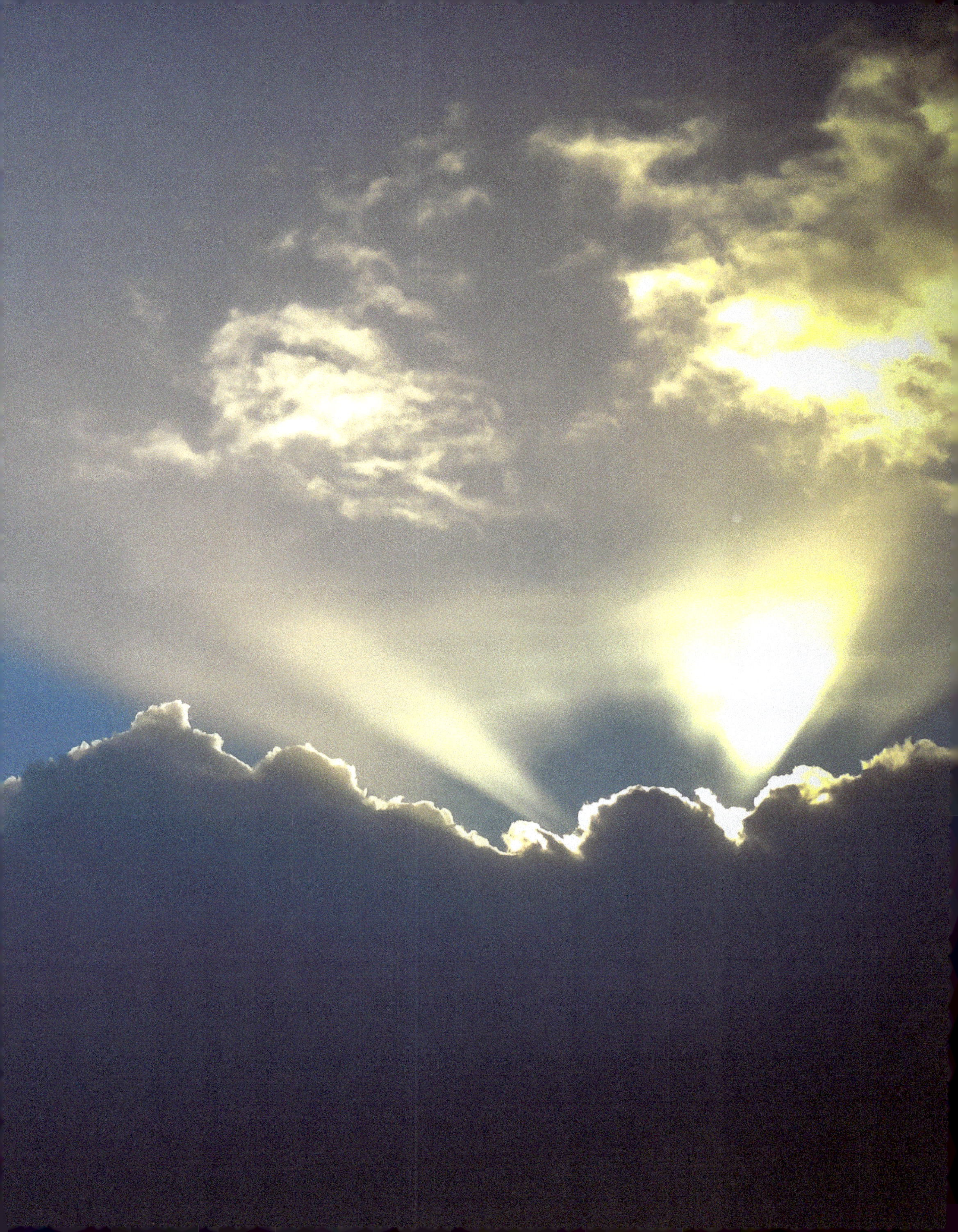

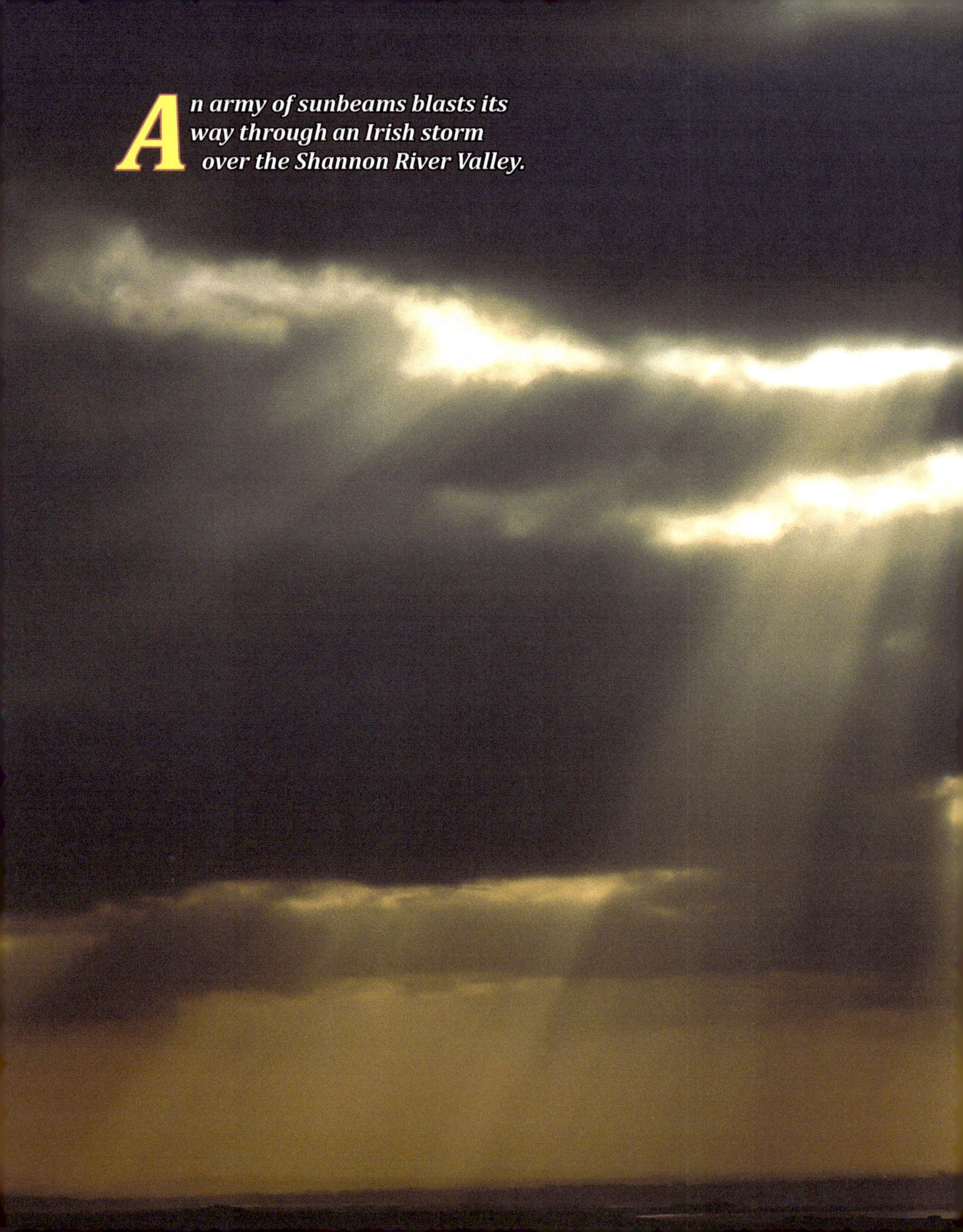

An army of sunbeams blasts its
way through an Irish storm
over the Shannon River Valley.

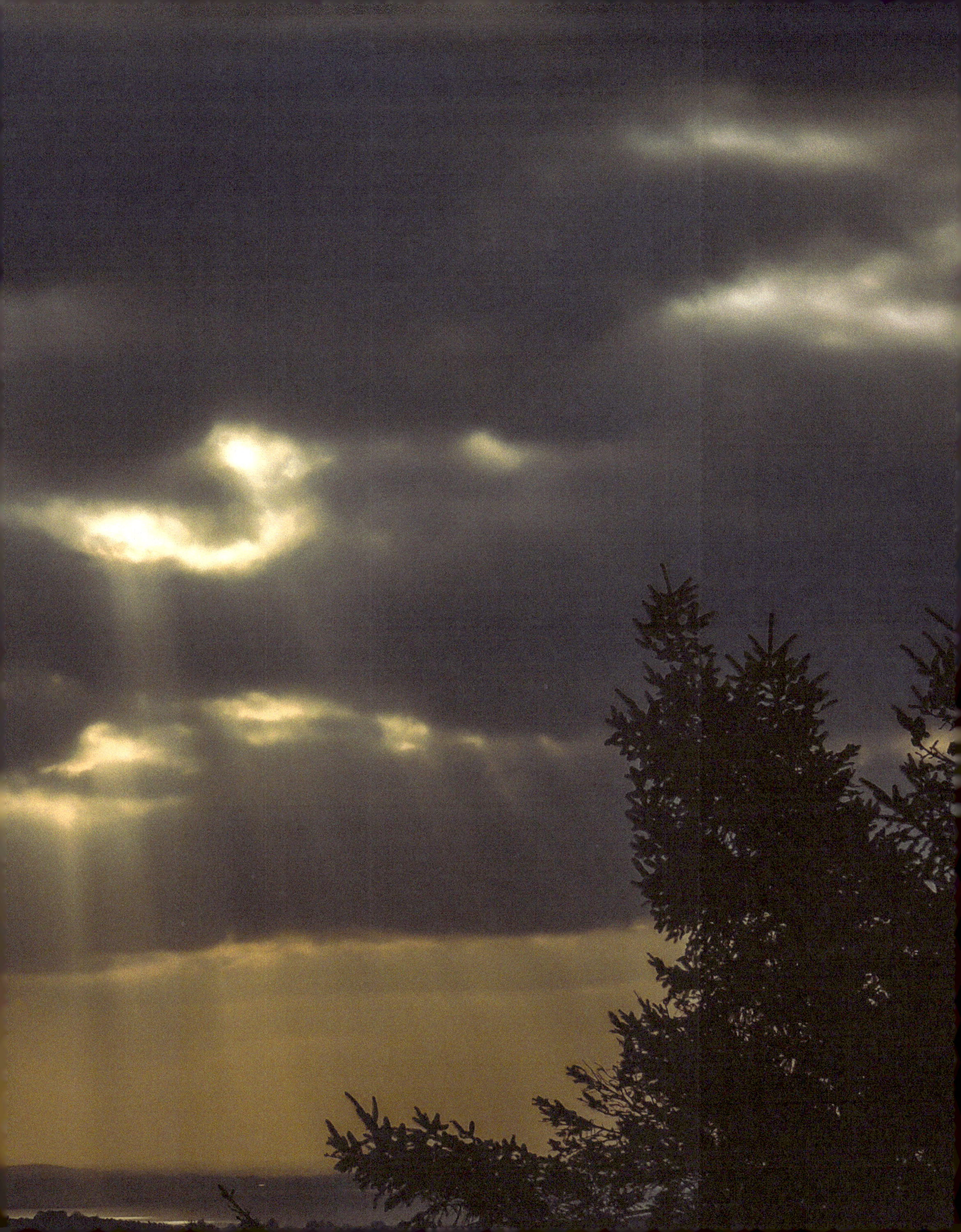

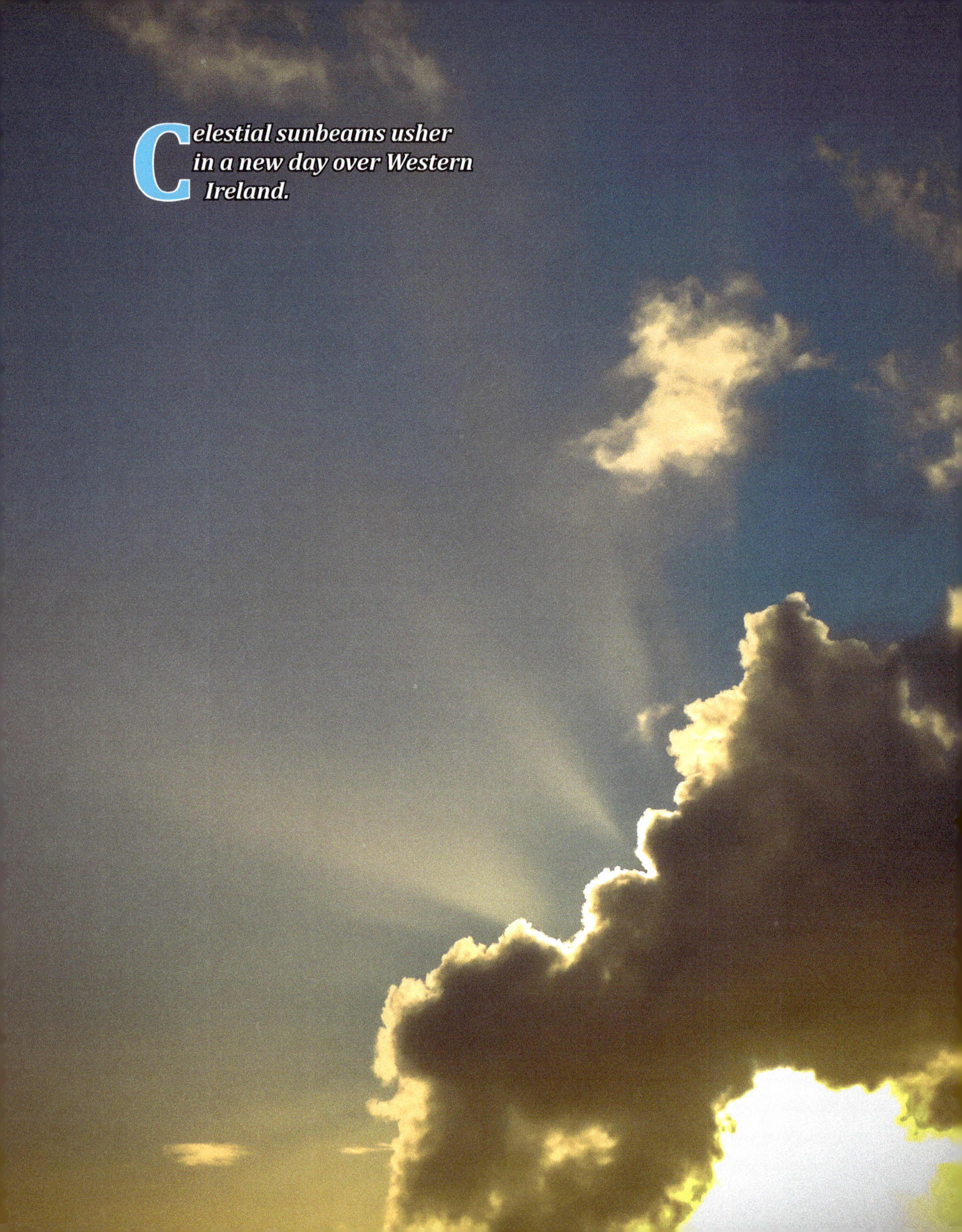

Celestial sunbeams usher
in a new day over Western
Ireland.

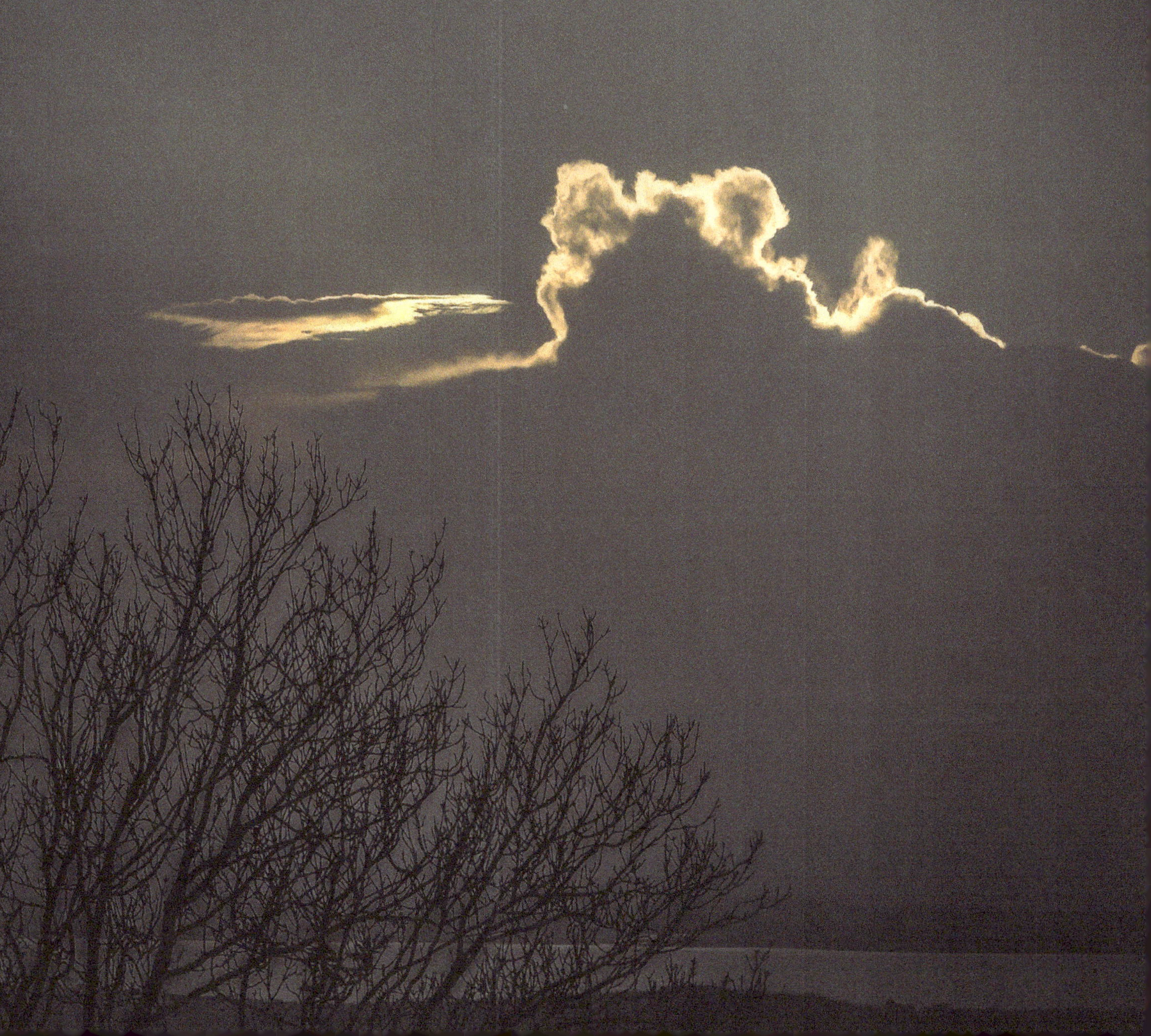

The morning sun chisels a crisp edge to a wintery storm front over County Clare's River Fergus.

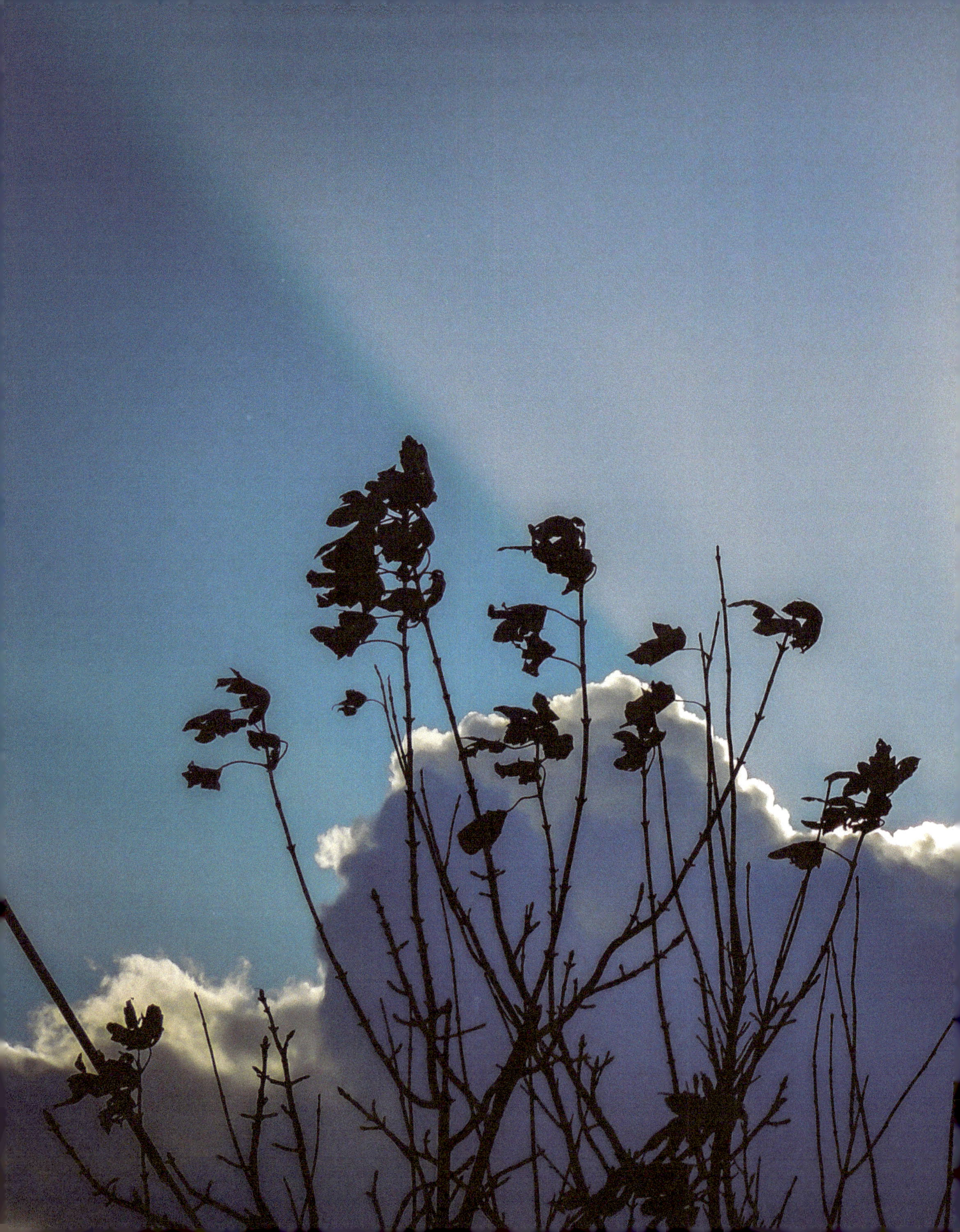

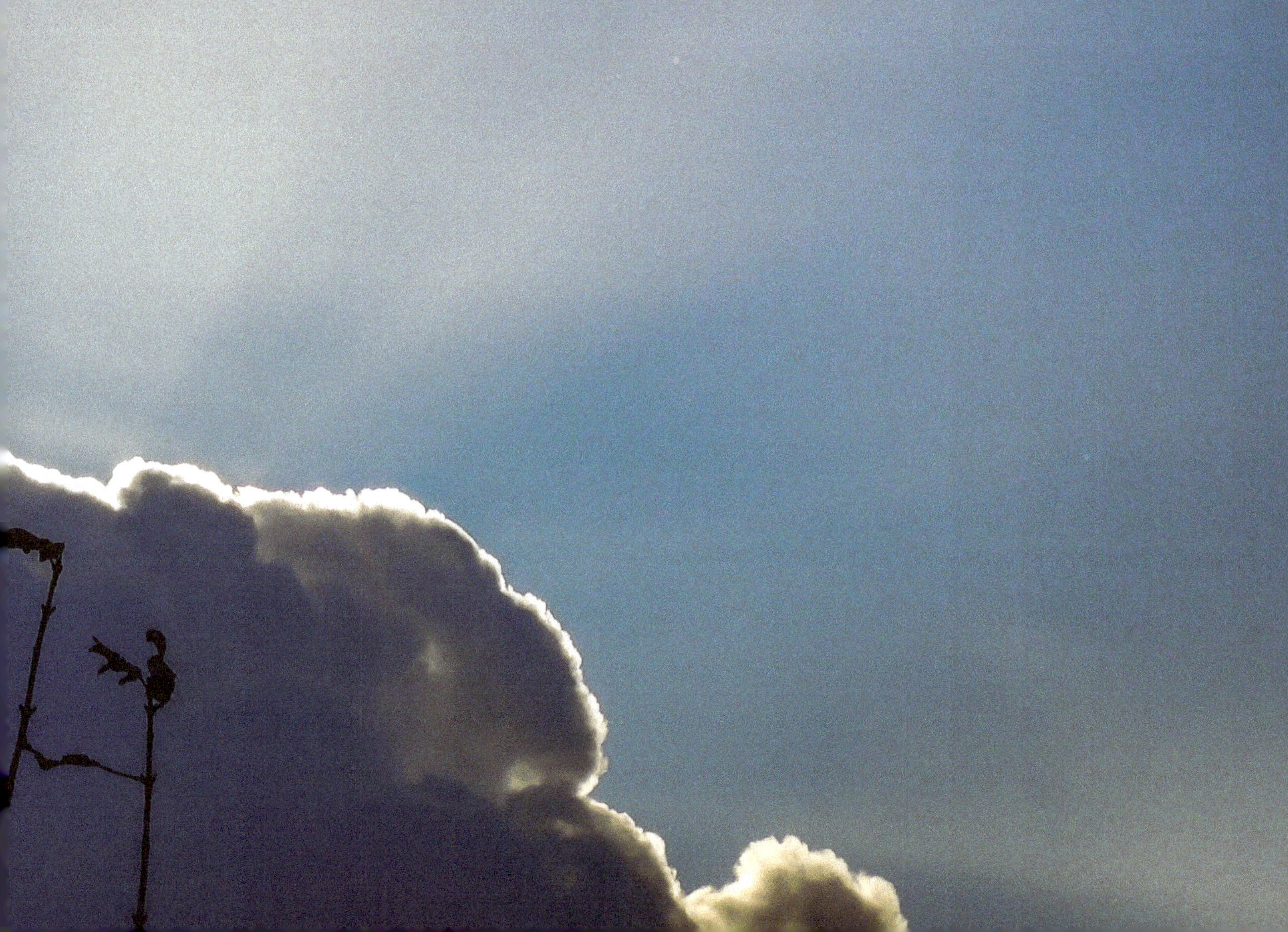

Fall foliage clings to these branches
in a stiff breeze as sunbeams emerge
from a passing cloud in blue skies
over County Clare.

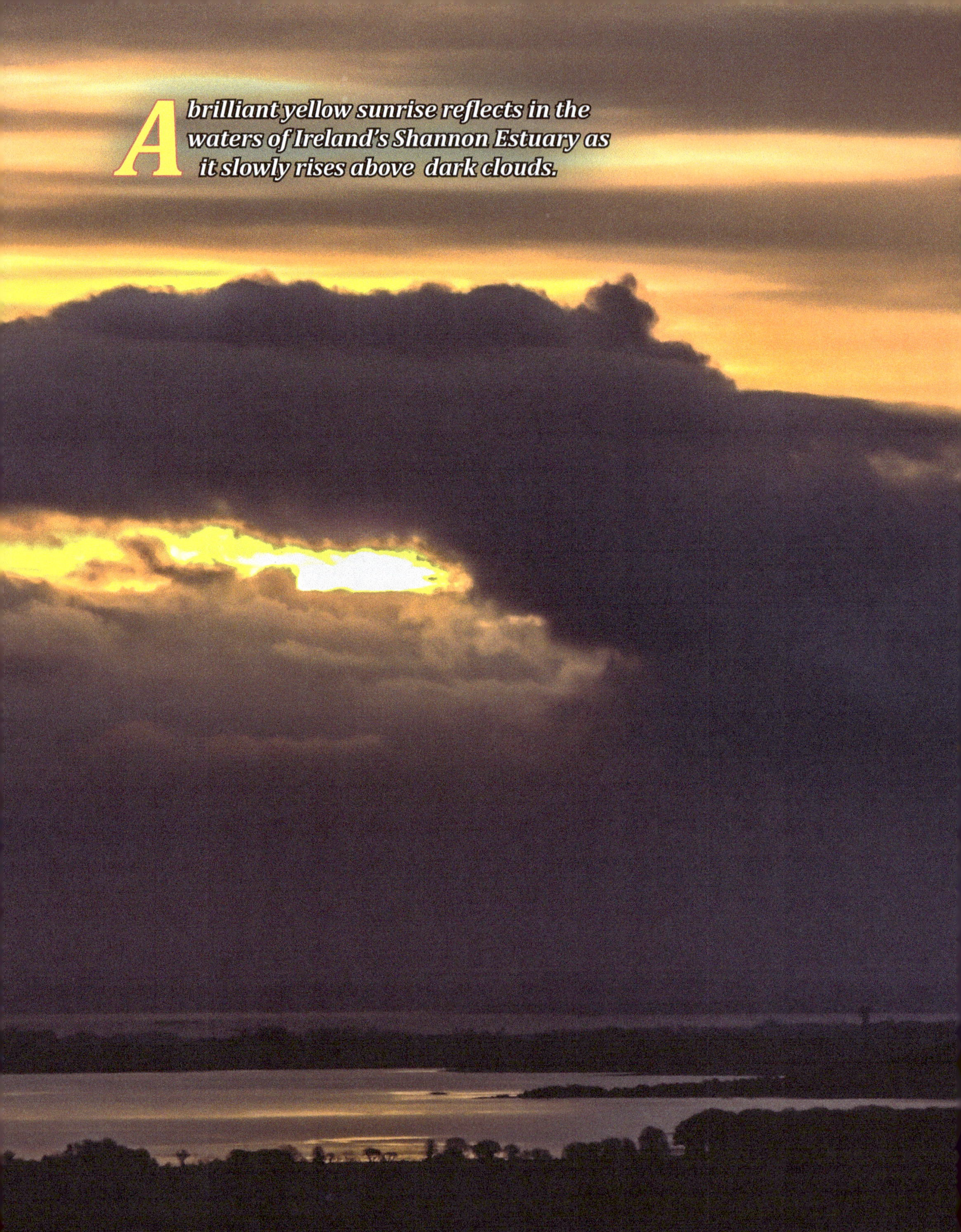

A brilliant yellow sunrise reflects in the
waters of Ireland's Shannon Estuary as
it slowly rises above dark clouds.

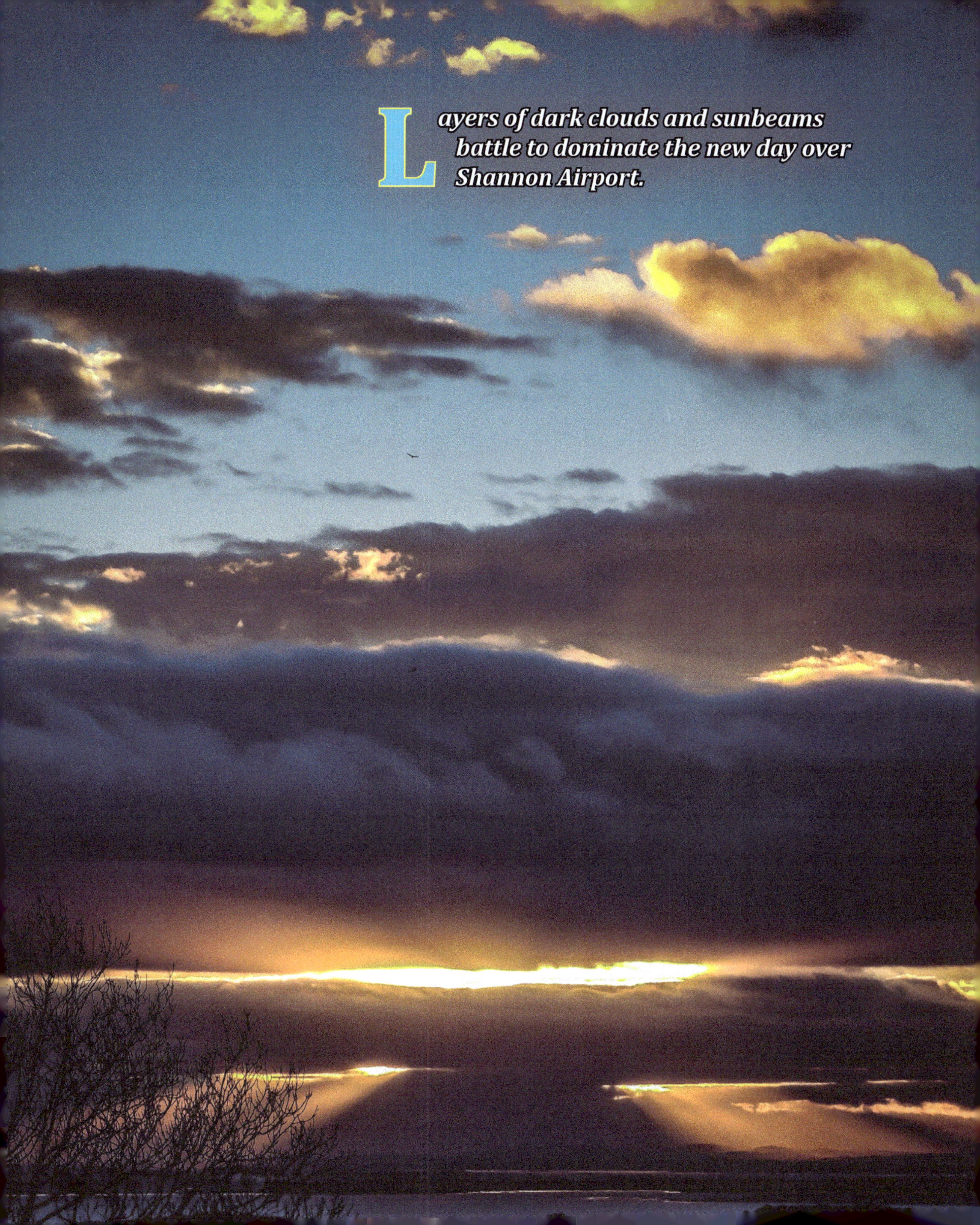

Layers of dark clouds and sunbeams battle to dominate the new day over Shannon Airport.

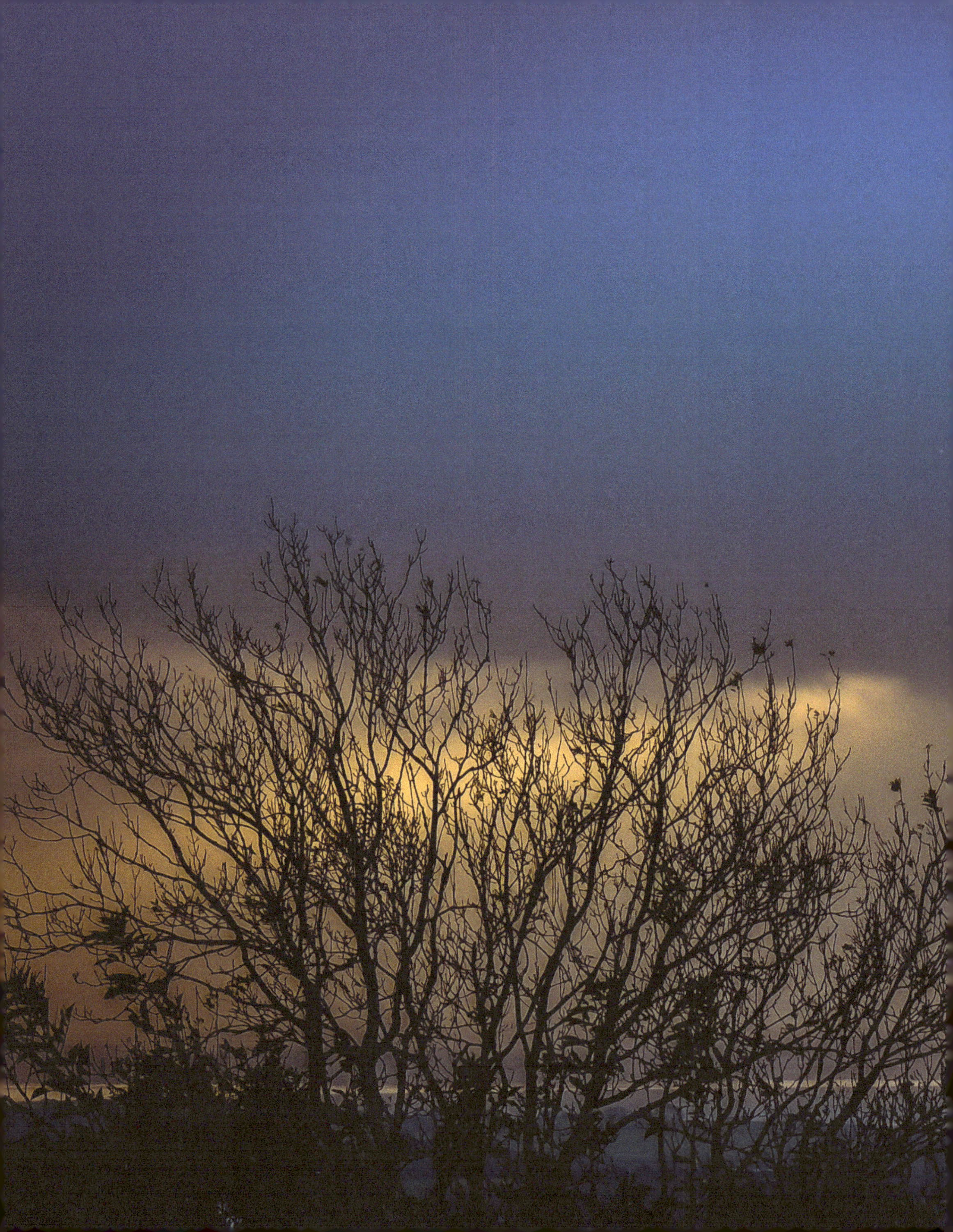

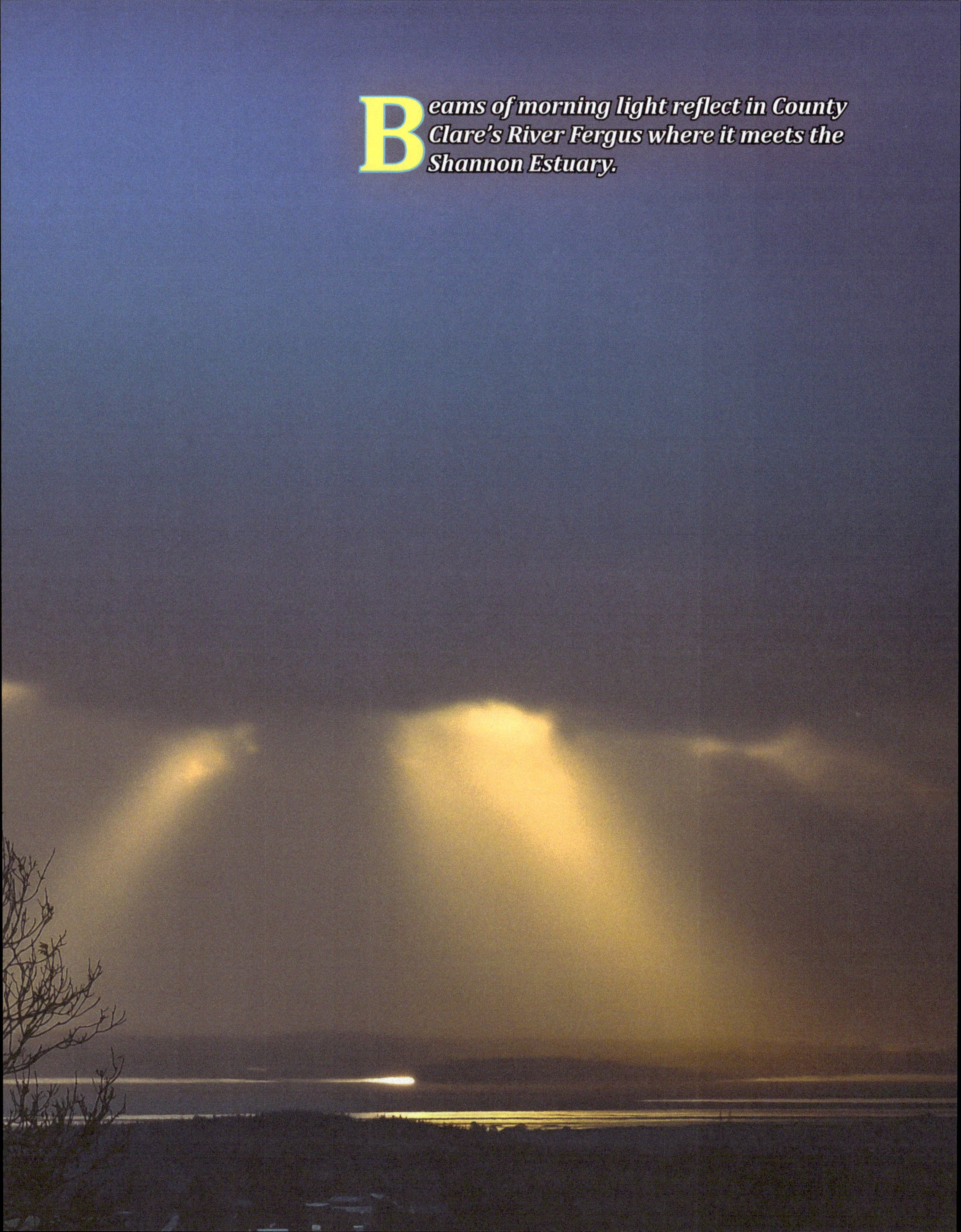

Beams of morning light reflect in County Clare's River Fergus where it meets the Shannon Estuary.

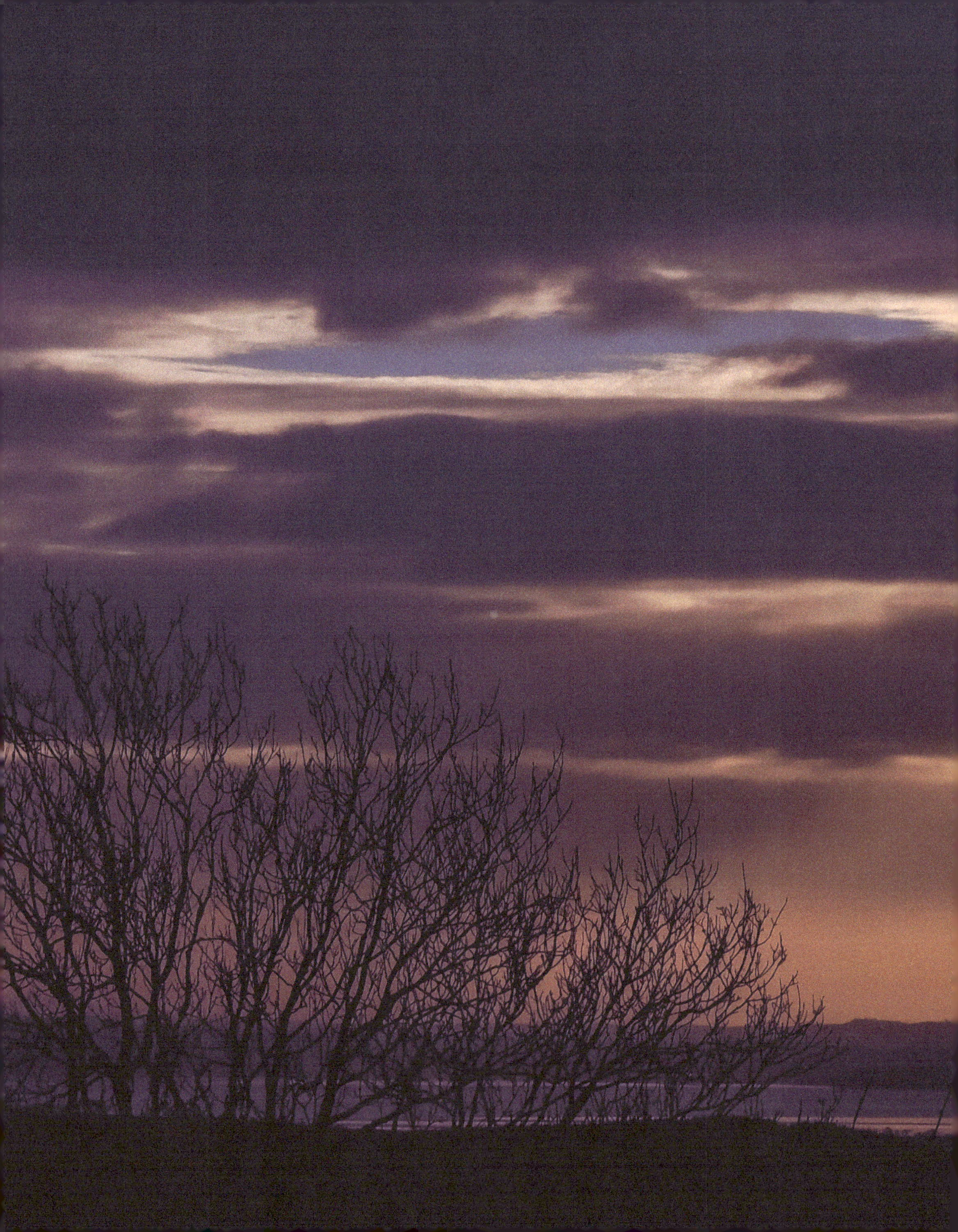

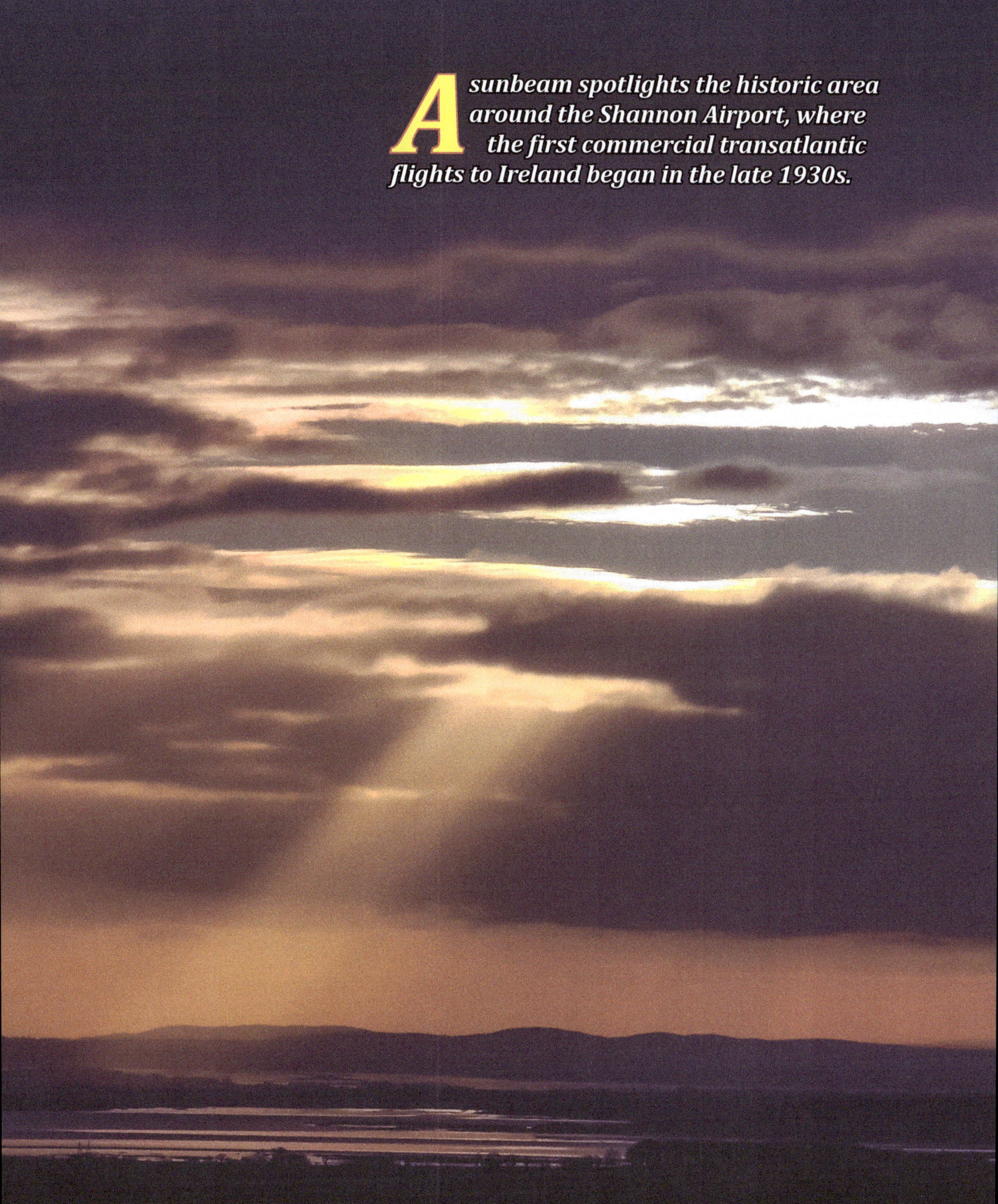

A sunbeam spotlights the historic area around the Shannon Airport, where the first commercial transatlantic flights to Ireland began in the late 1930s.

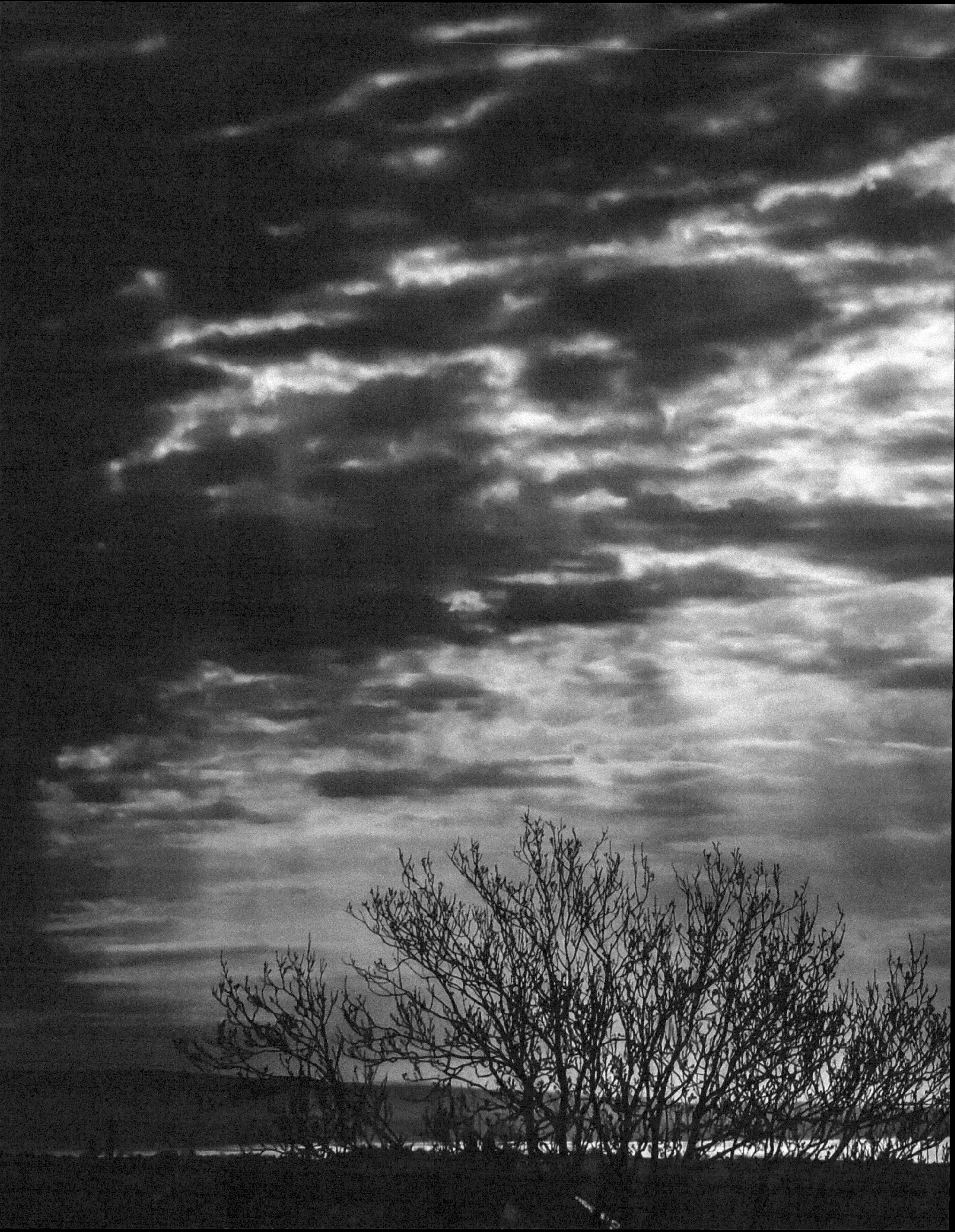

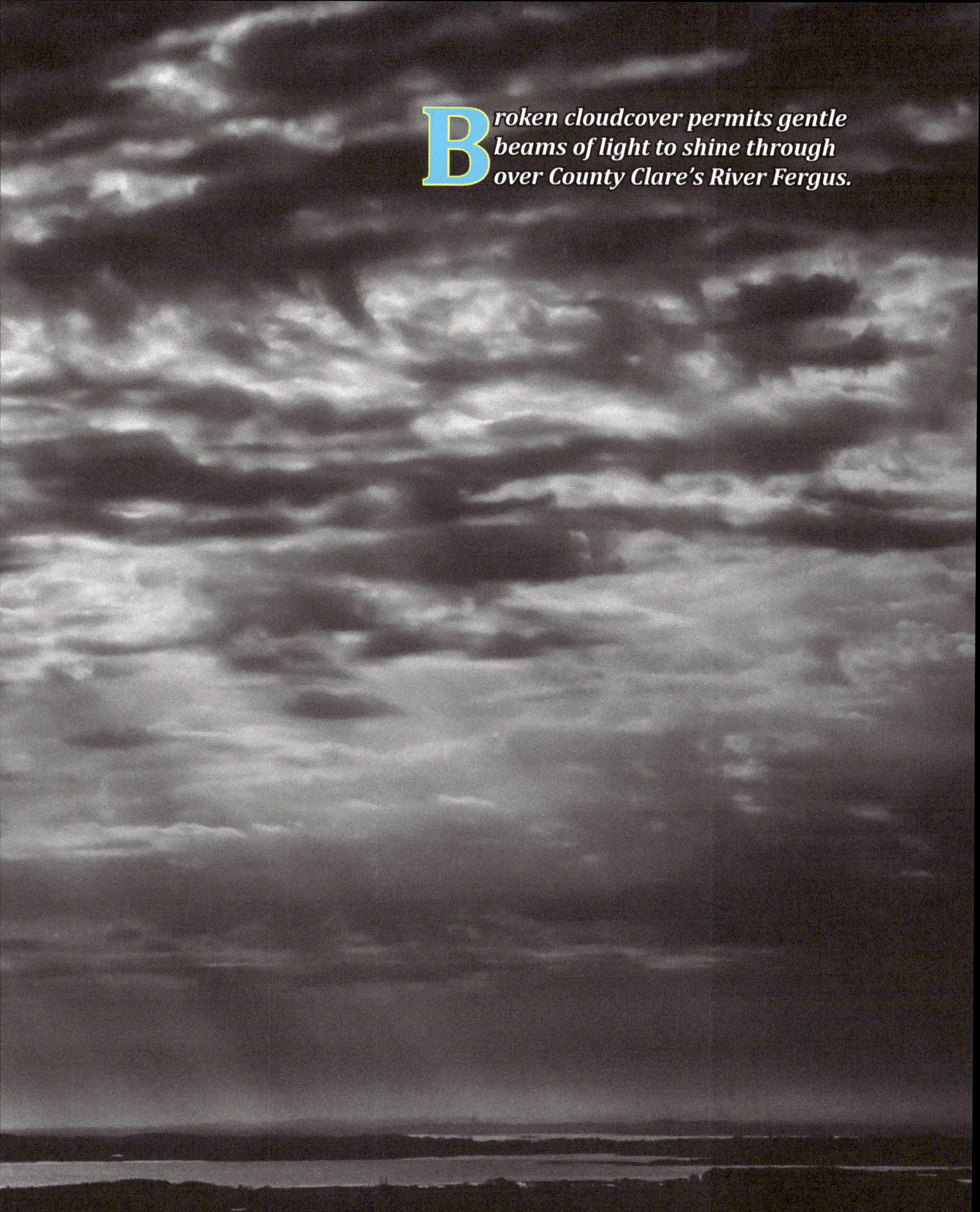

Broken cloudcover permits gentle
beams of light to shine through
over County Clare's River Fergus.

Distant sunbeams shine over County Limerick beyond the waters of the Shannon Estuary, once plied by Vikings, missionaries and traders.

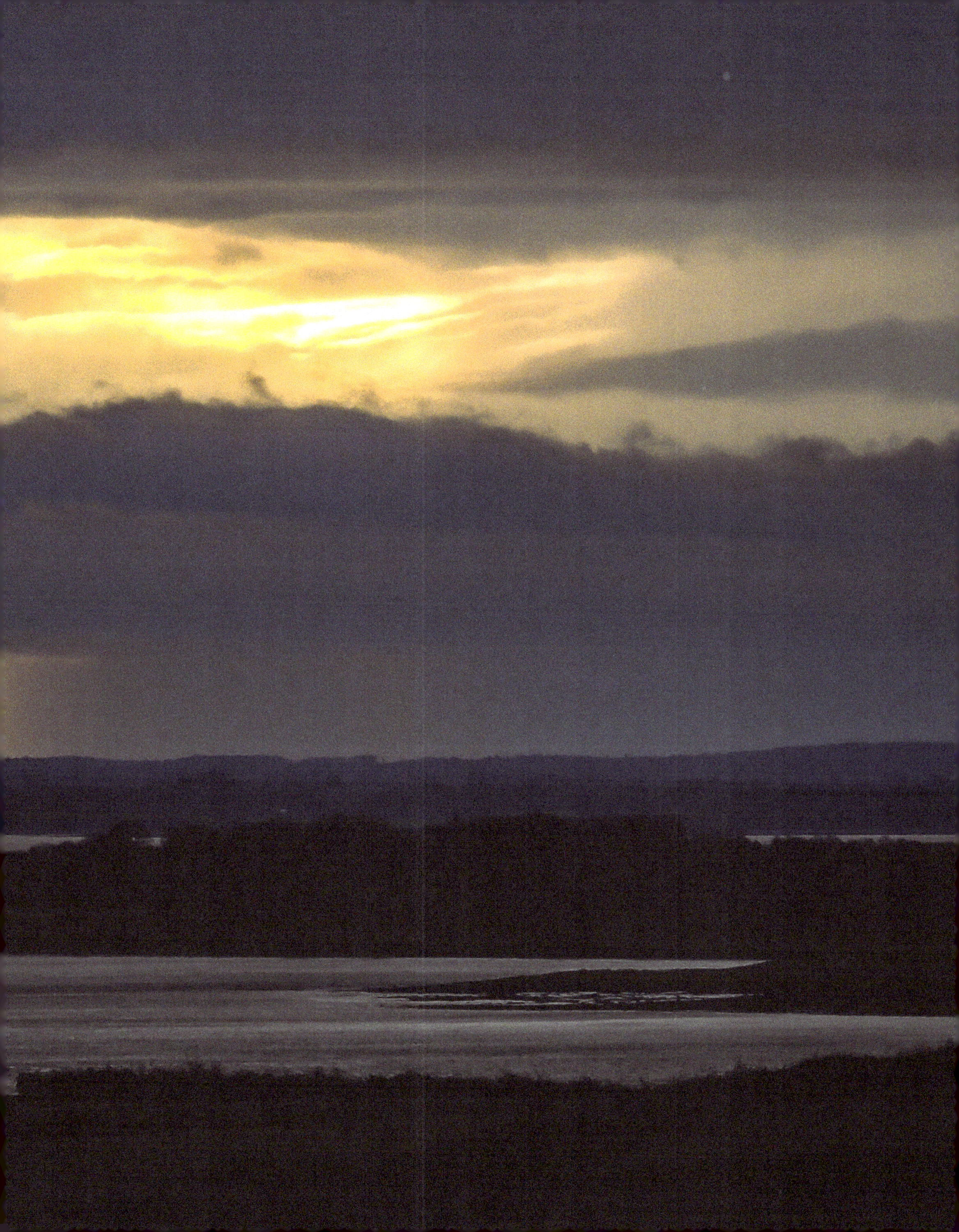

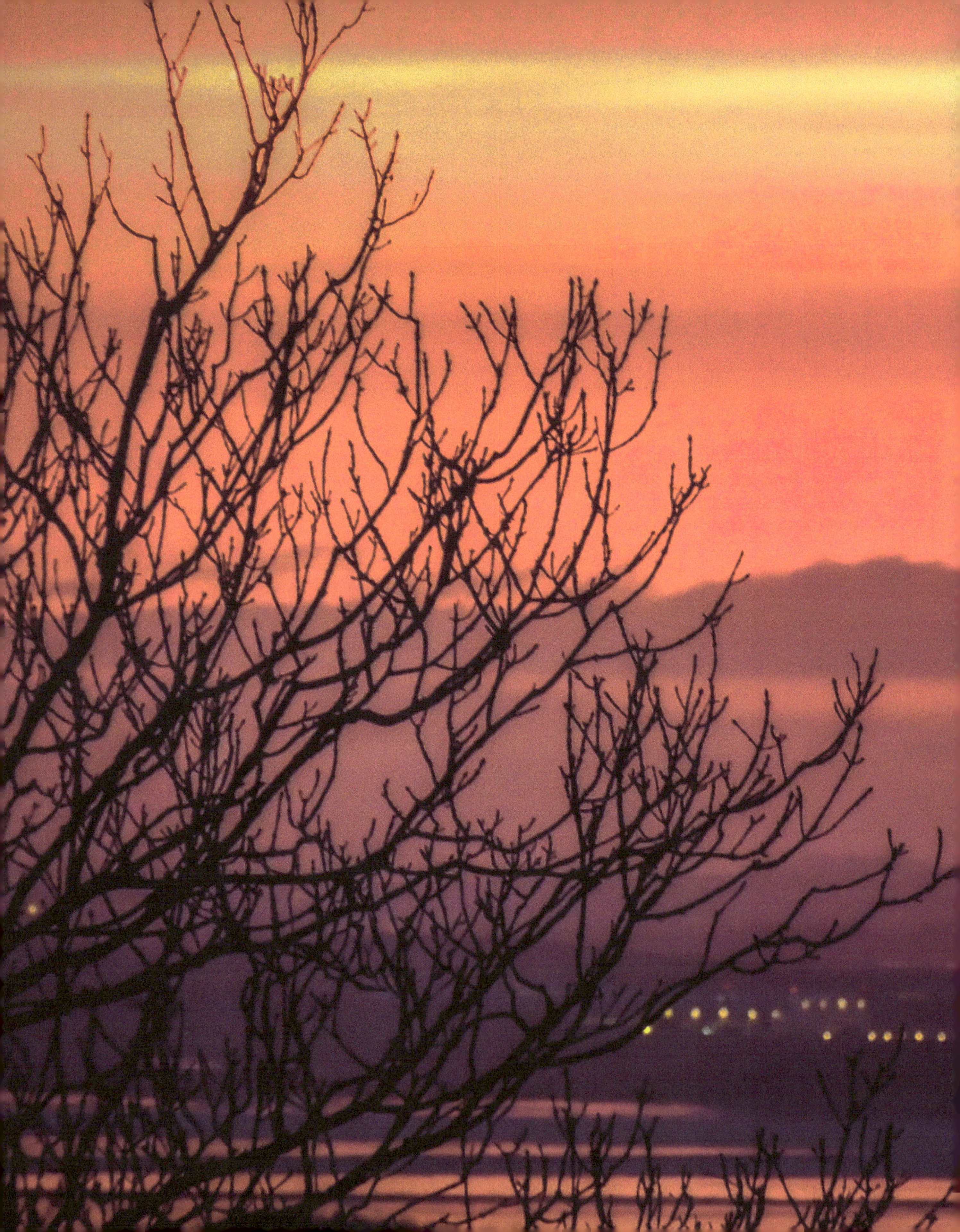

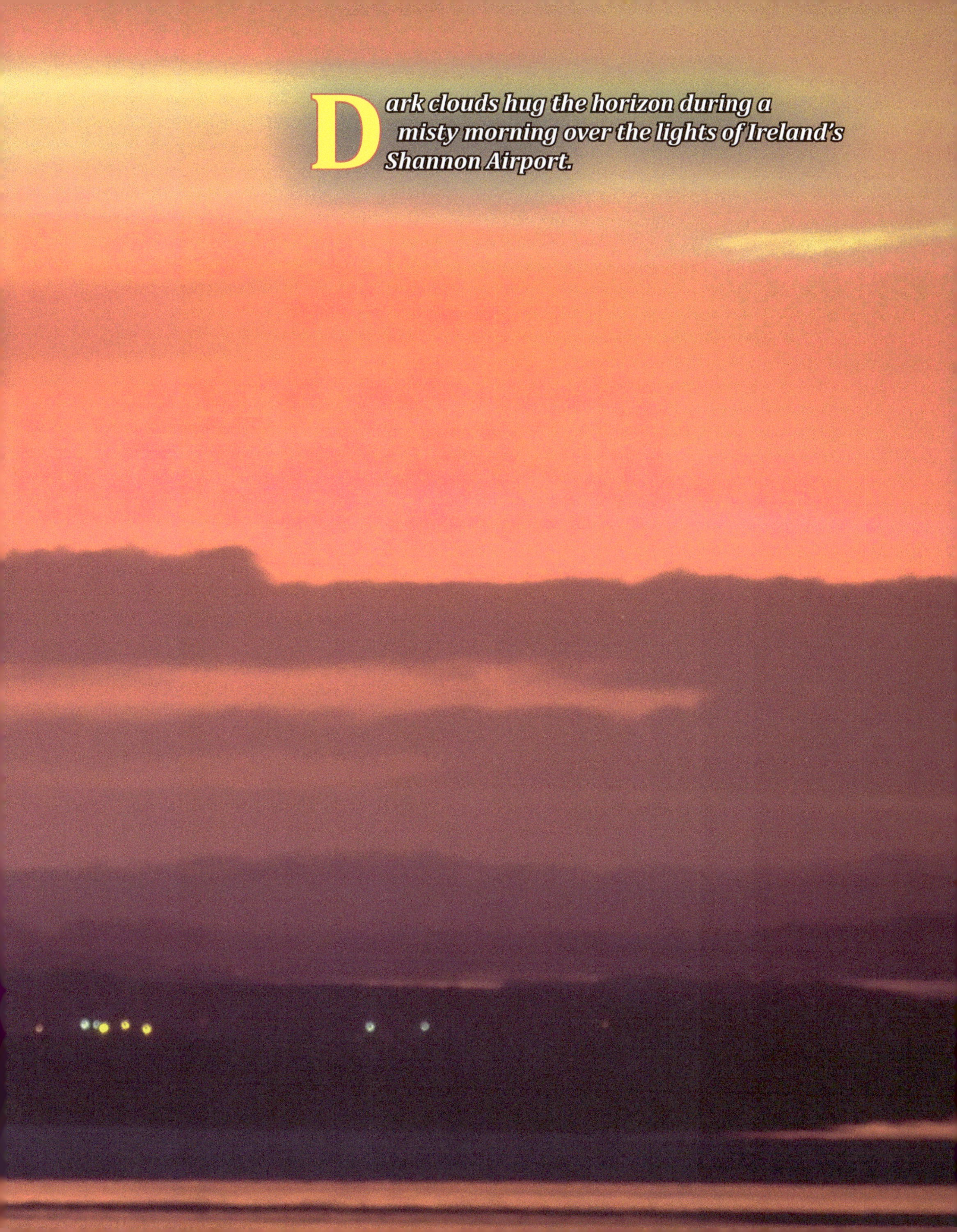

Dark clouds hug the horizon during a misty morning over the lights of Ireland's Shannon Airport.

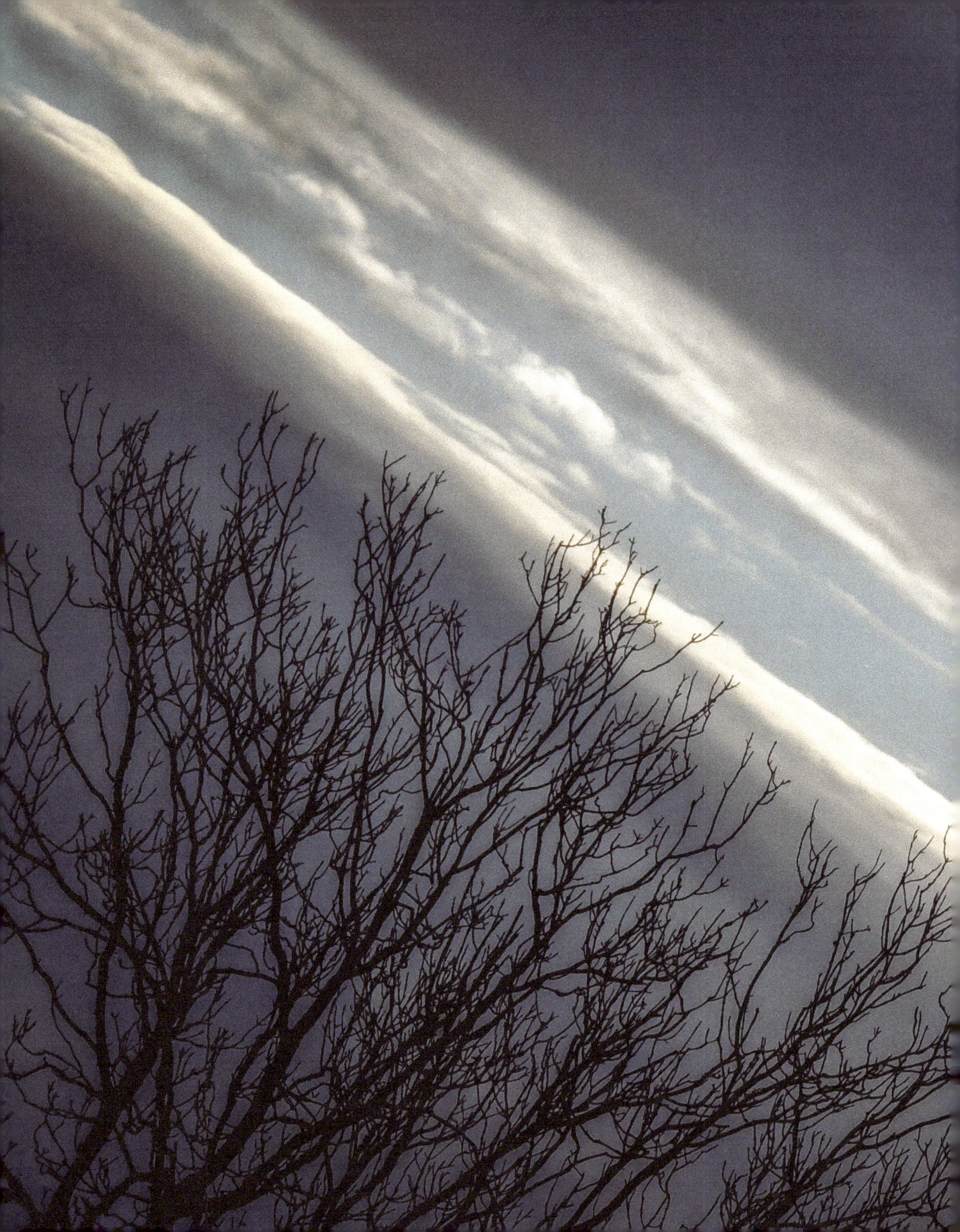

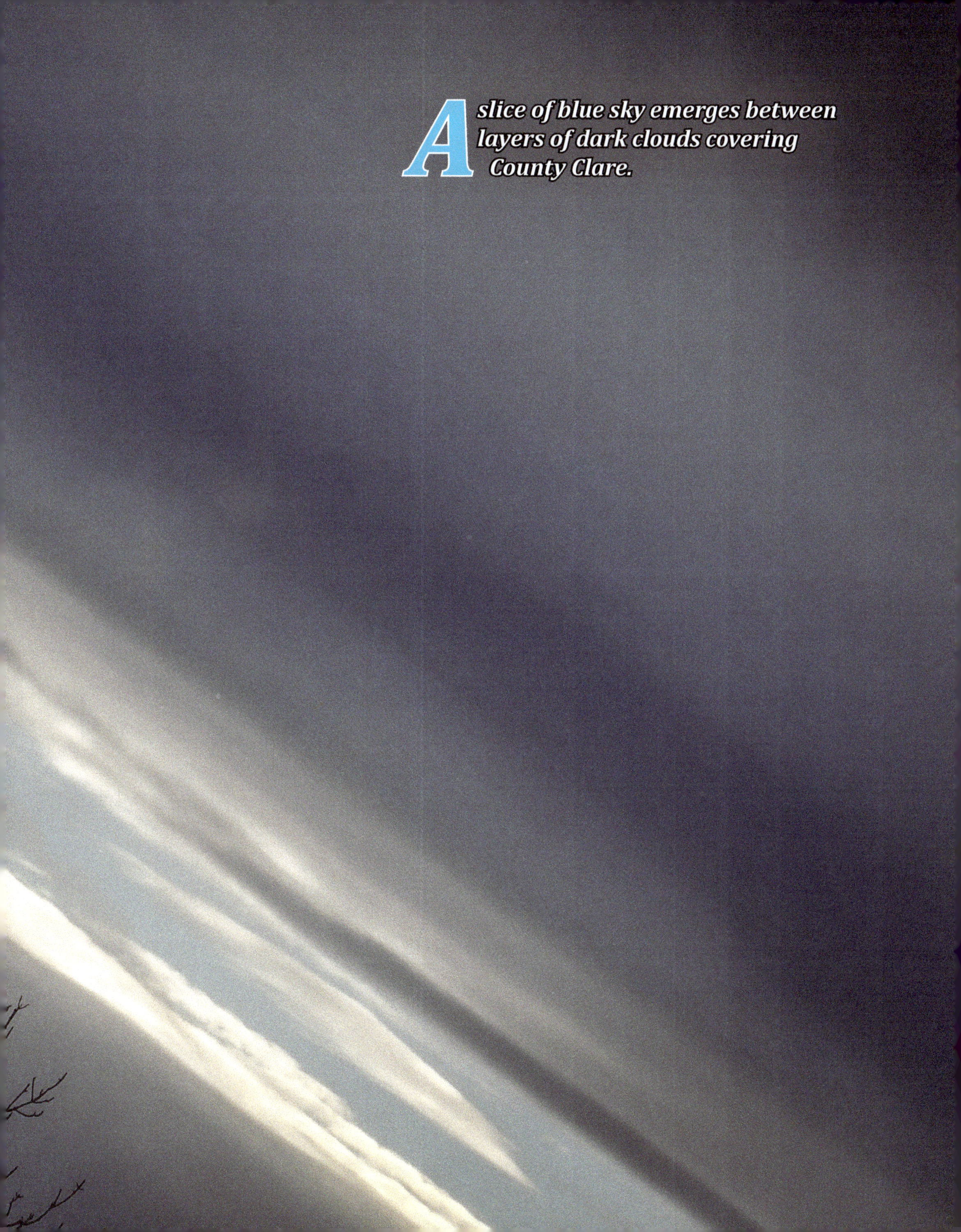

A slice of blue sky emerges between layers of dark clouds covering County Clare.

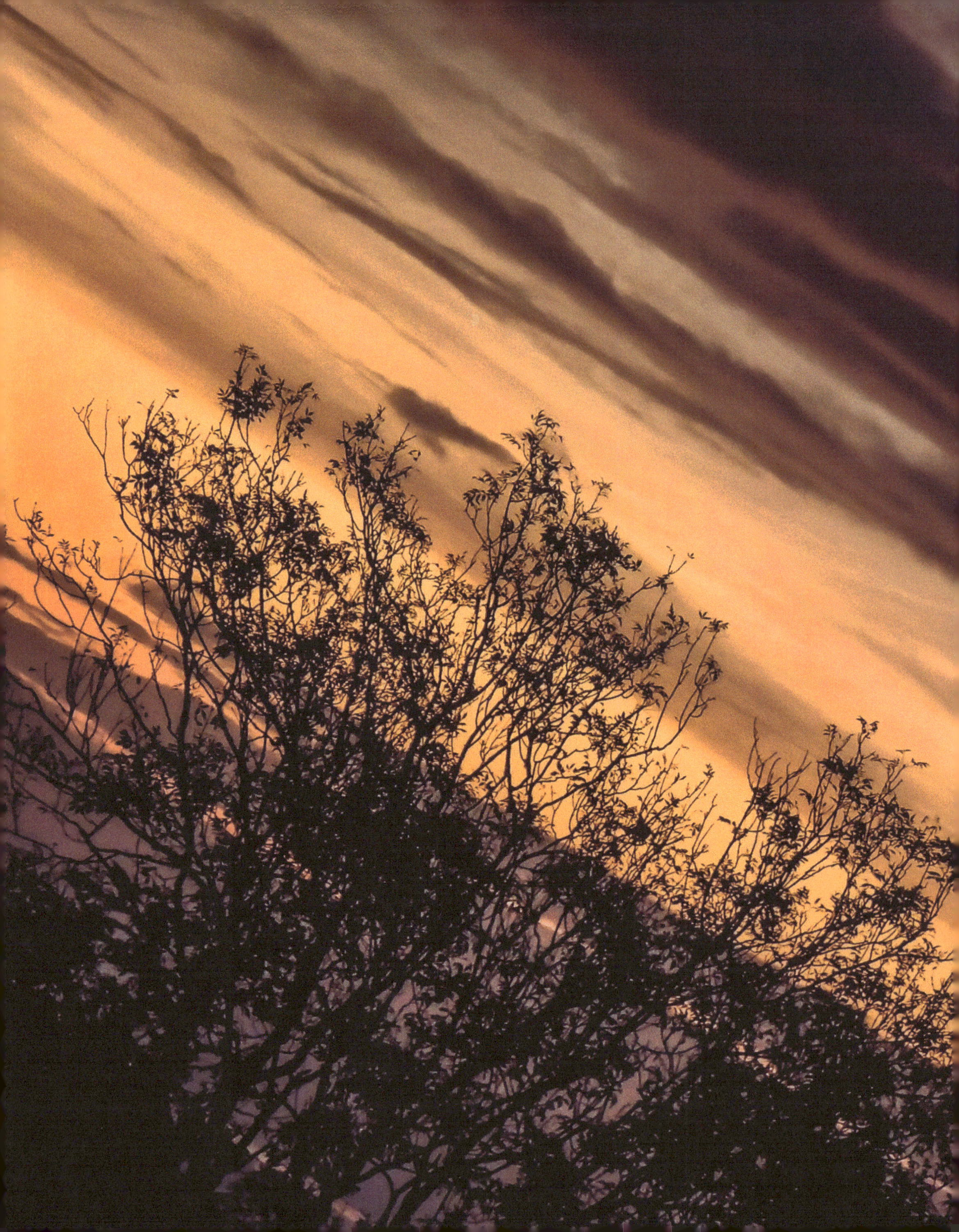

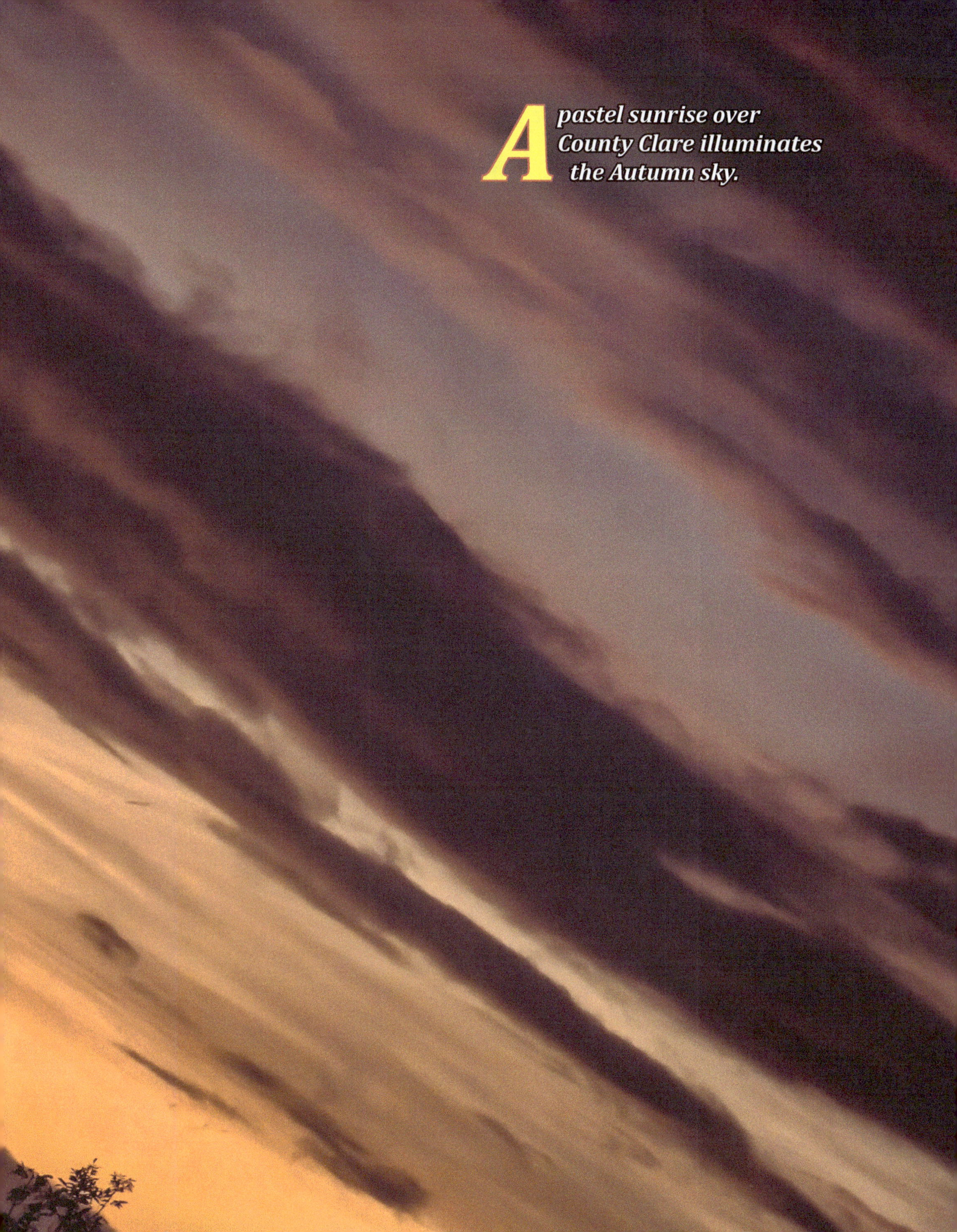

A pastel sunrise over County Clare illuminates the Autumn sky.

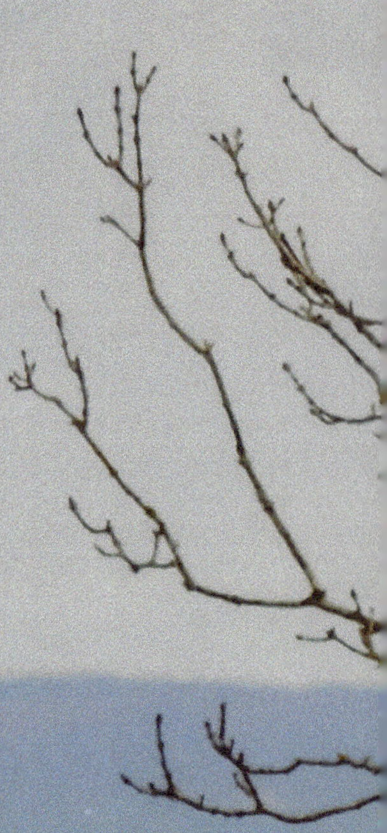

From its perch in a leafless tree in the hills above Lissycasey in County Clare, a bird surveys the River Fergus just before the waters enter the Shannon Estuary and travel out to the Atlantic Ocean.

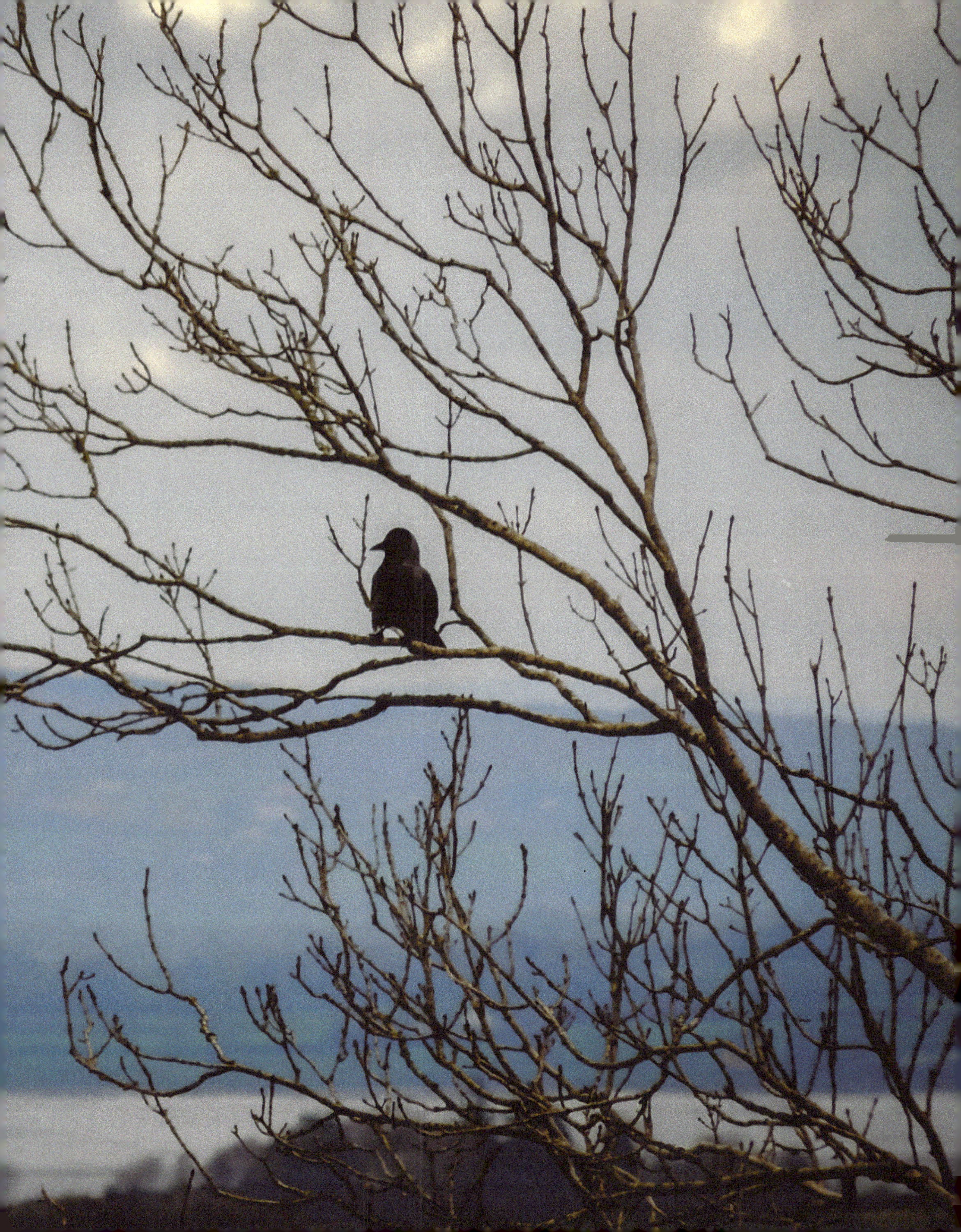

Here's a splendid example of the mercurial nature of Irish weather, as a late winter hail storm blows in from the Atlantic to obscure sunny blue skies over County Clare and the Shannon Estuary.

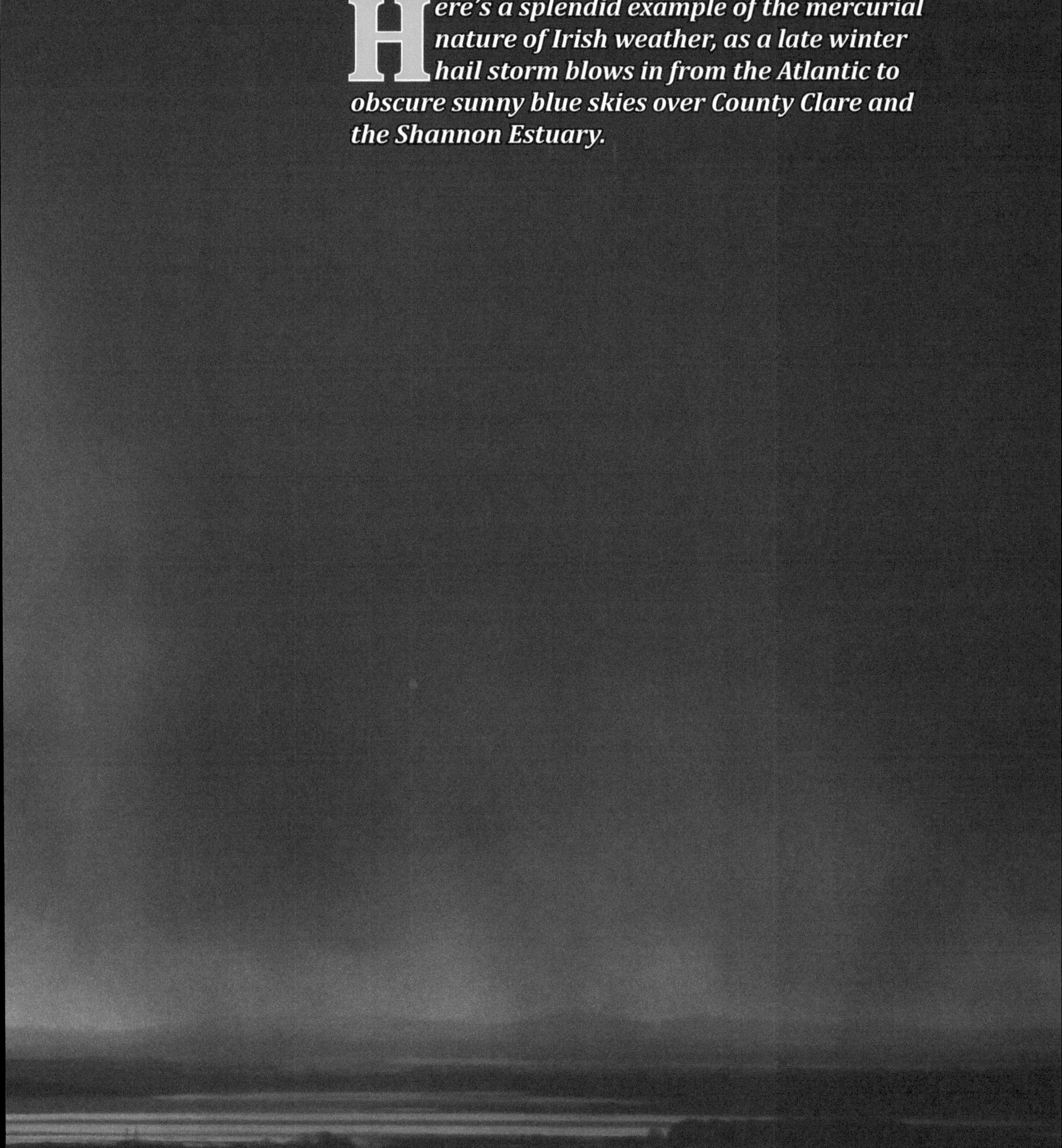

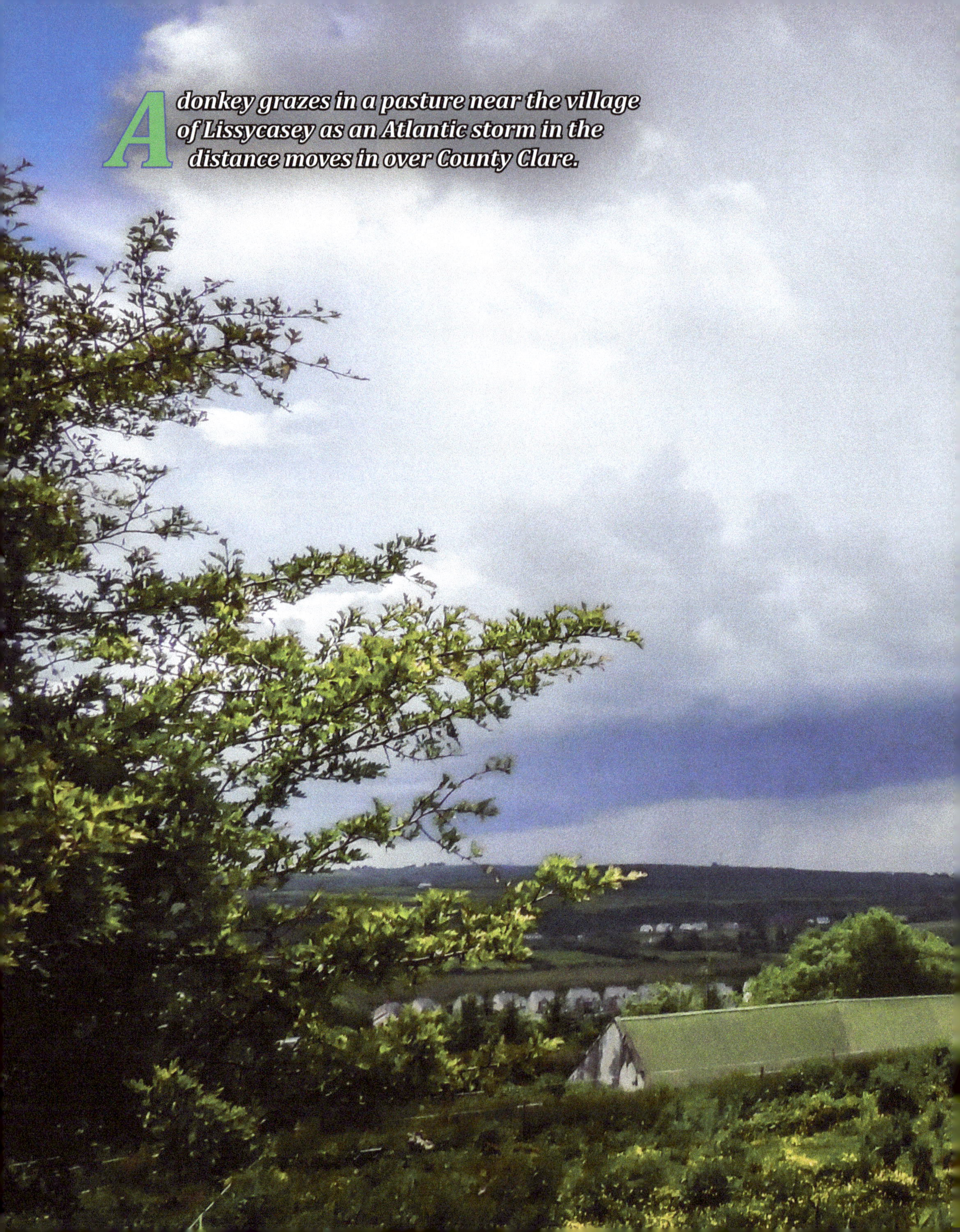

A donkey grazes in a pasture near the village of Lissycasey as an Atlantic storm in the distance moves in over County Clare.

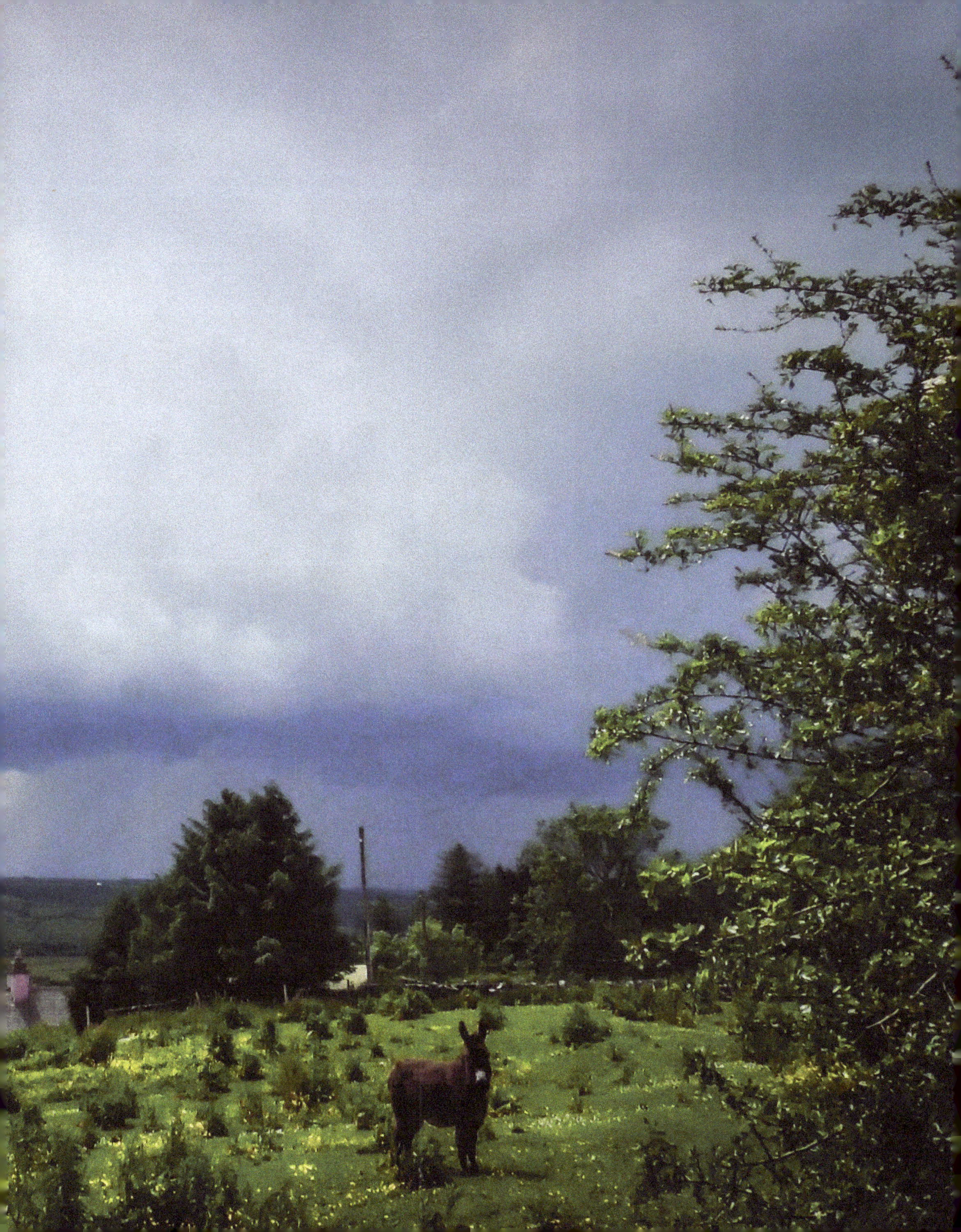

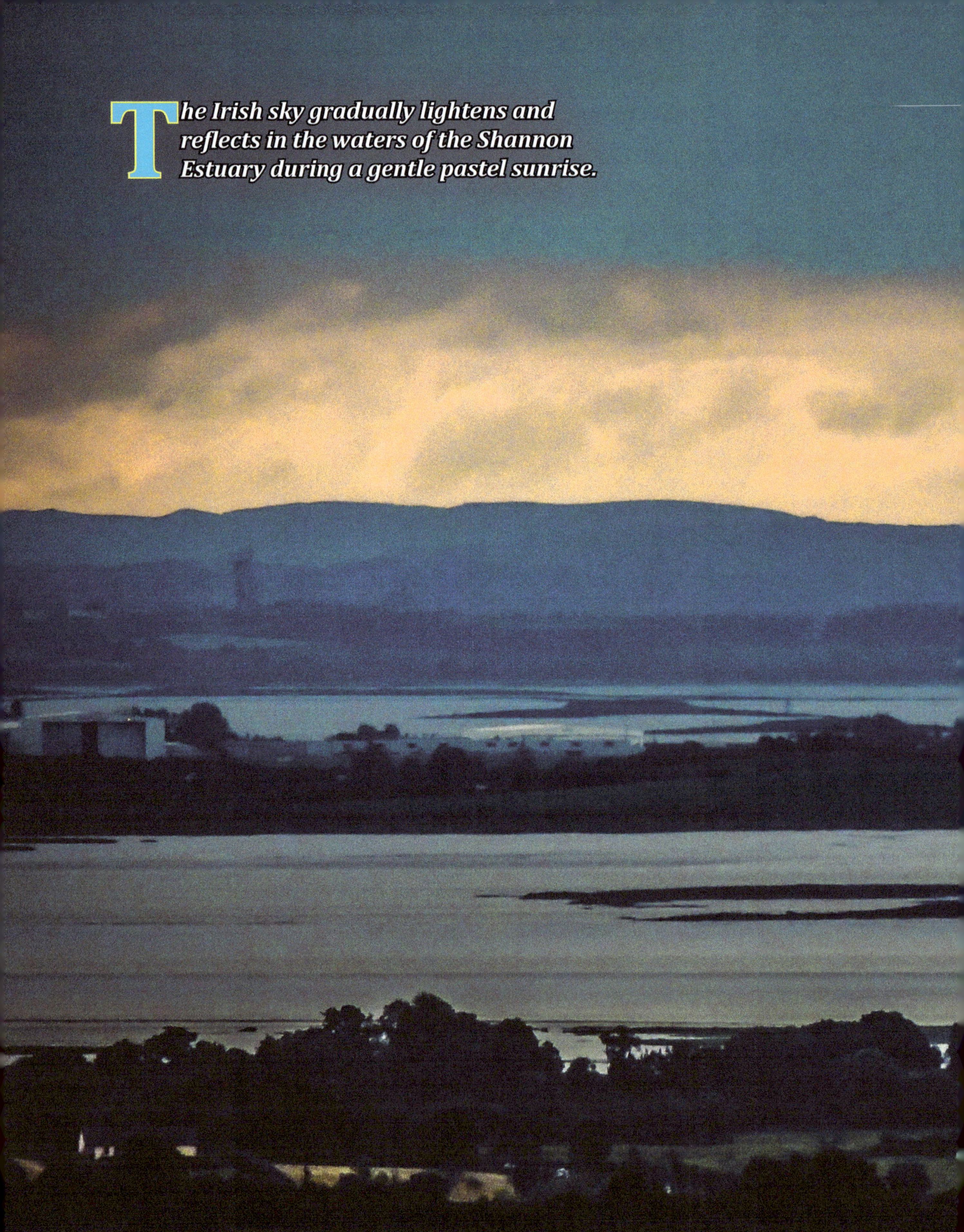

The Irish sky gradually lightens and reflects in the waters of the Shannon Estuary during a gentle pastel sunrise.

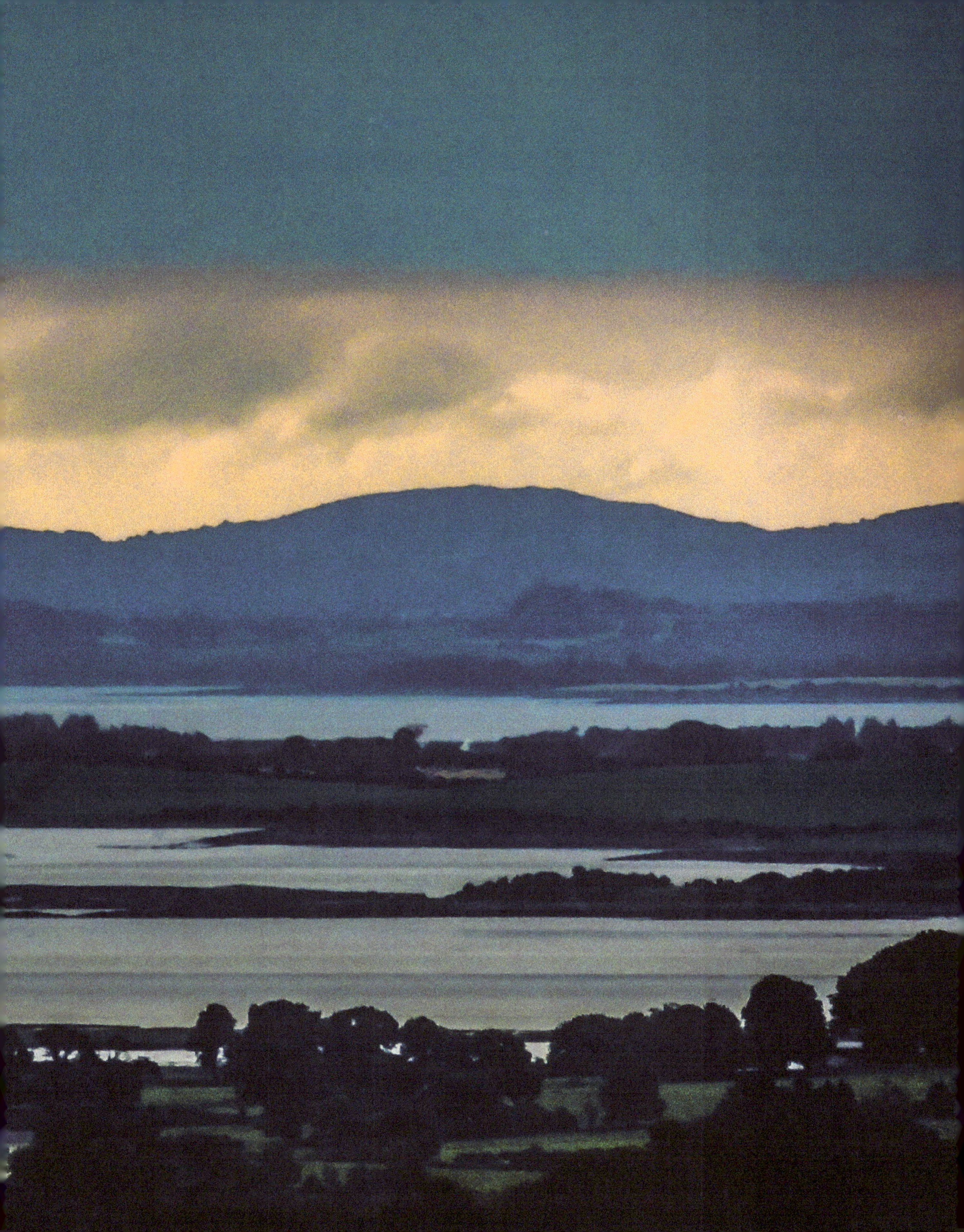

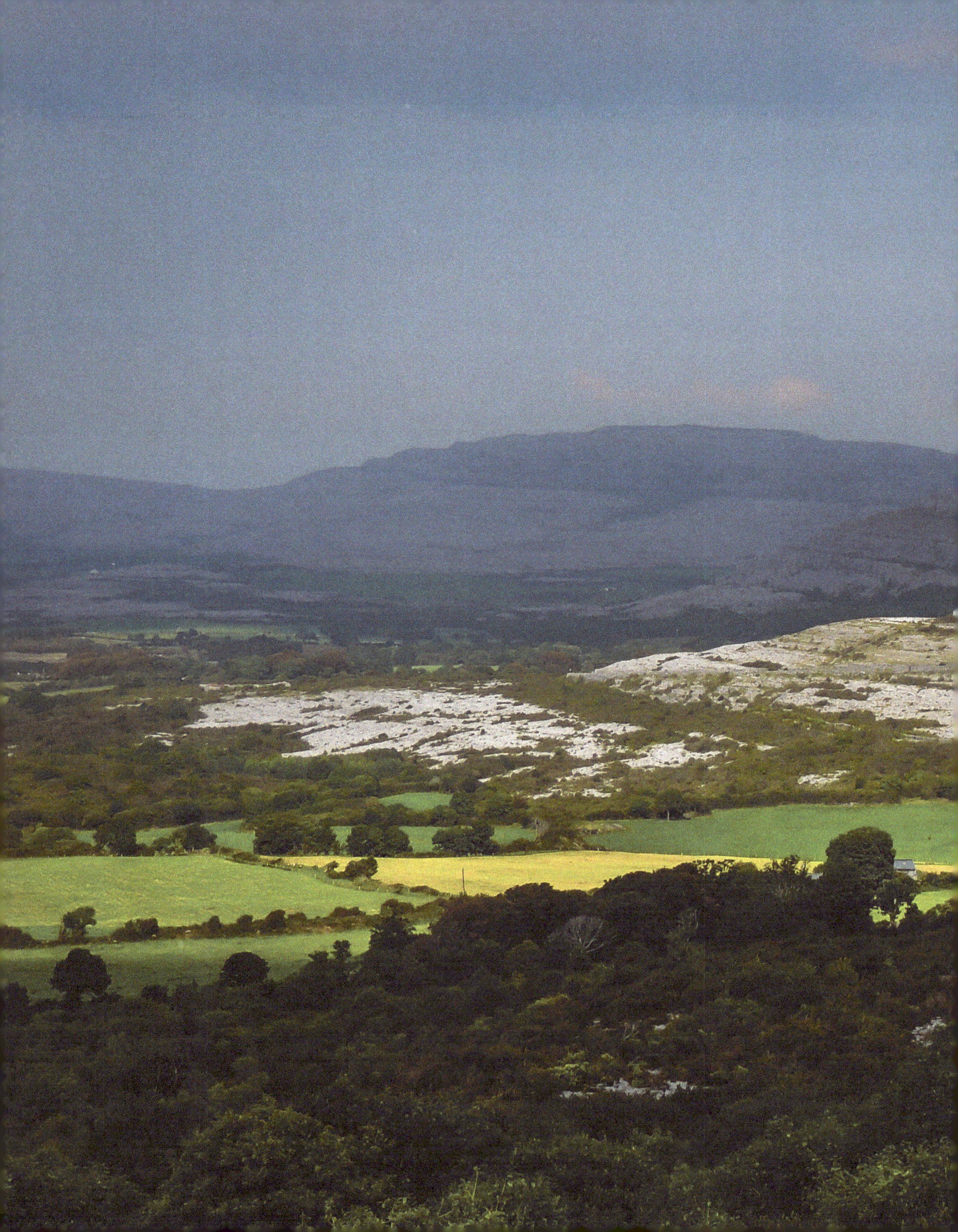

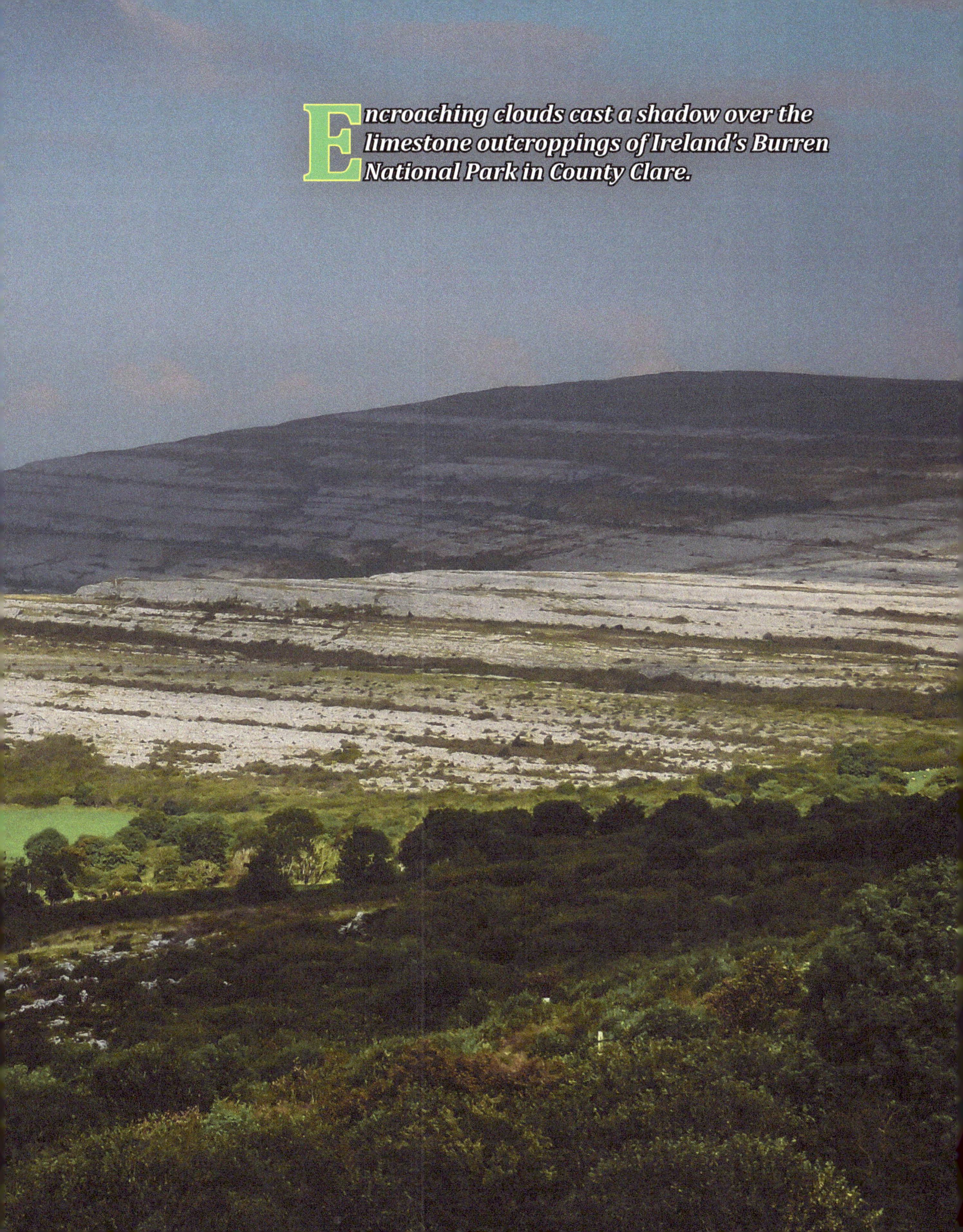

Encroaching clouds cast a shadow over the limestone outcroppings of Ireland's Burren National Park in County Clare.

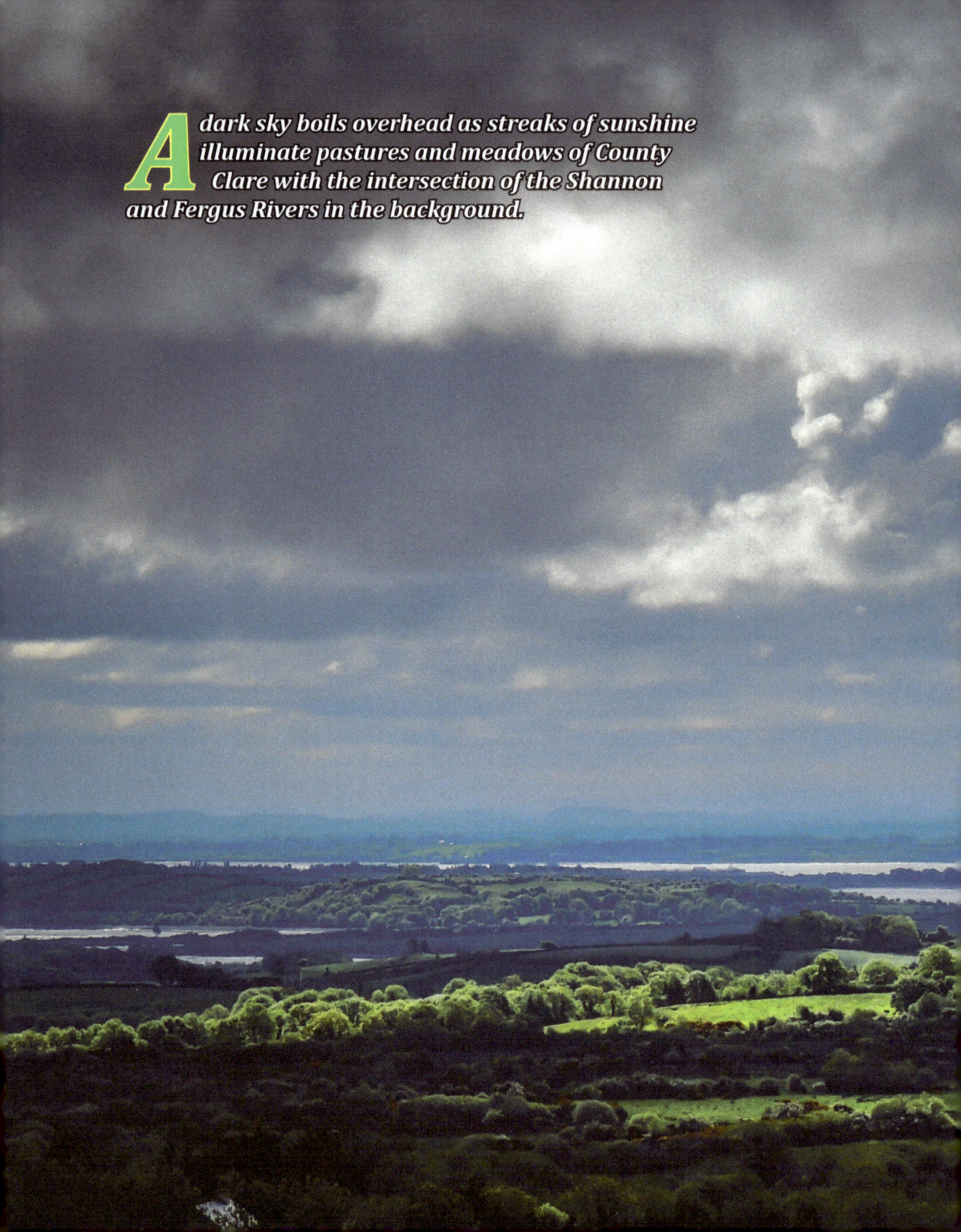
A dark sky boils overhead as streaks of sunshine illuminate pastures and meadows of County Clare with the intersection of the Shannon and Fergus Rivers in the background.

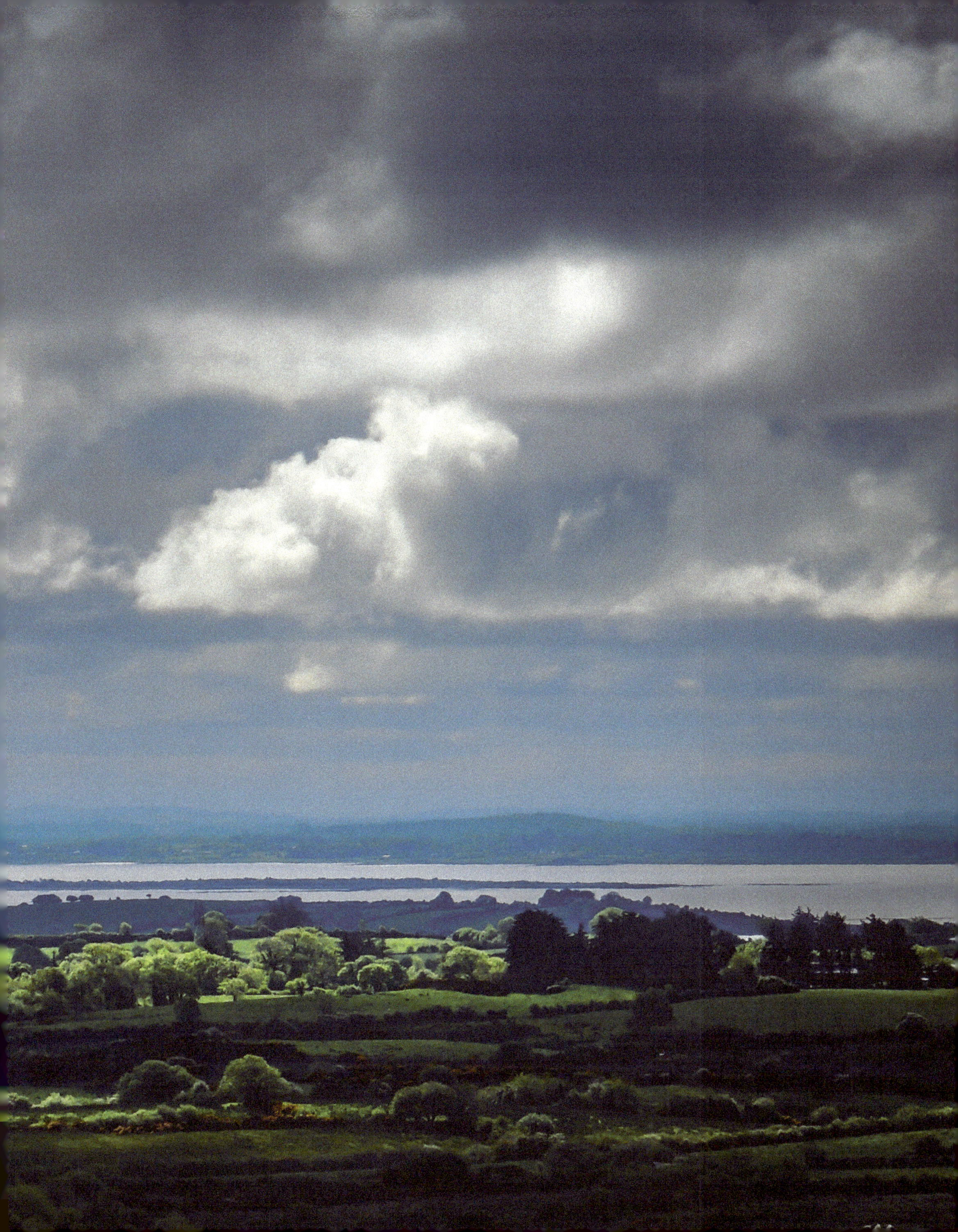

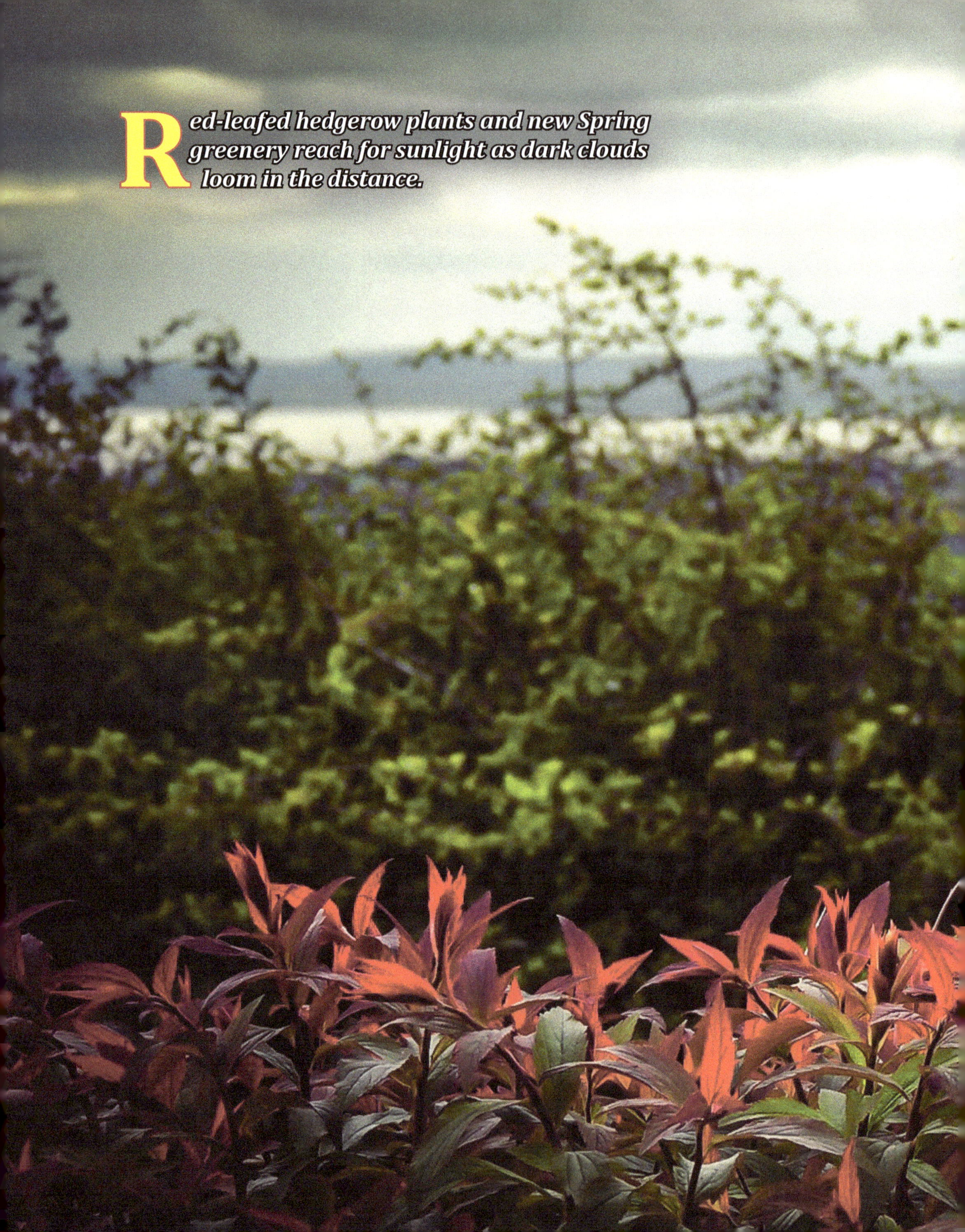
Red-leafed hedgerow plants and new Spring greenery reach for sunlight as dark clouds loom in the distance.

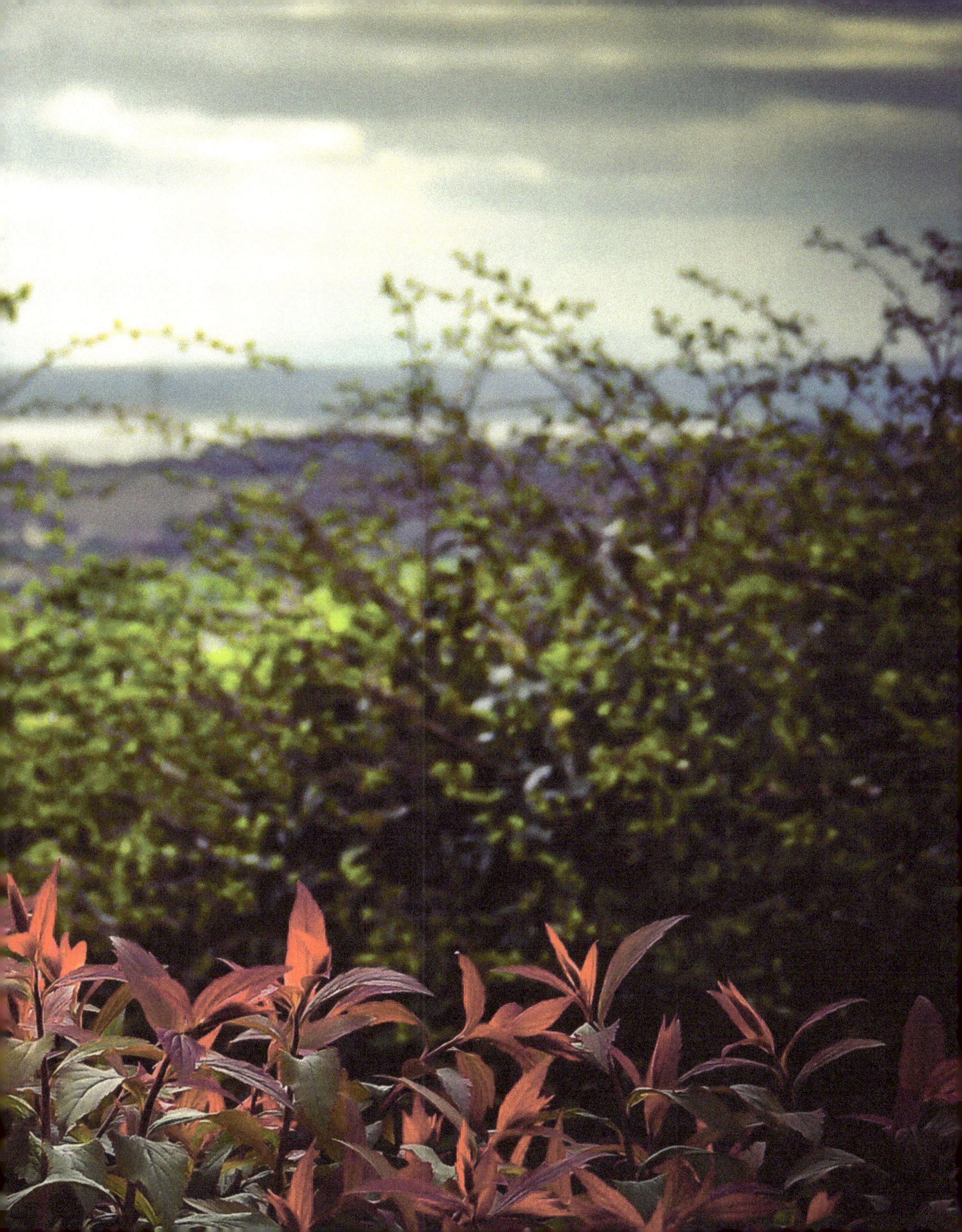

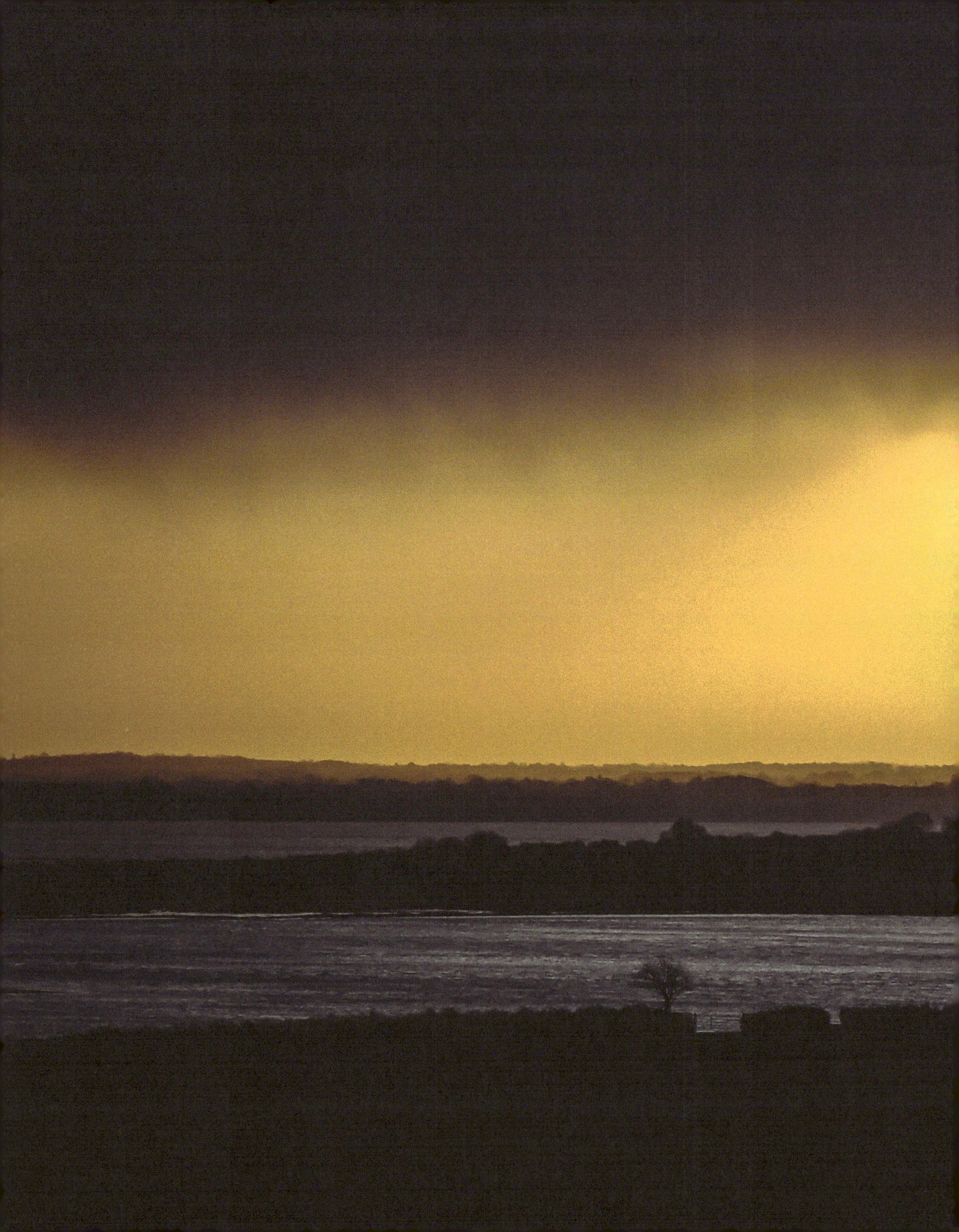

One of Ireland's intense Winter storms sweeps in at sunrise over the Shannon Estuary where it divides counties Clare and Limerick.

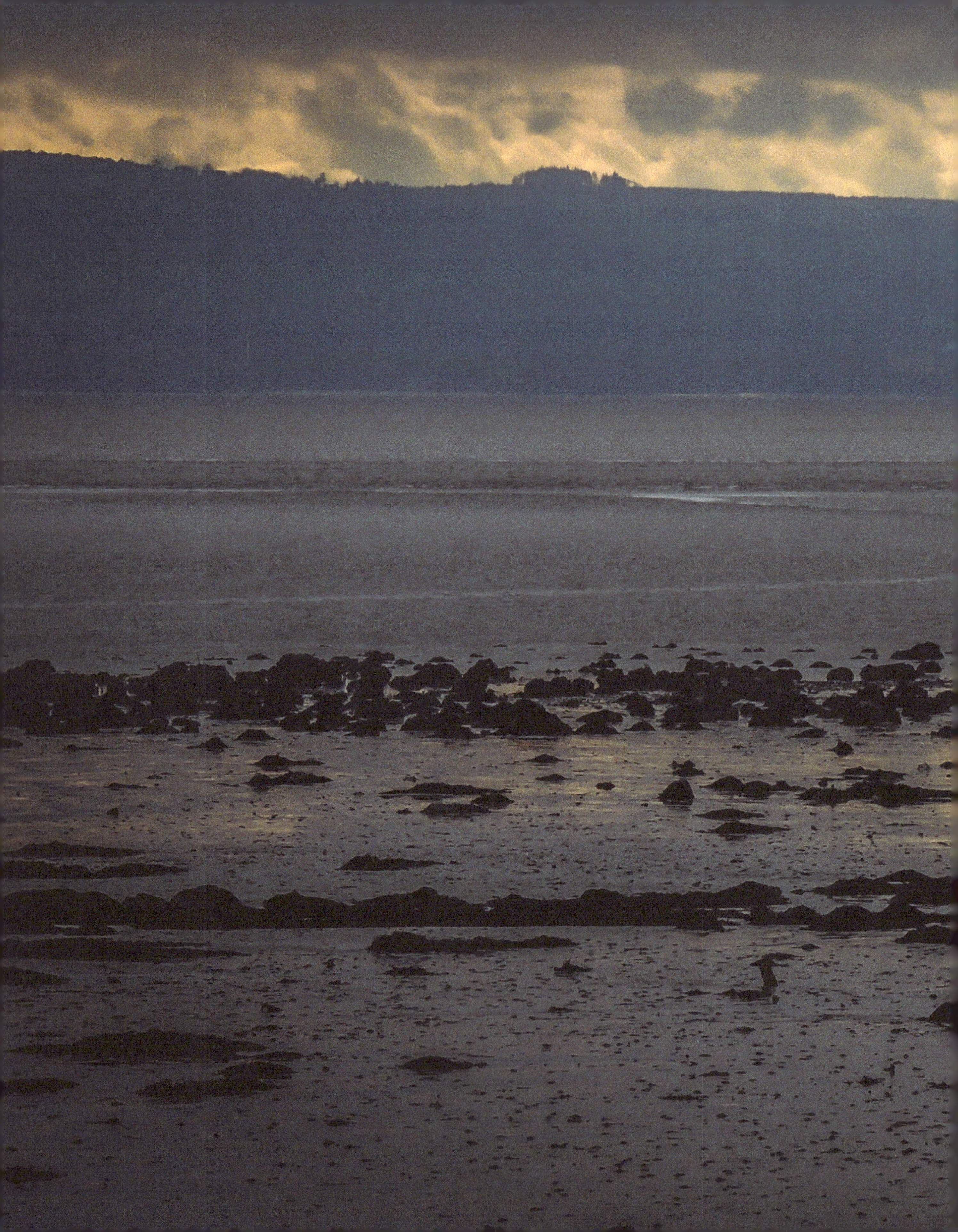

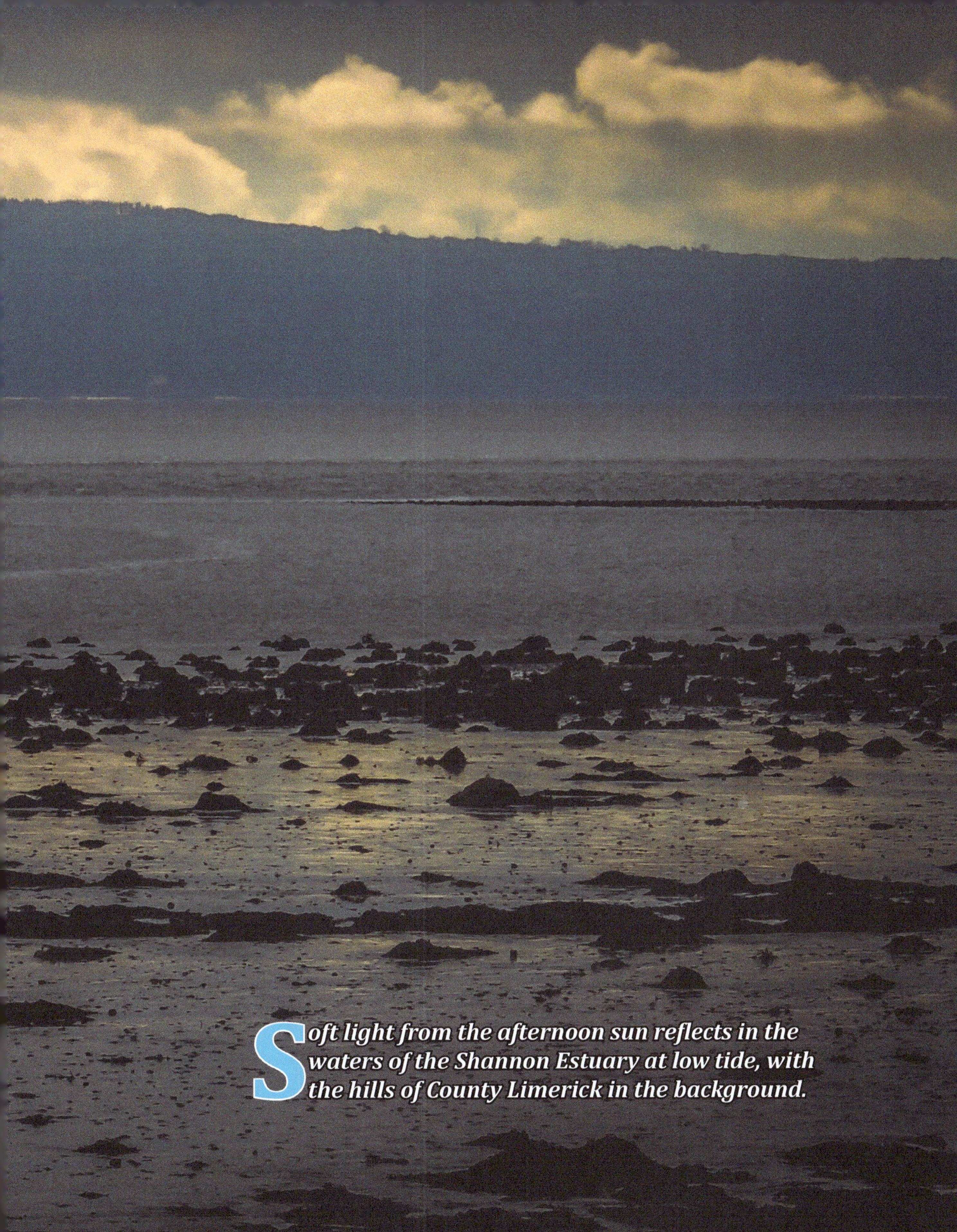

Soft light from the afternoon sun reflects in the waters of the Shannon Estuary at low tide, with the hills of County Limerick in the background.

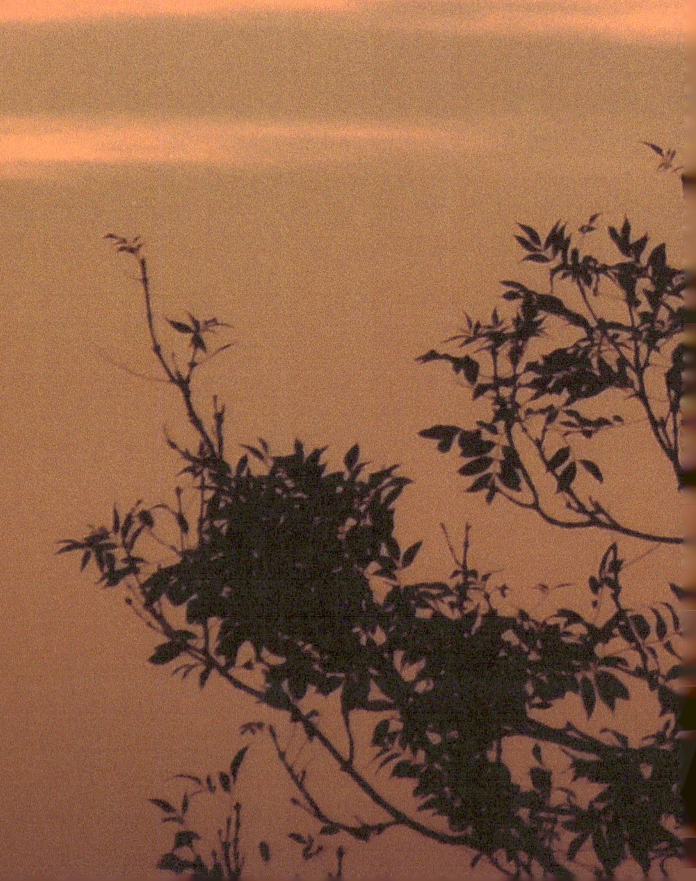

A pink and orange Autumn sky coaxes this tree to shed its old leaves and prepare for winter in County Clare.

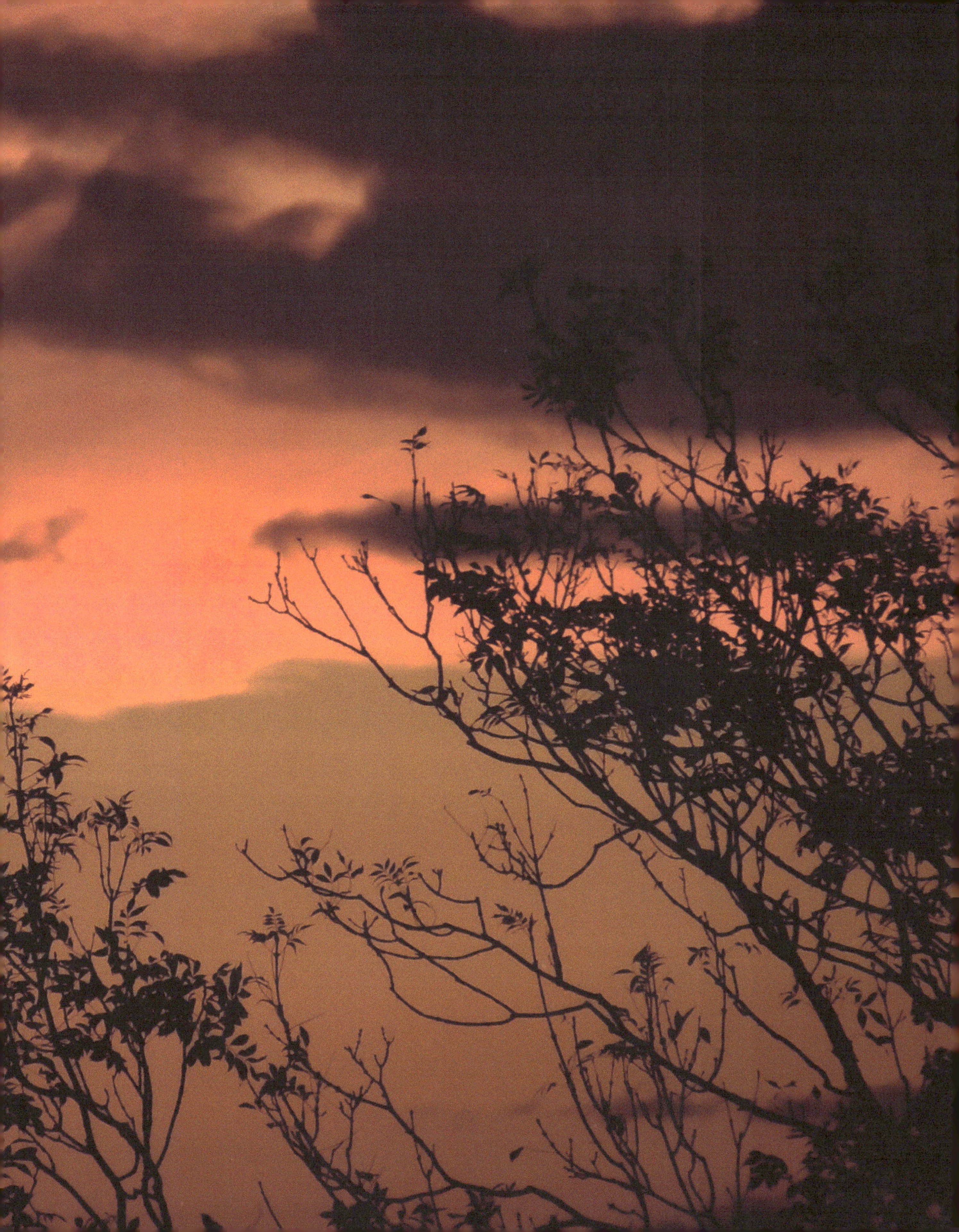

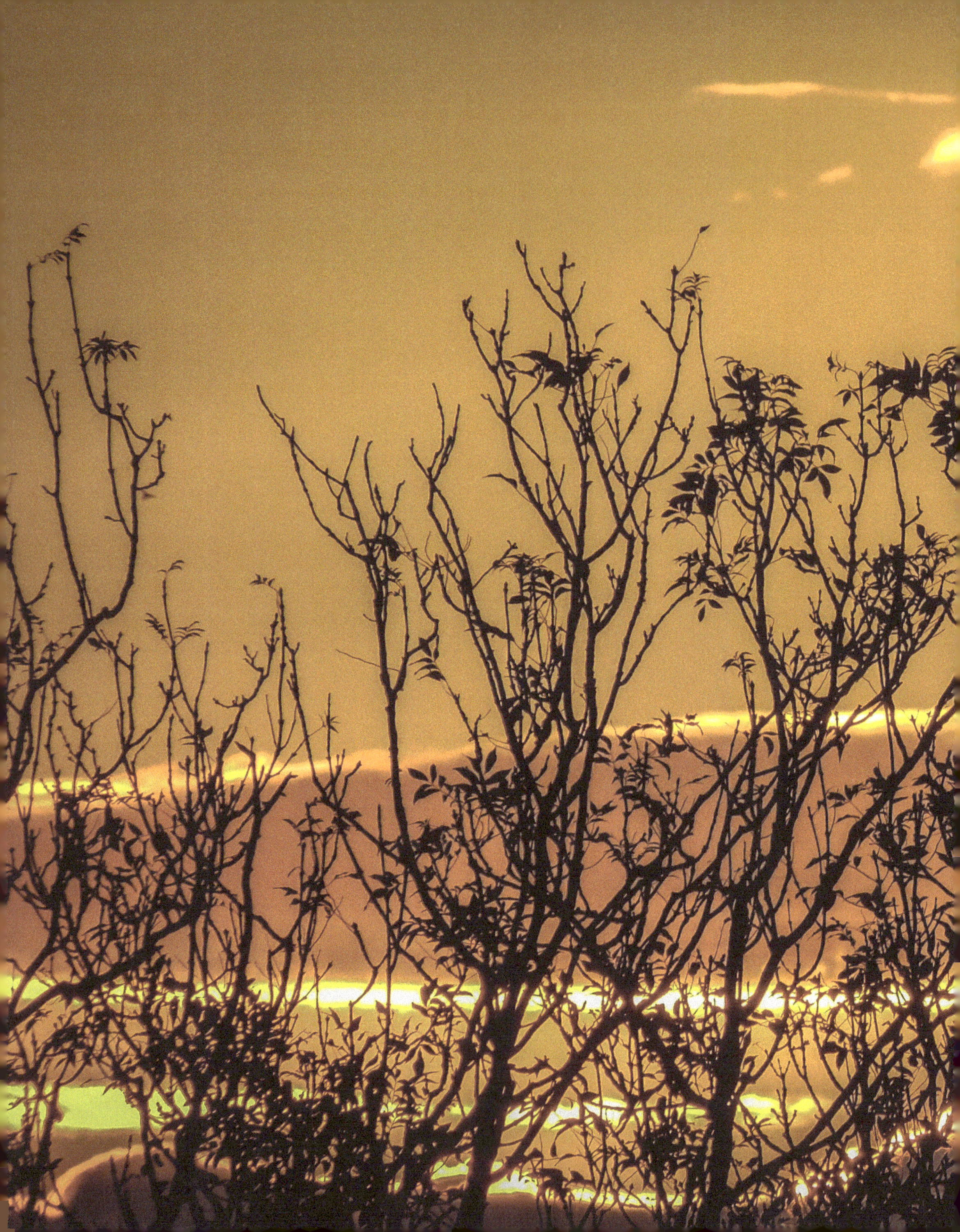

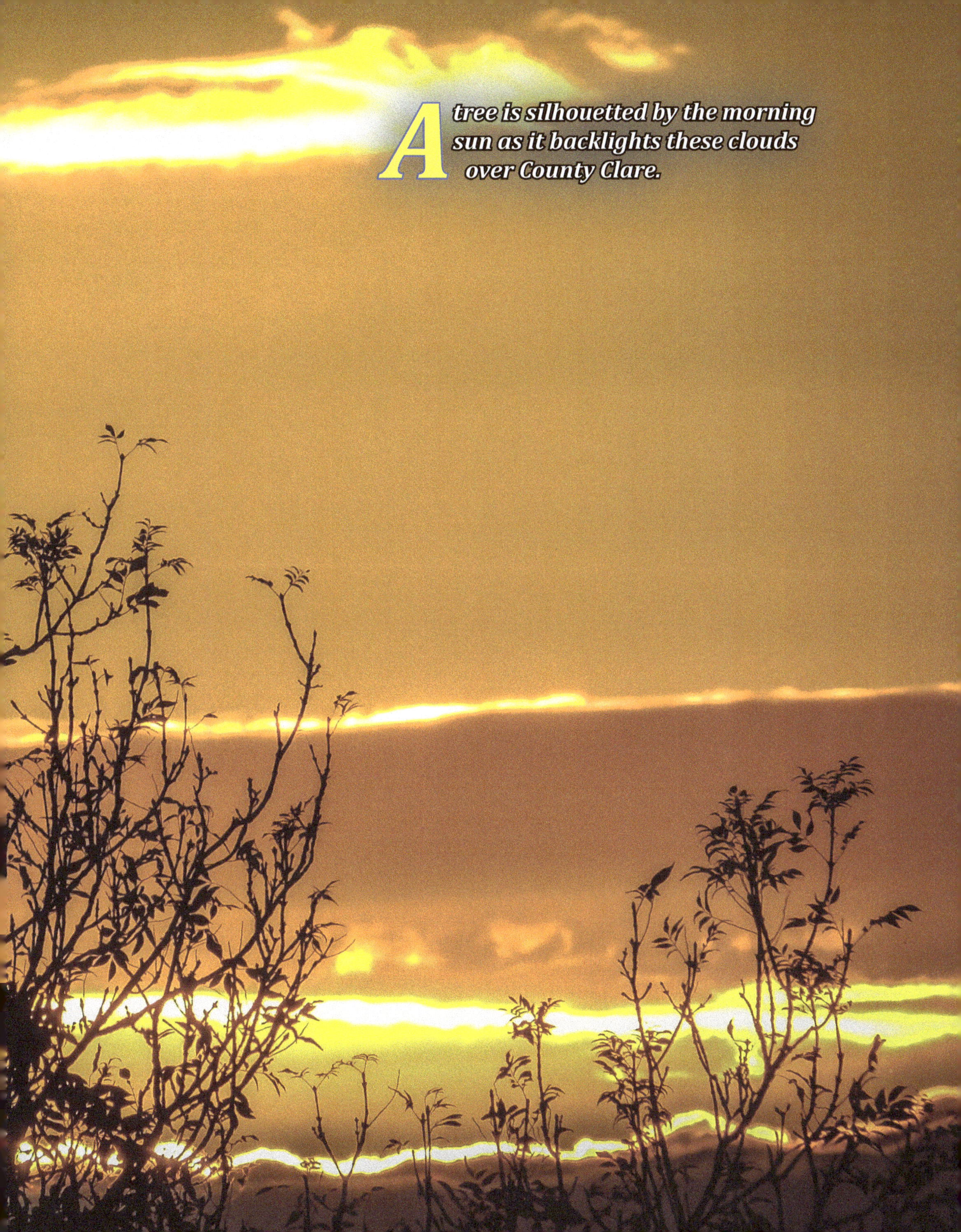
A tree is silhouetted by the morning sun as it backlights these clouds over County Clare.

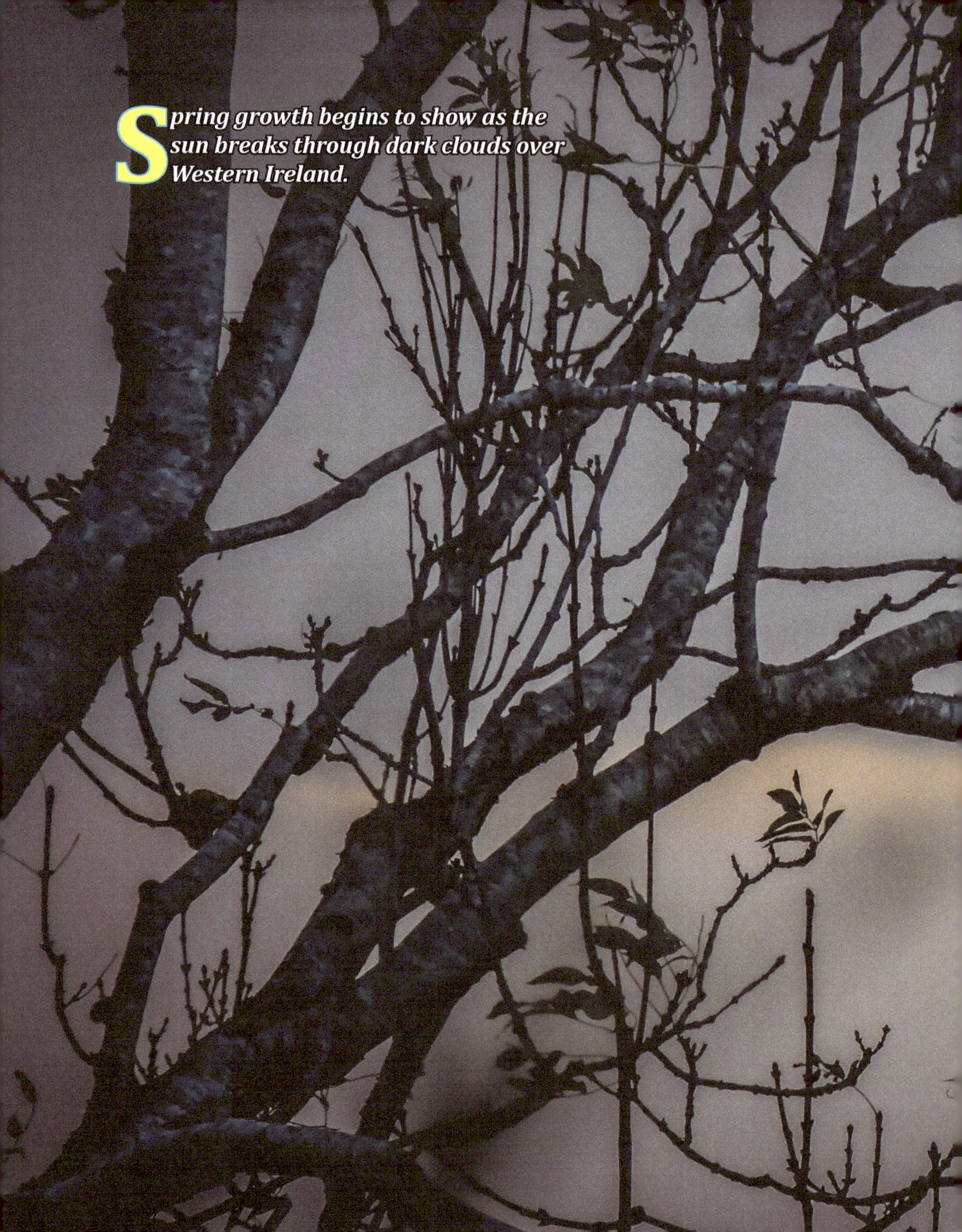

Spring growth begins to show as the sun breaks through dark clouds over Western Ireland.

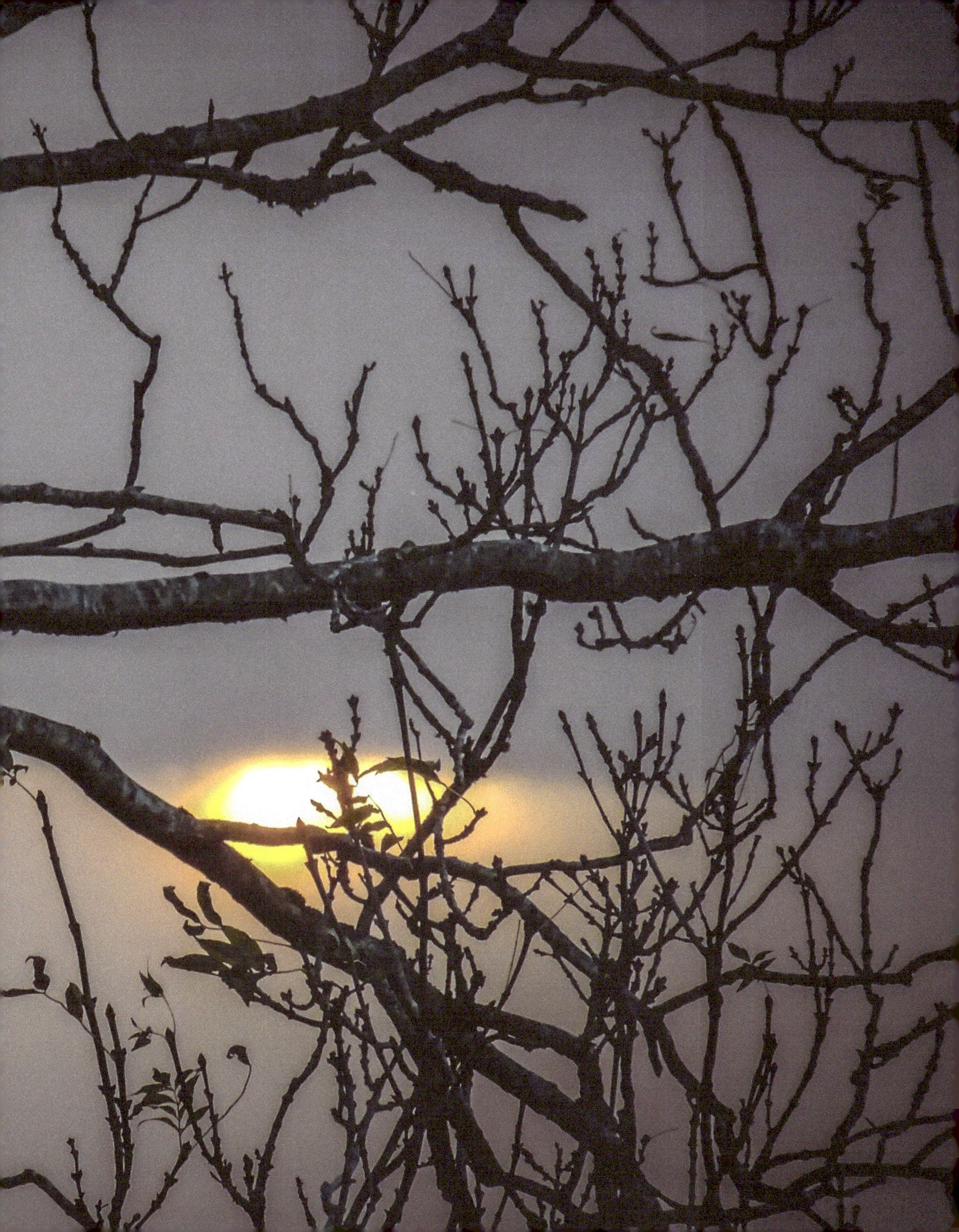

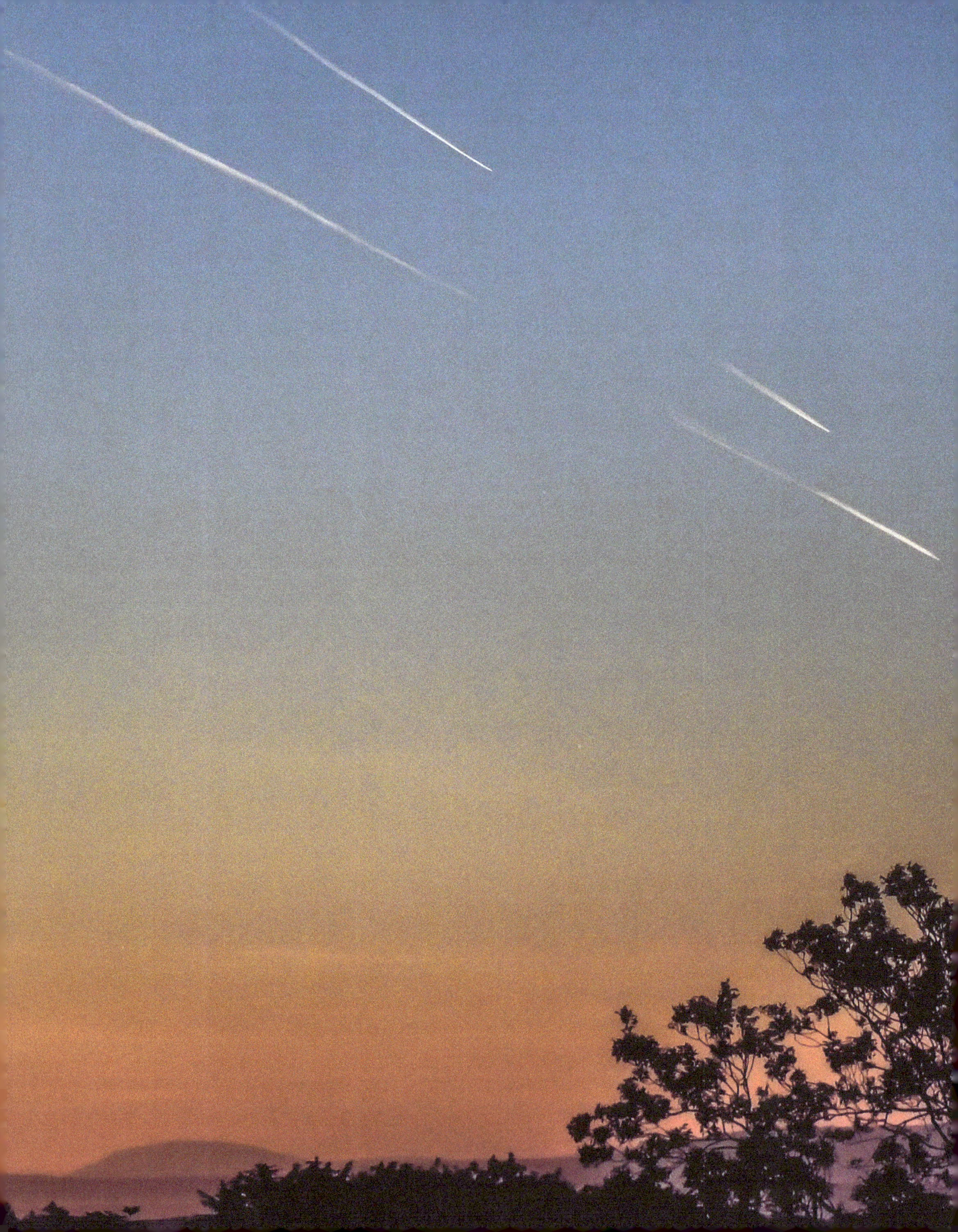

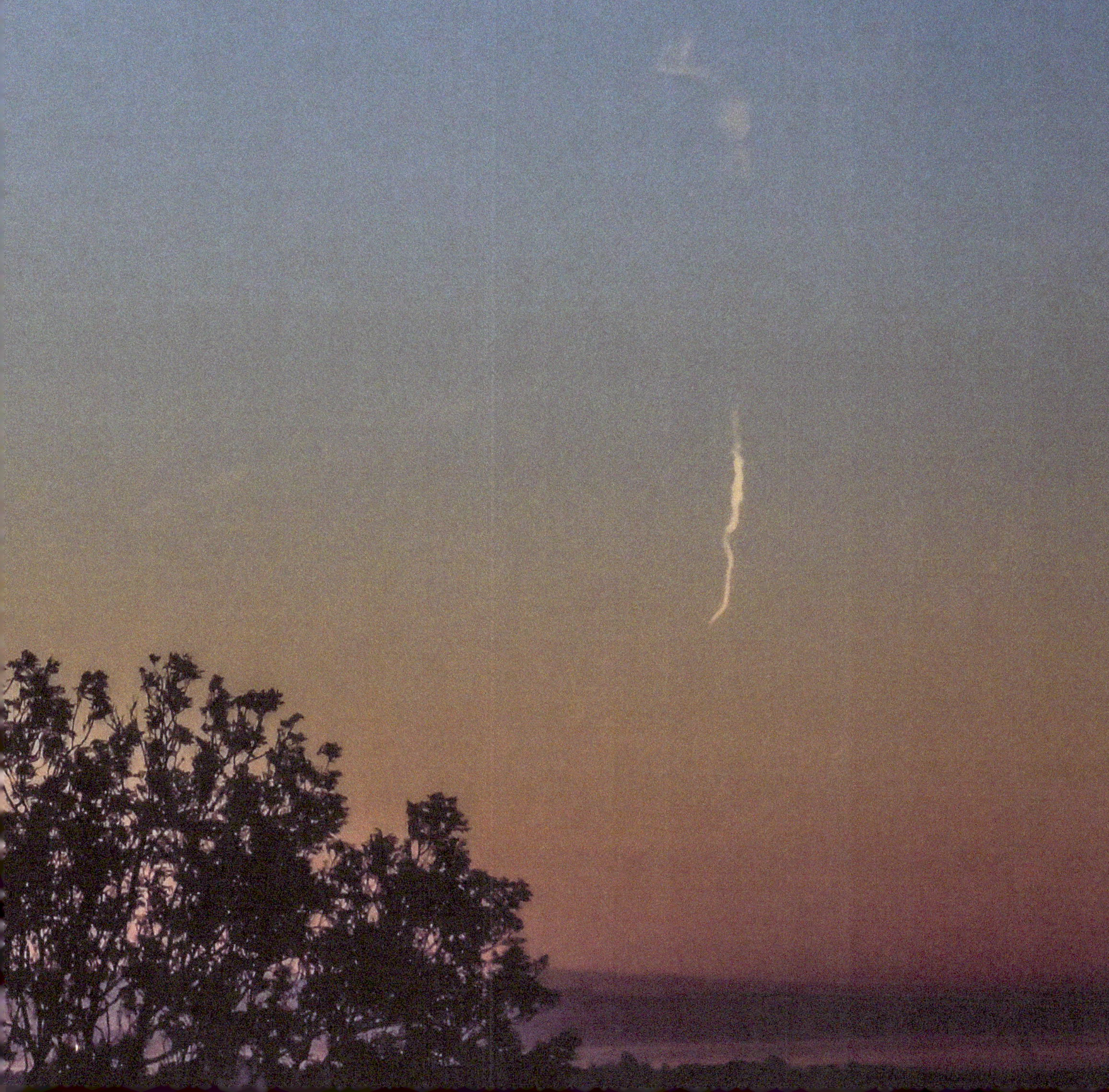

Trails from eastbound jets streak the
morning sky over Western Ireland as
an orange glow on the horizon signals
the rising sun.

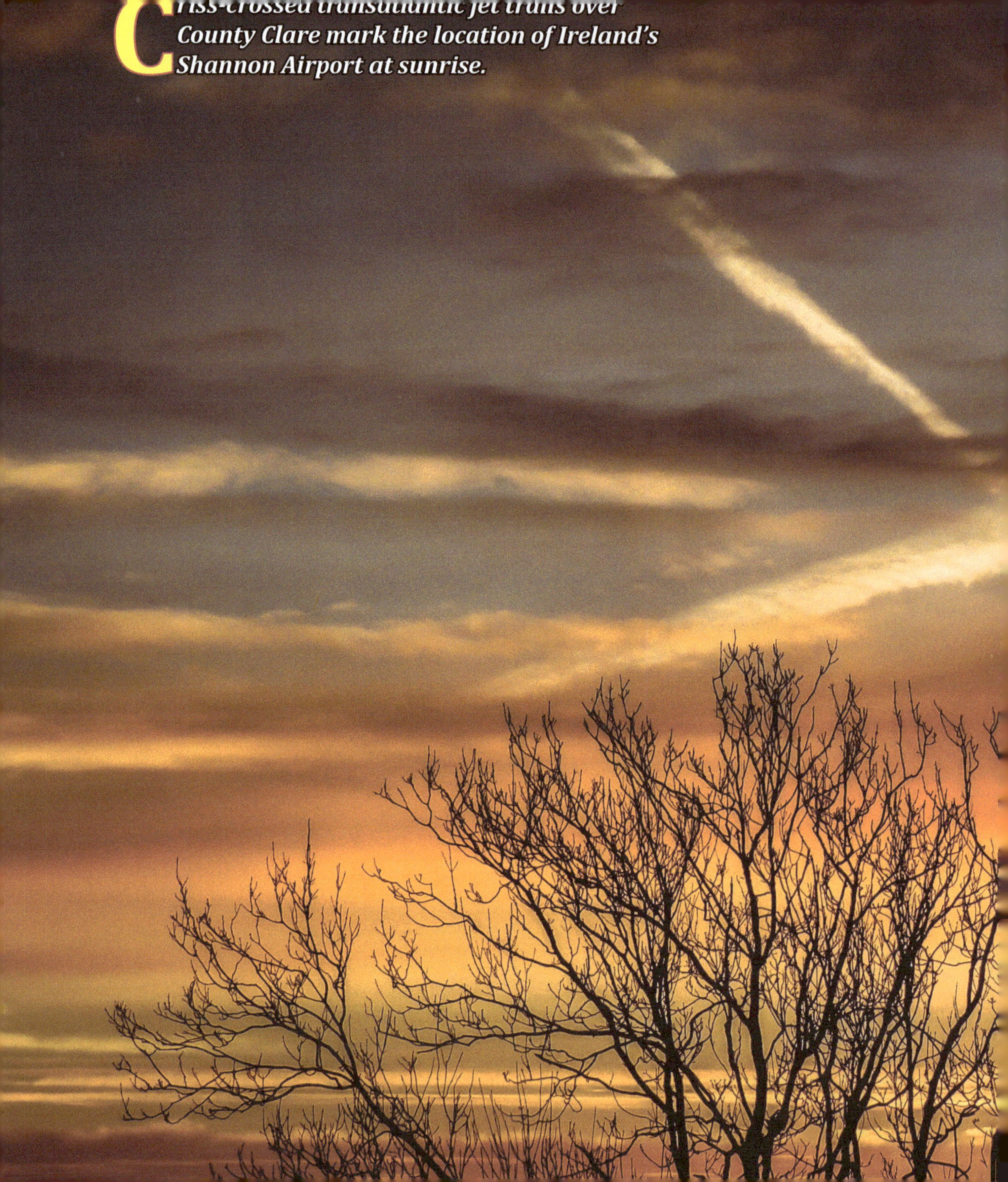
Criss-crossed transatlantic jet trails over County Clare mark the location of Ireland's Shannon Airport at sunrise.

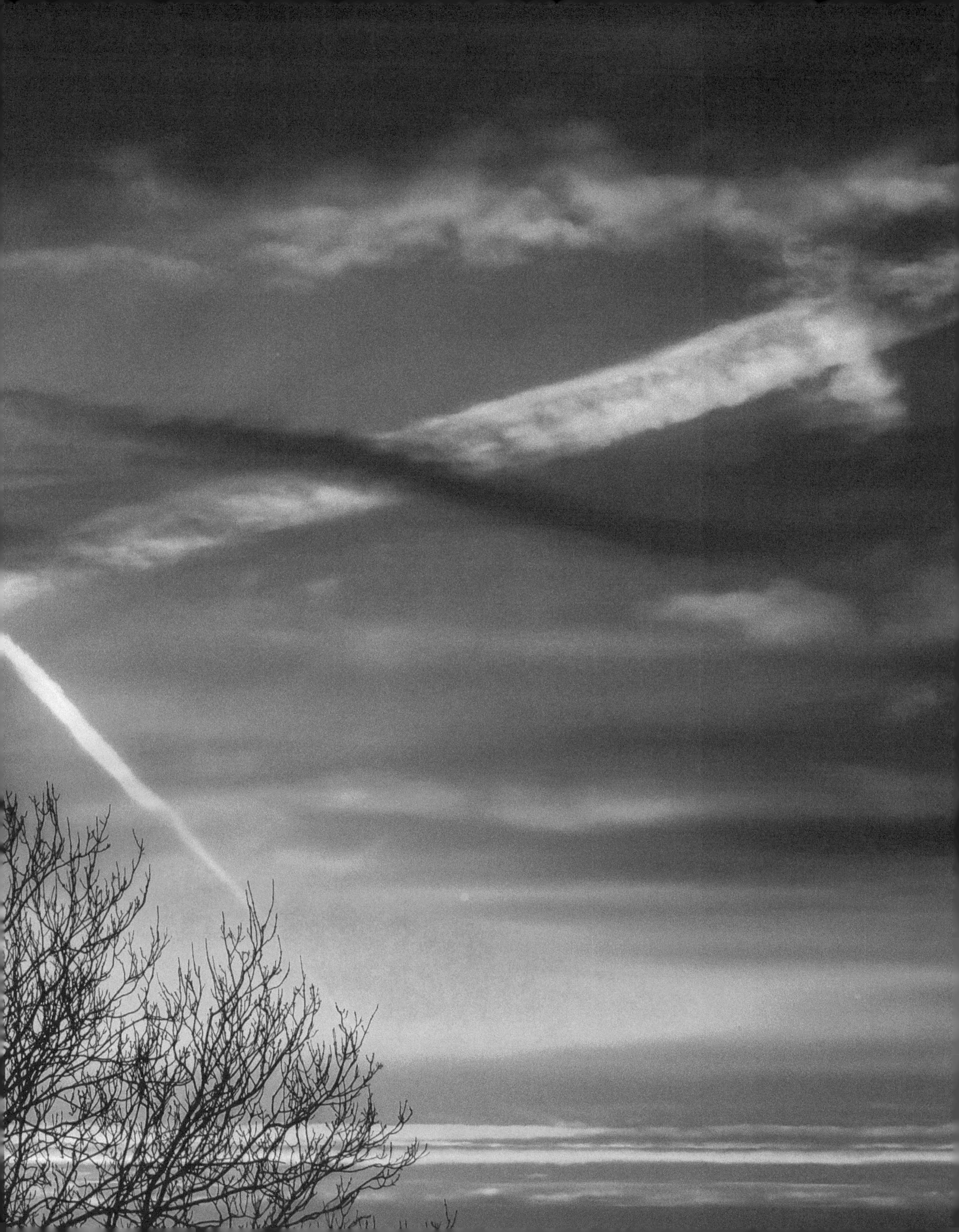

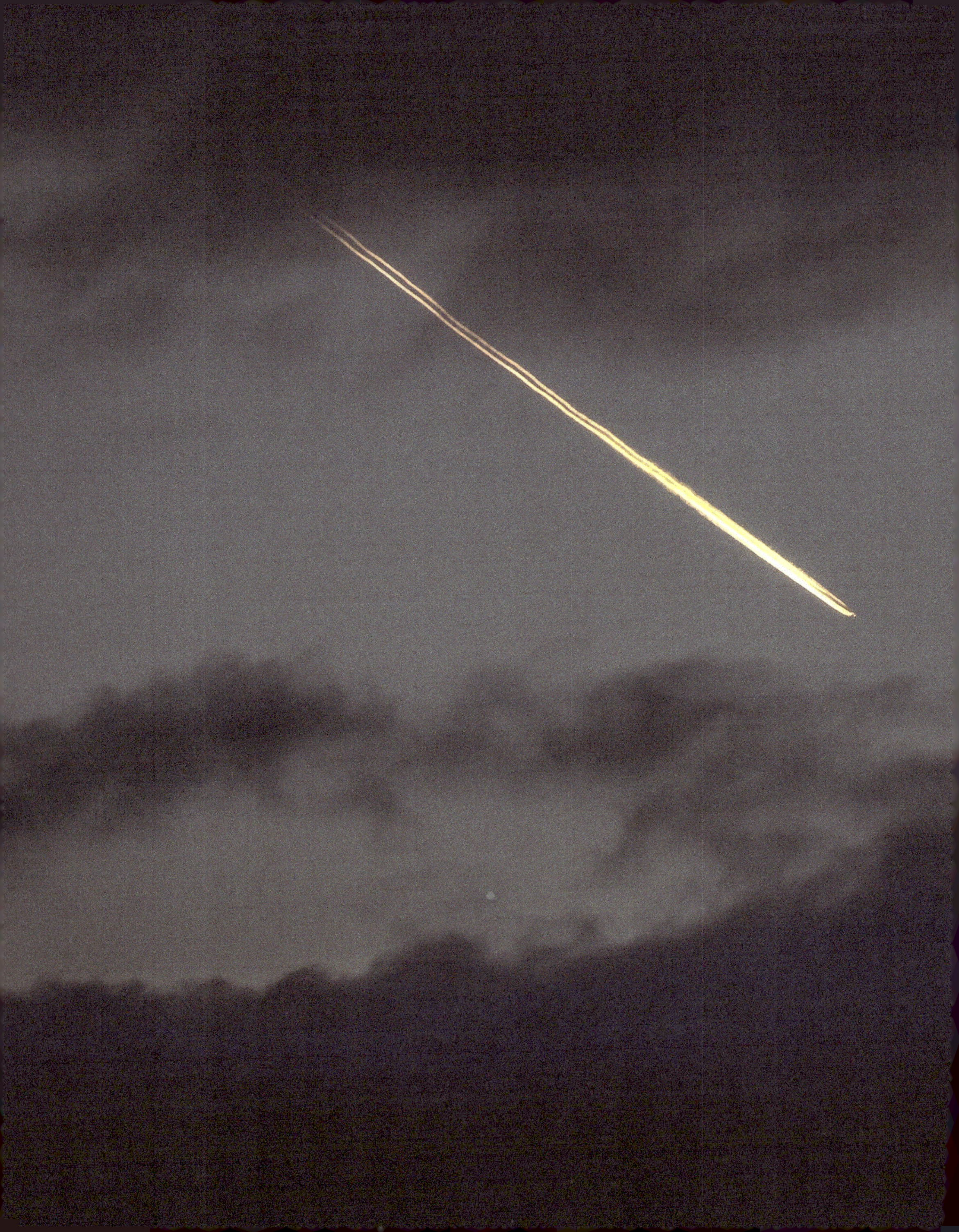

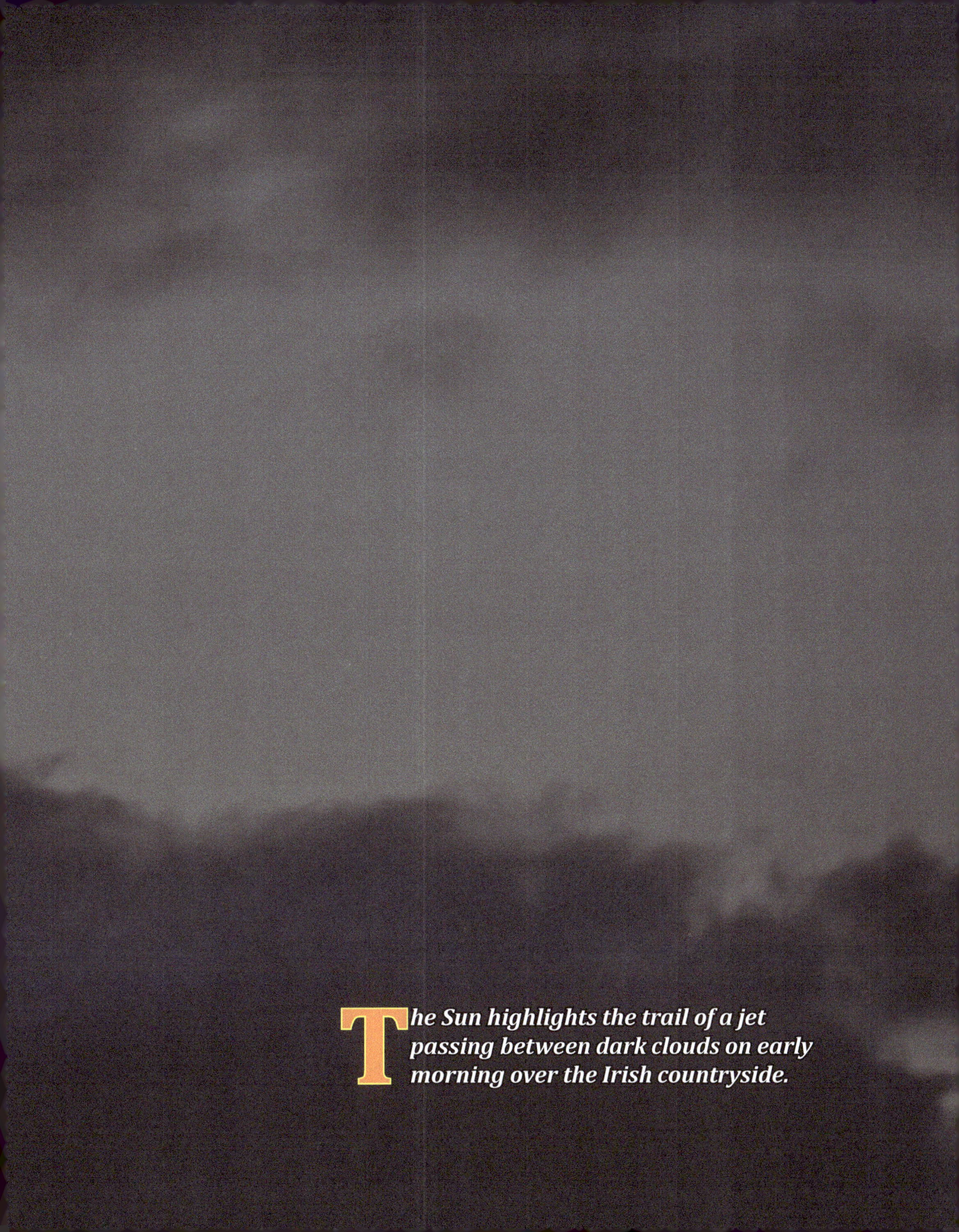

The Sun highlights the trail of a jet passing between dark clouds on early morning over the Irish countryside.

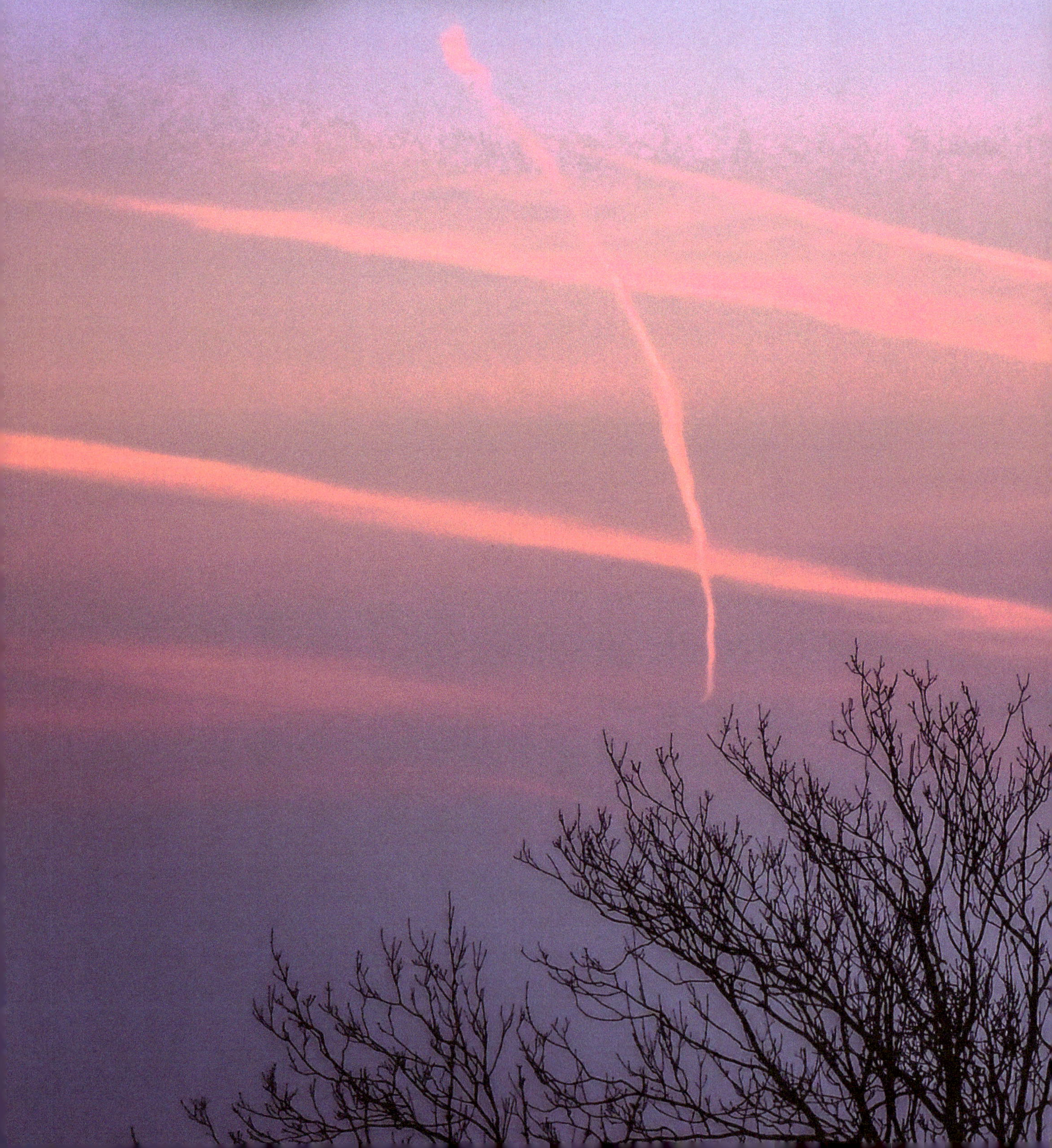
Pink jet trails paint the misty
morning sky over County Clare
at sunrise.

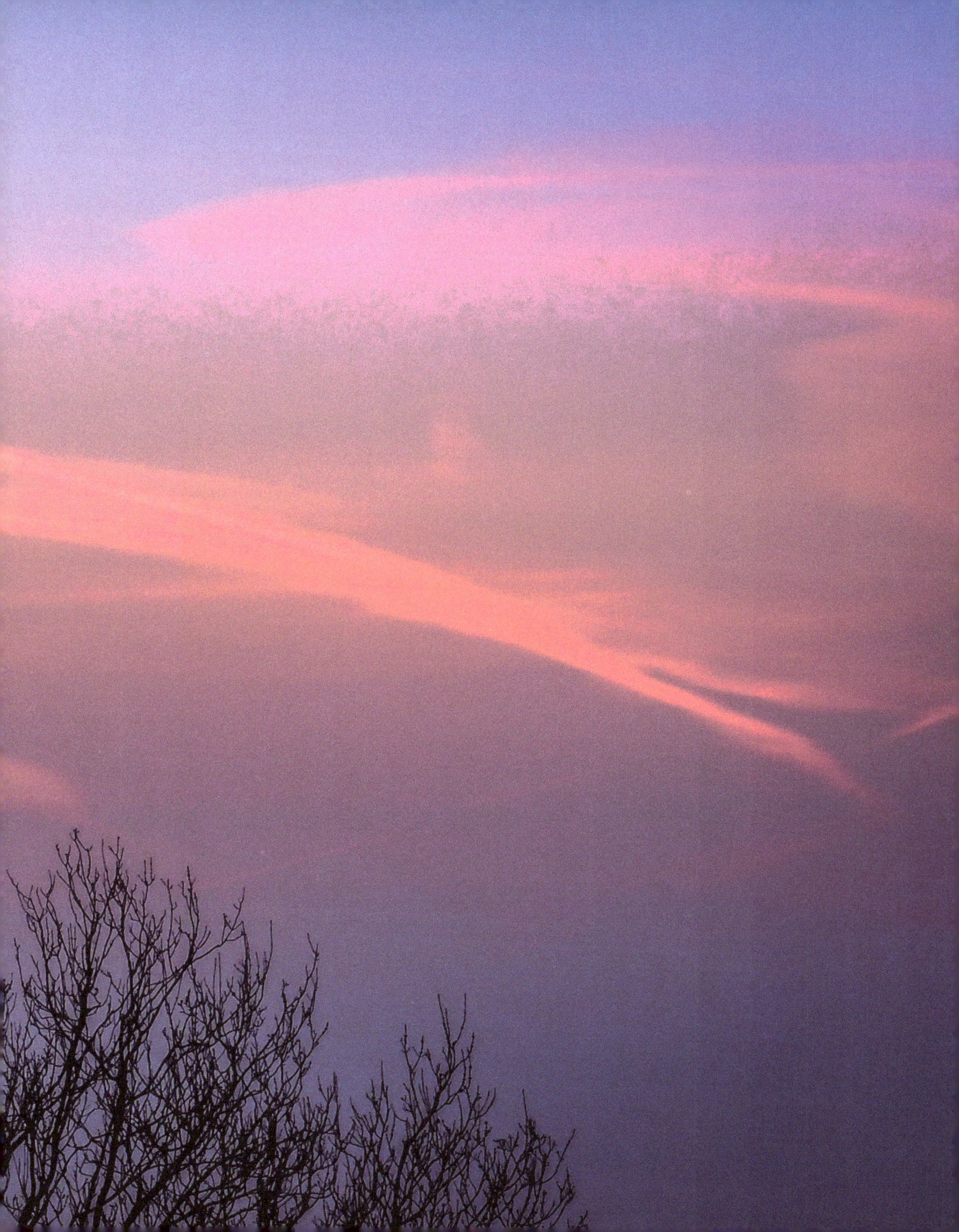

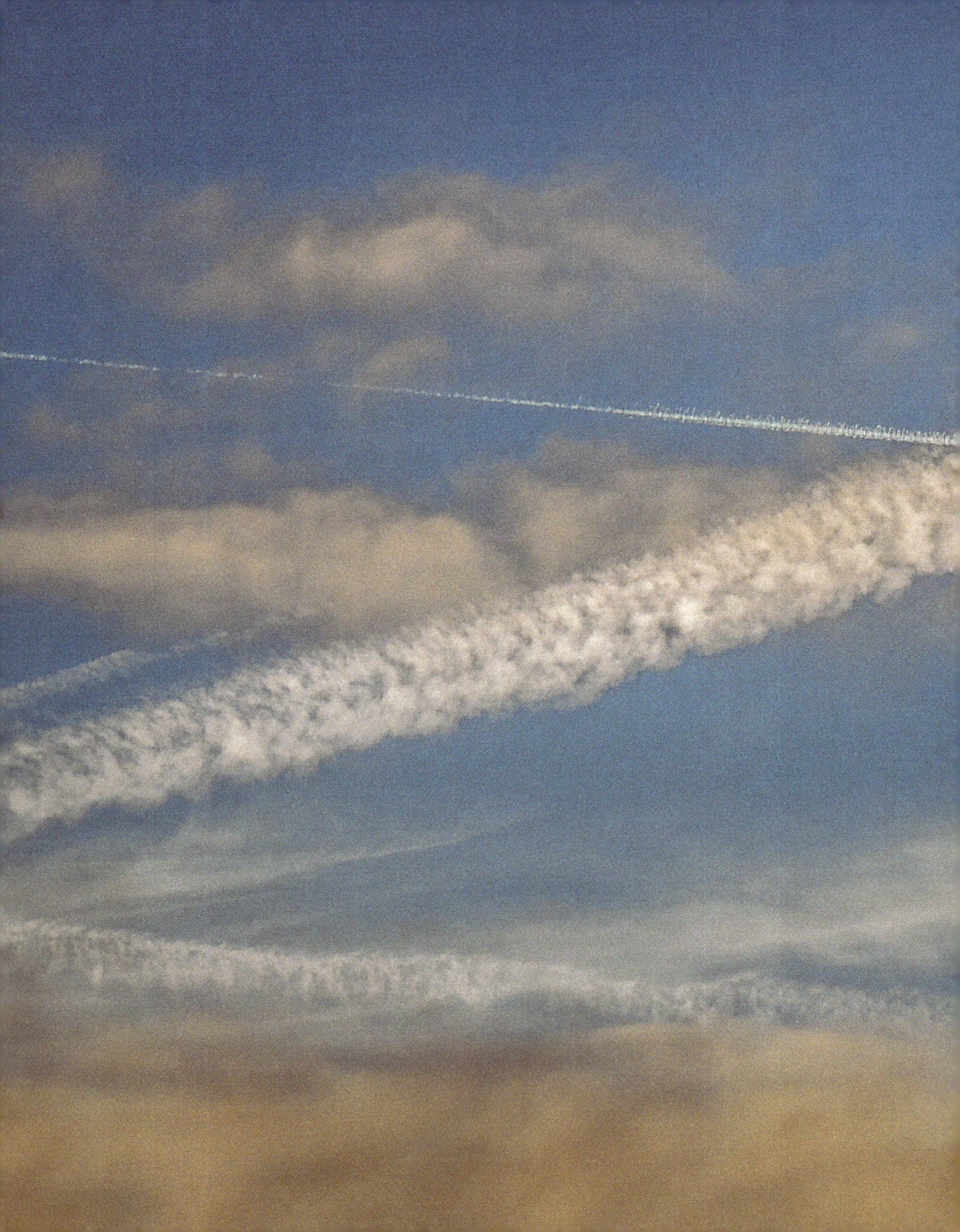

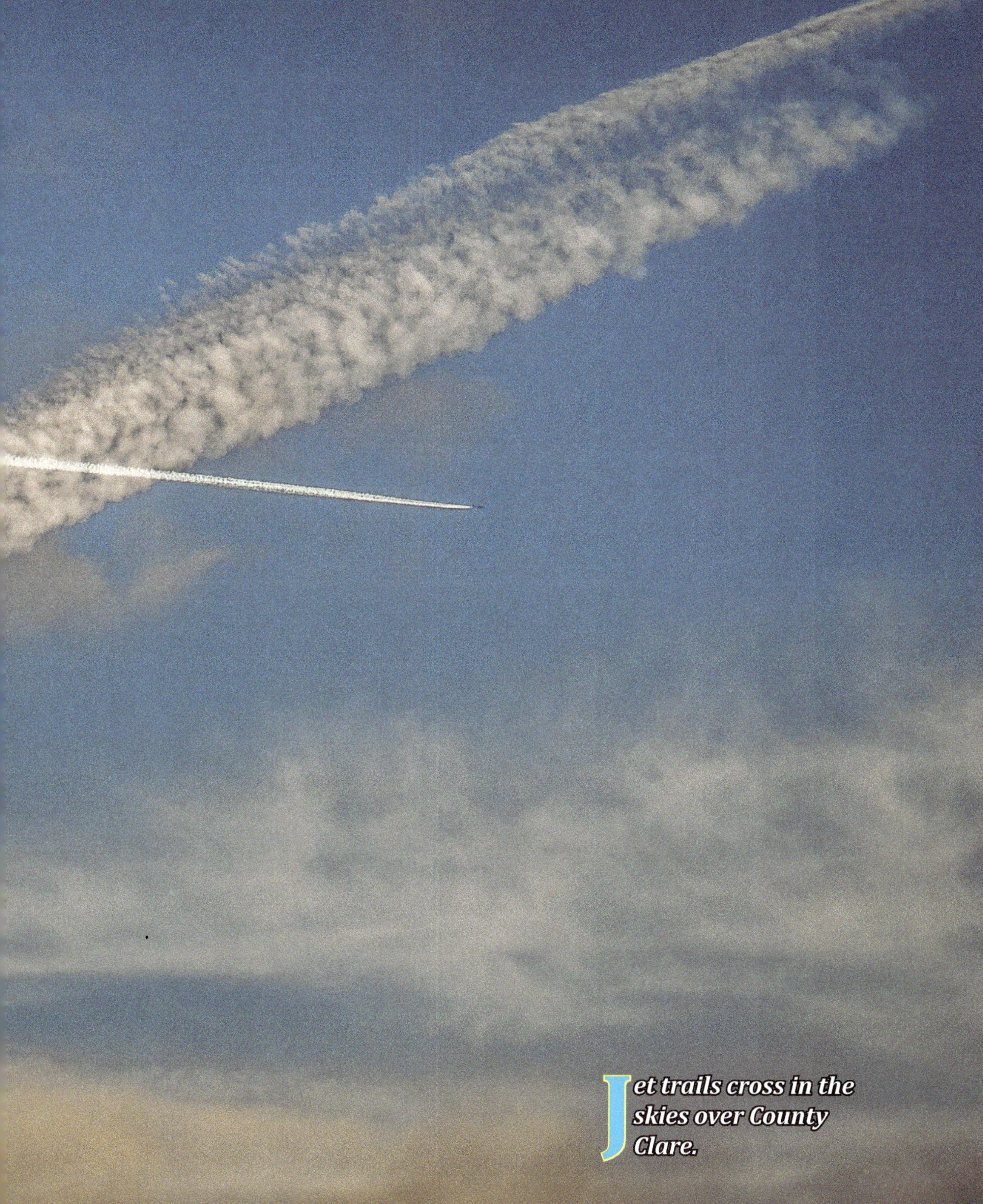

Jet trails cross in the skies over County Clare.

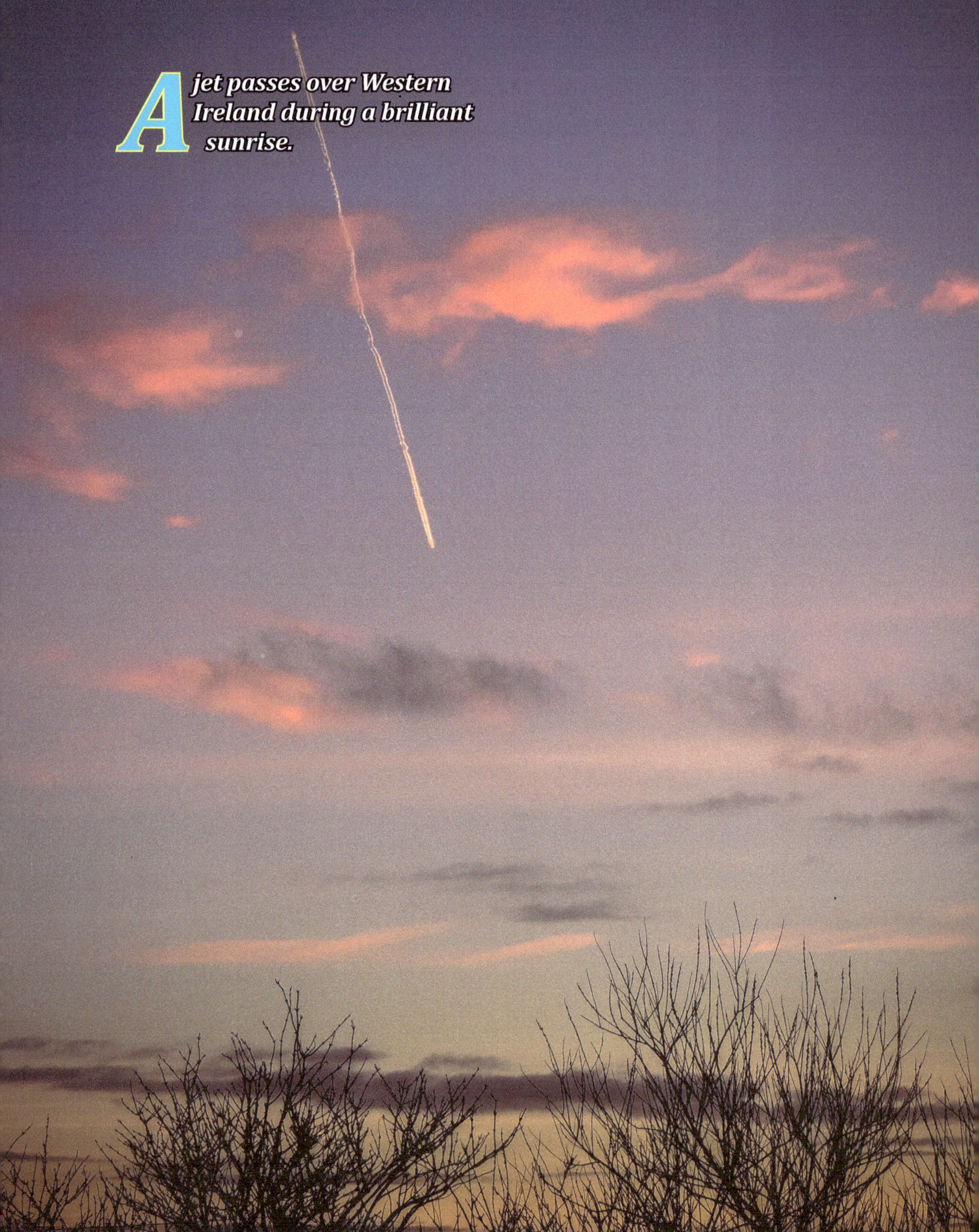
A jet passes over Western Ireland during a brilliant sunrise.

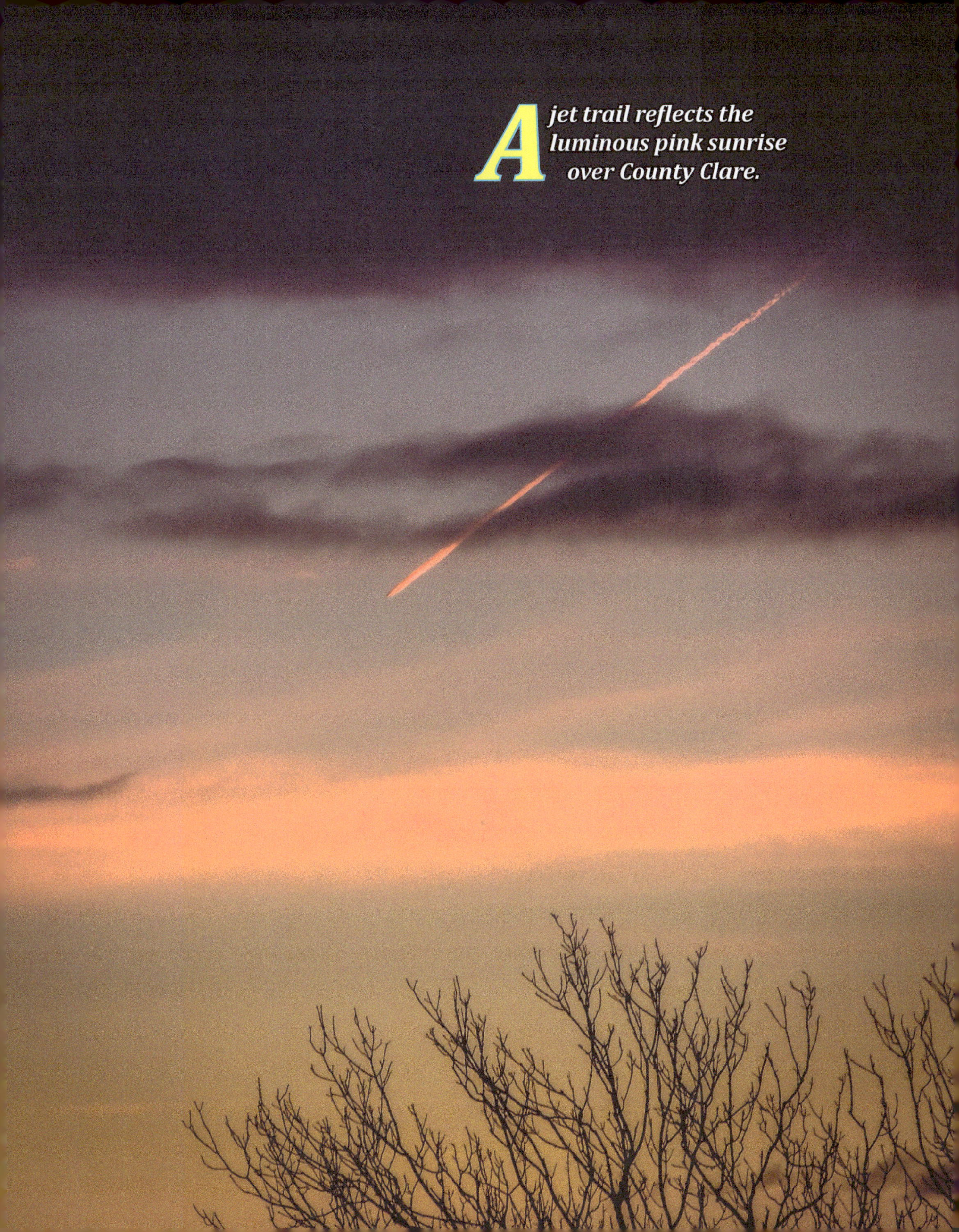

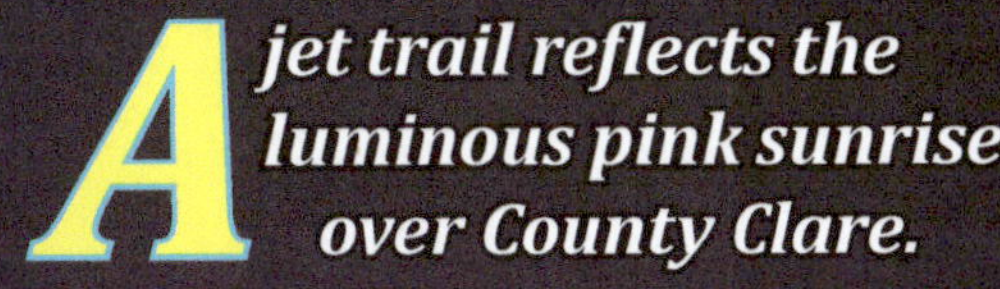

A jet trail reflects the luminous pink sunrise over County Clare.

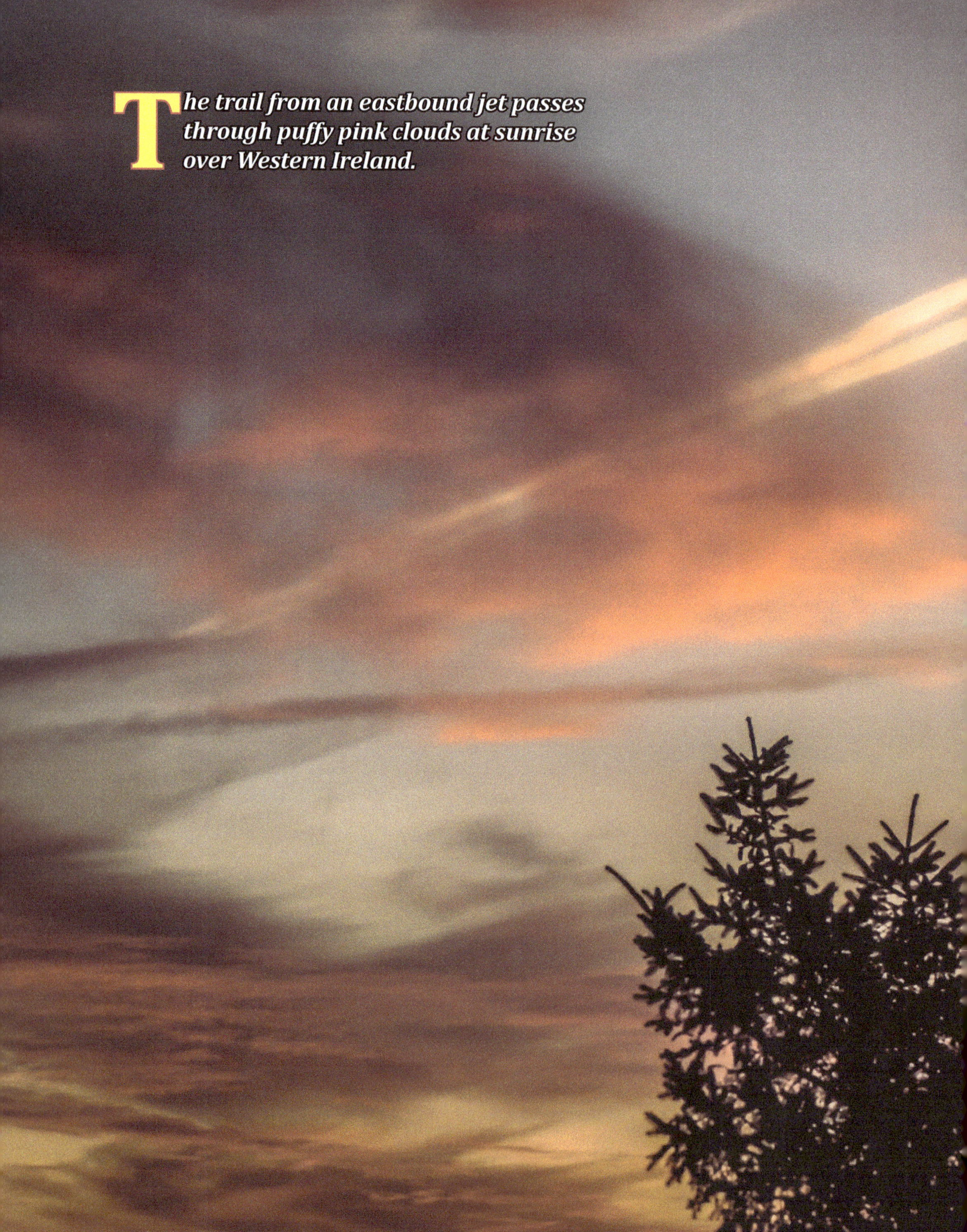

The trail from an eastbound jet passes through puffy pink clouds at sunrise over Western Ireland.

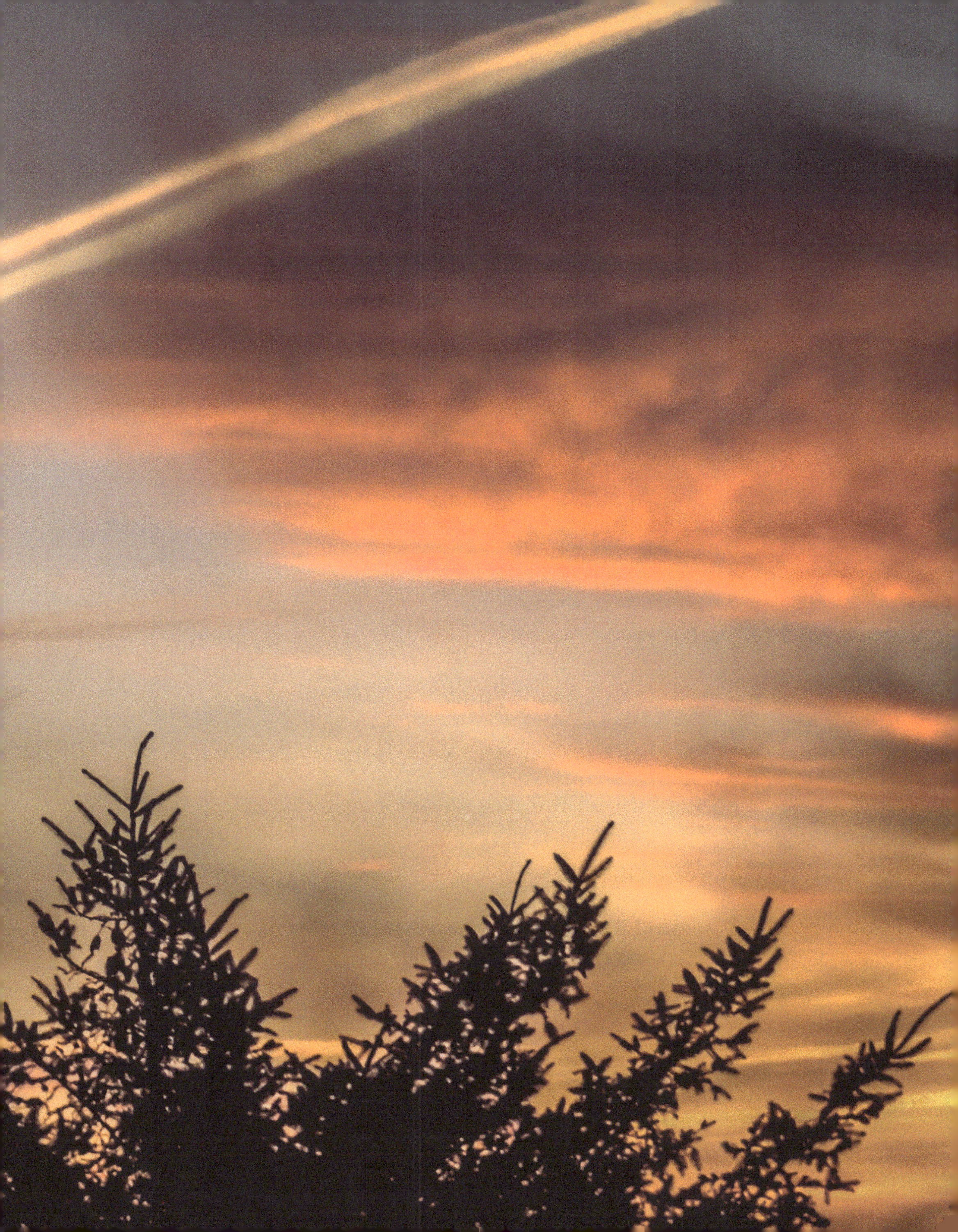

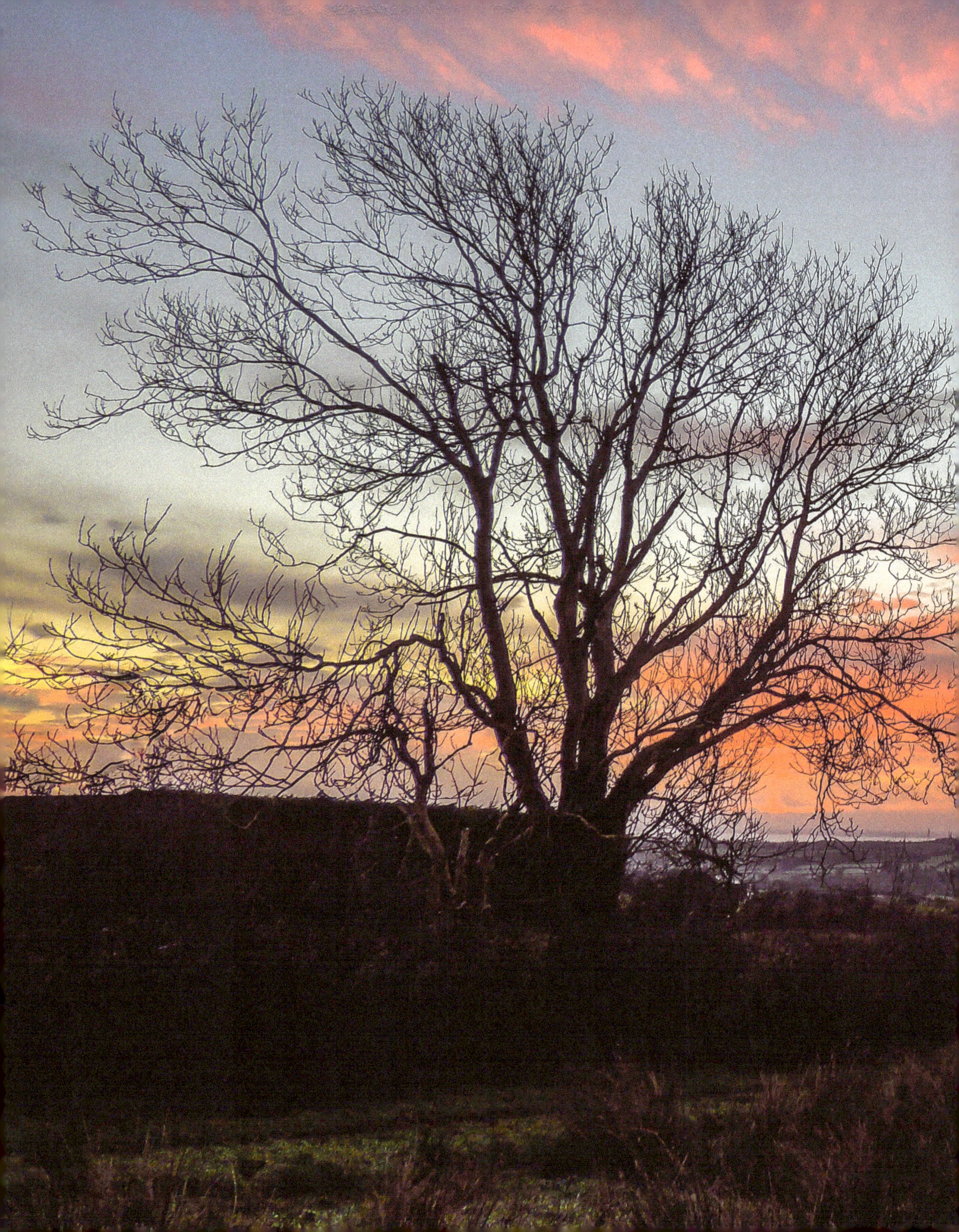

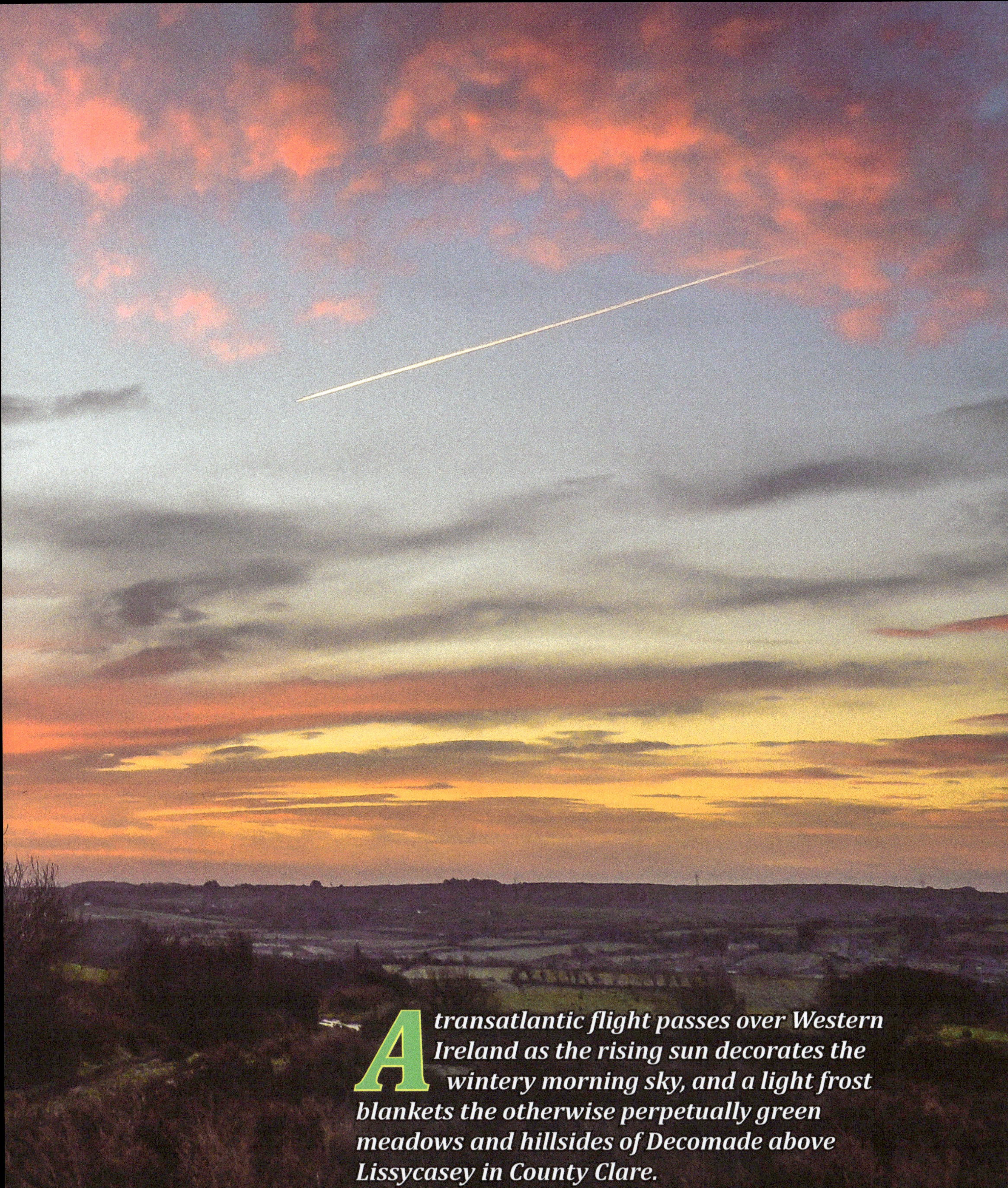

A transatlantic flight passes over Western Ireland as the rising sun decorates the wintery morning sky, and a light frost blankets the otherwise perpetually green meadows and hillsides of Decomade above Lissycasey in County Clare.

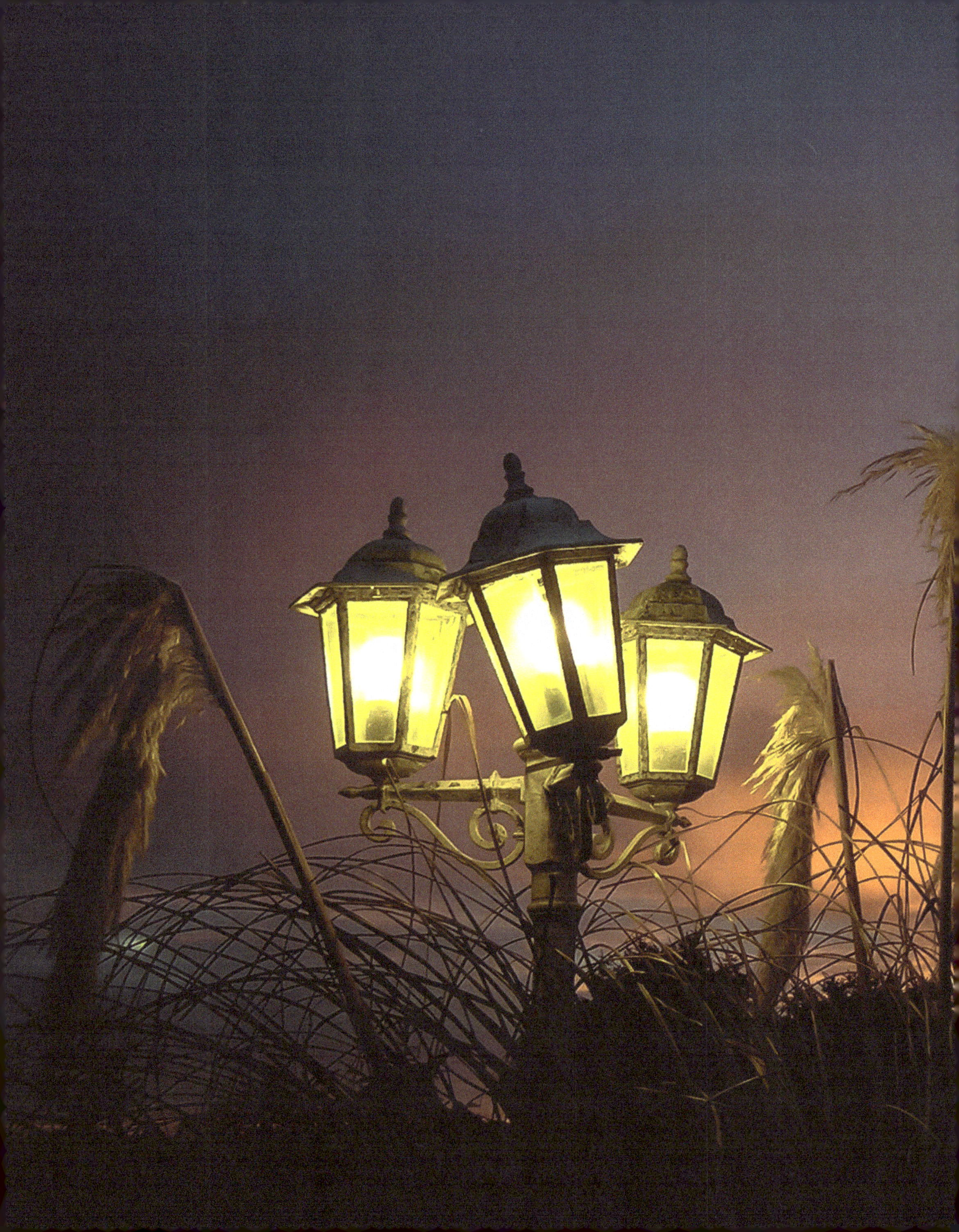

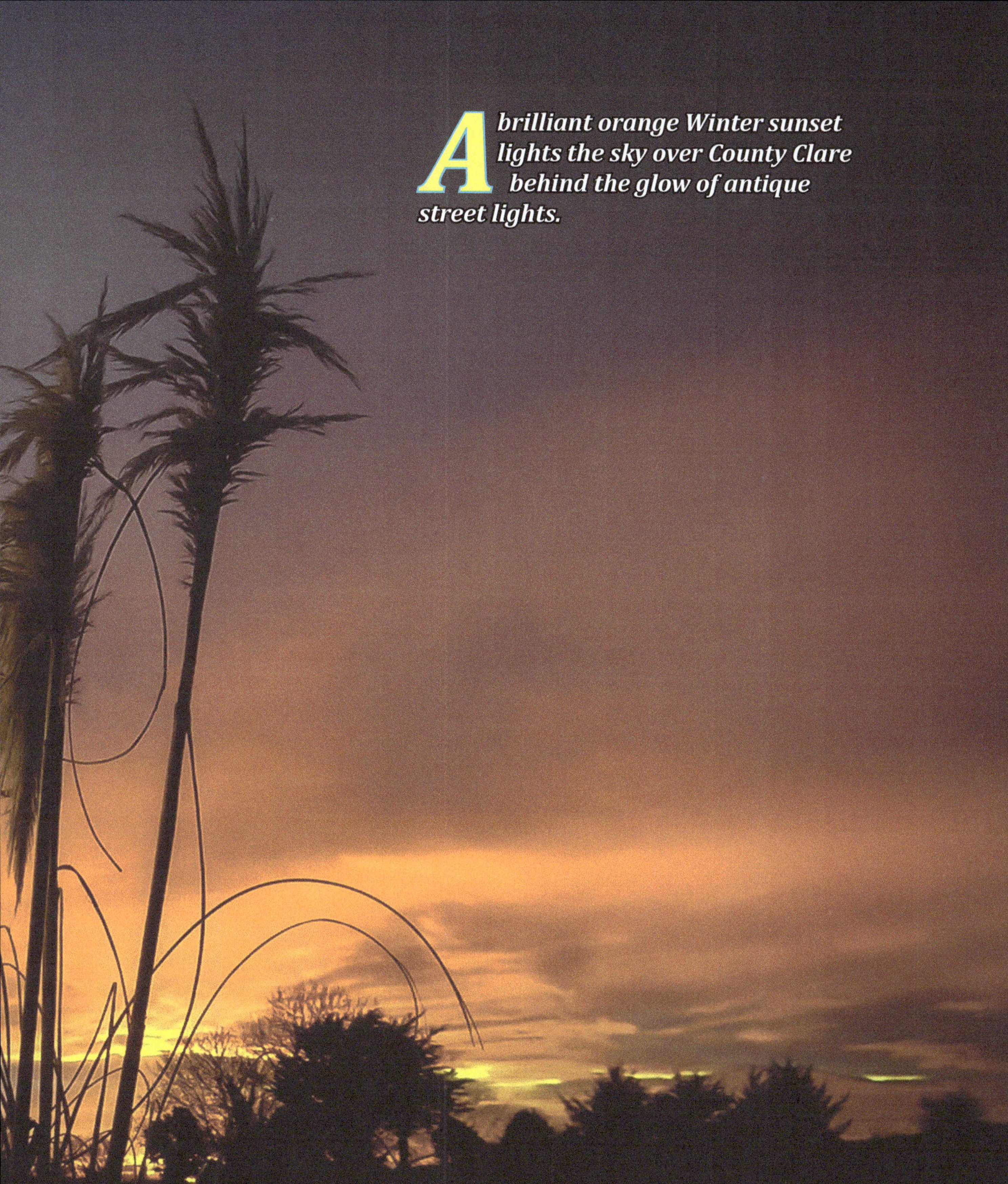
A brilliant orange Winter sunset
lights the sky over County Clare
behind the glow of antique
street lights.

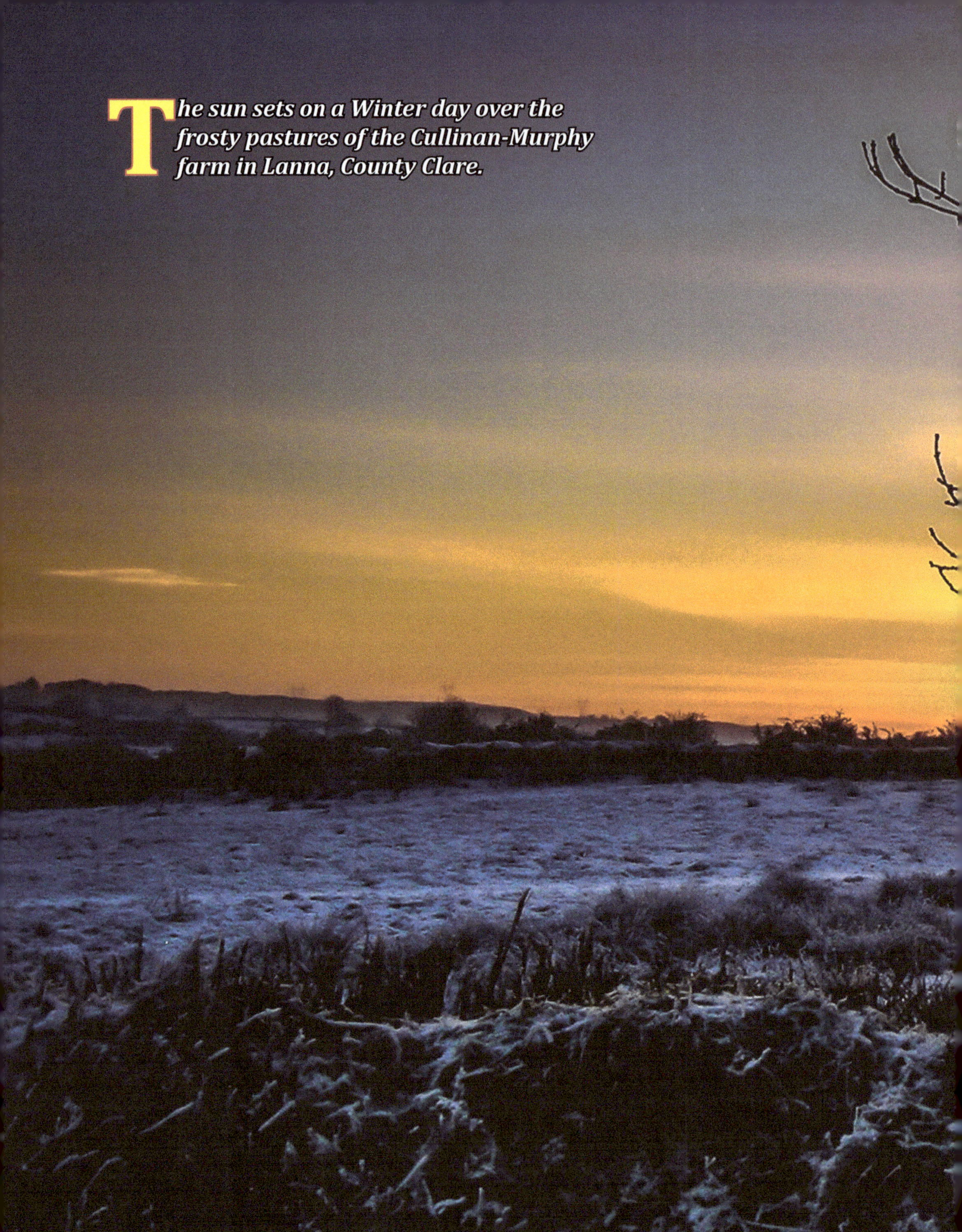

The sun sets on a Winter day over the frosty pastures of the Cullinan-Murphy farm in Lanna, County Clare.

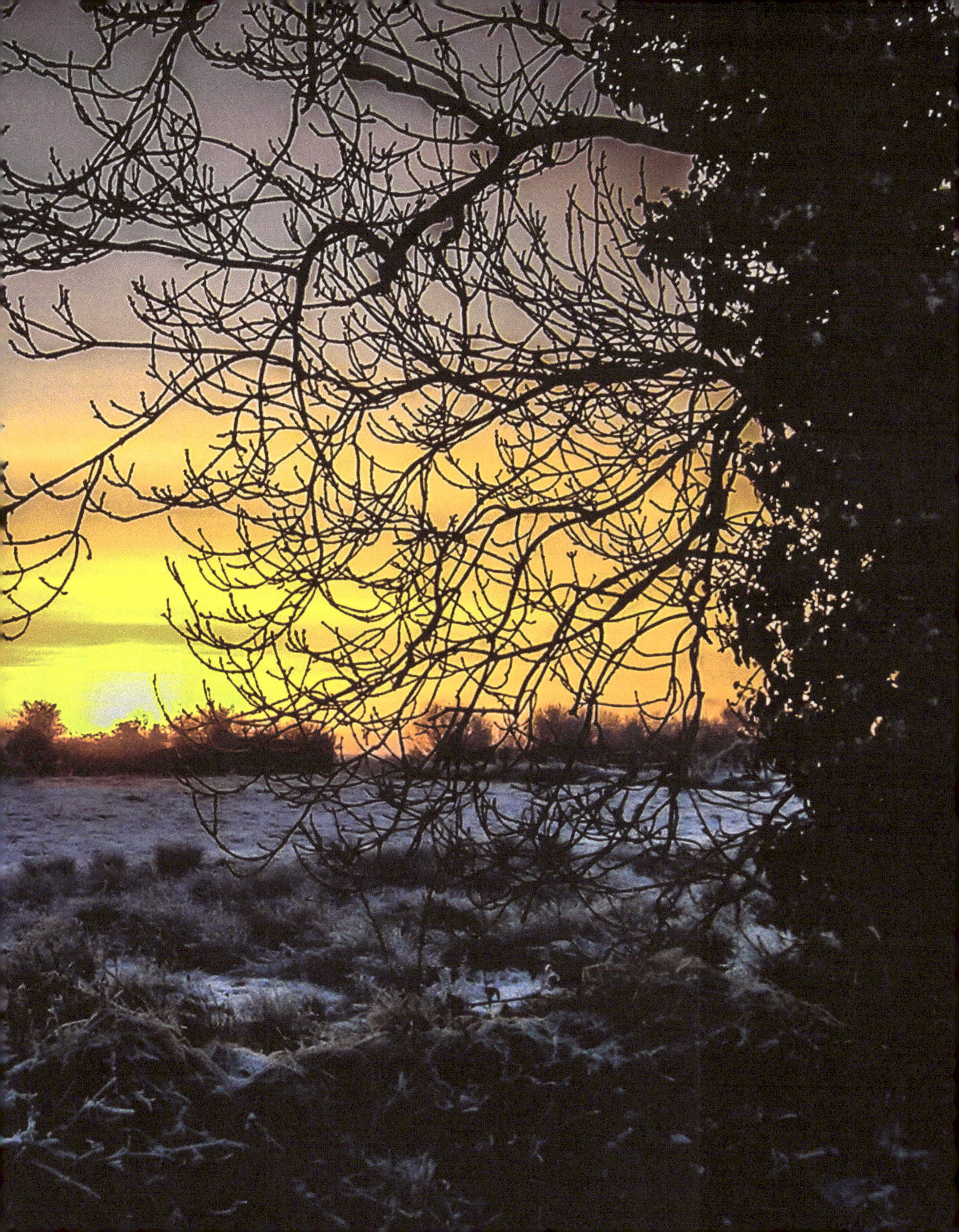

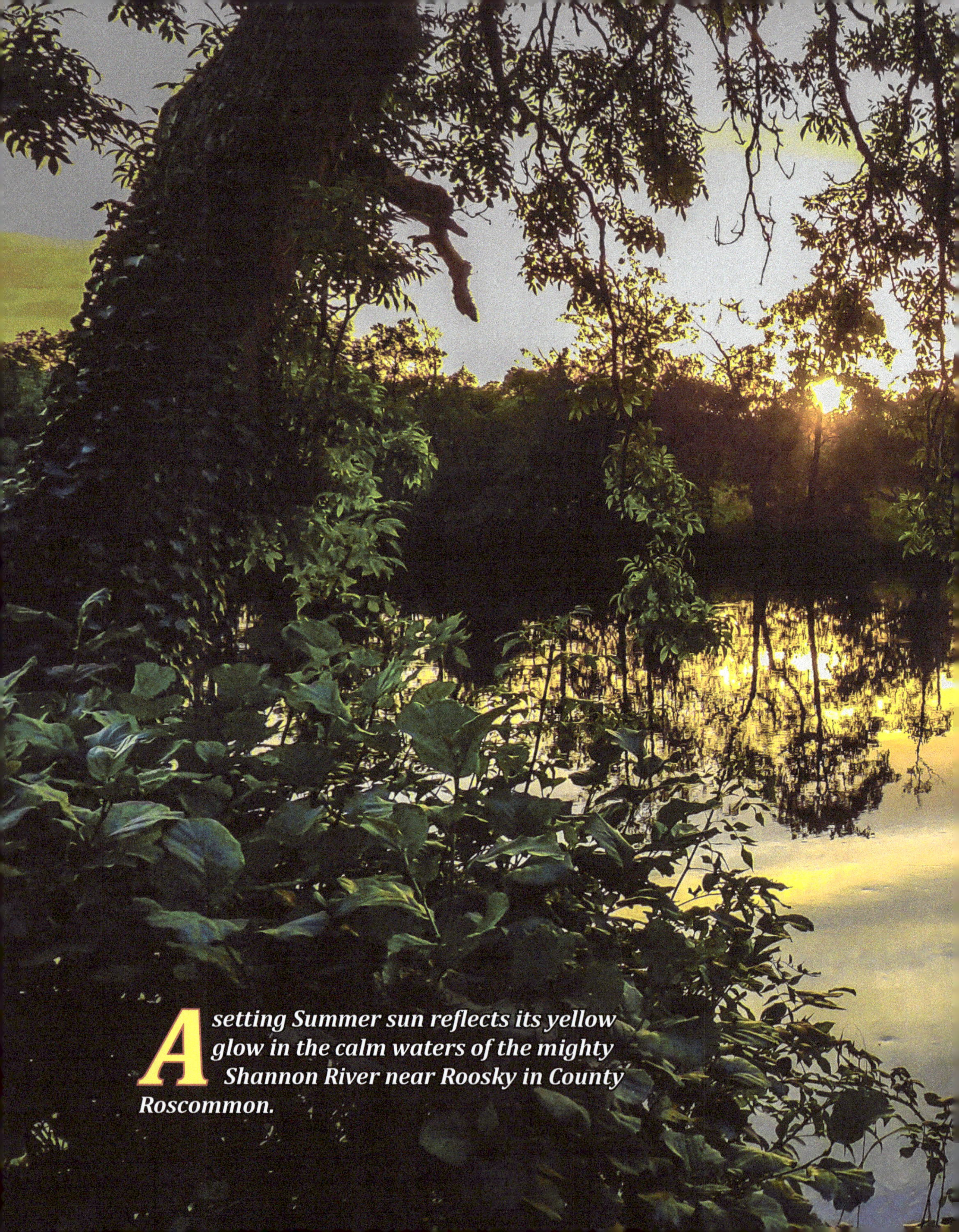

A setting Summer sun reflects its yellow glow in the calm waters of the mighty Shannon River near Roosky in County Roscommon.

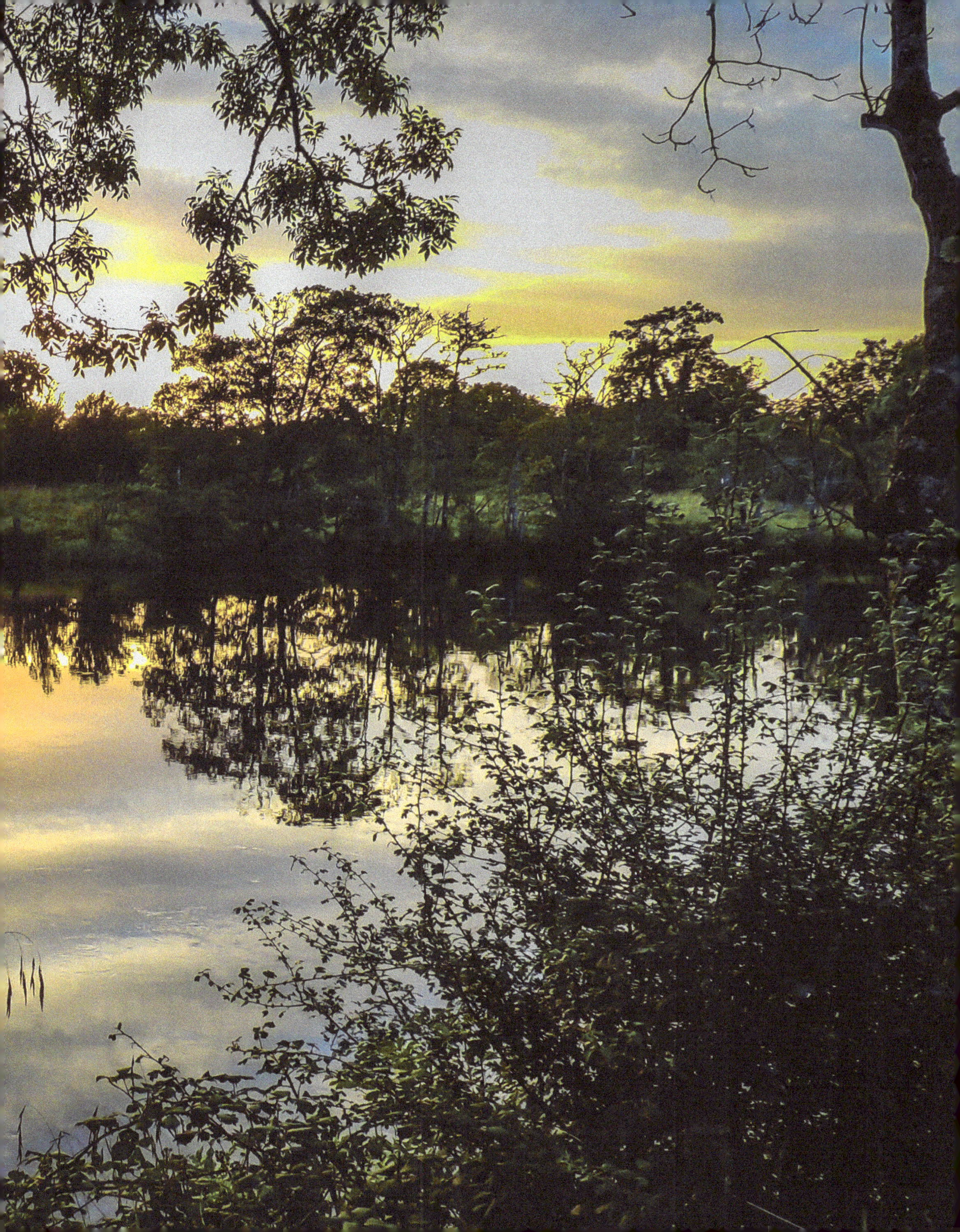

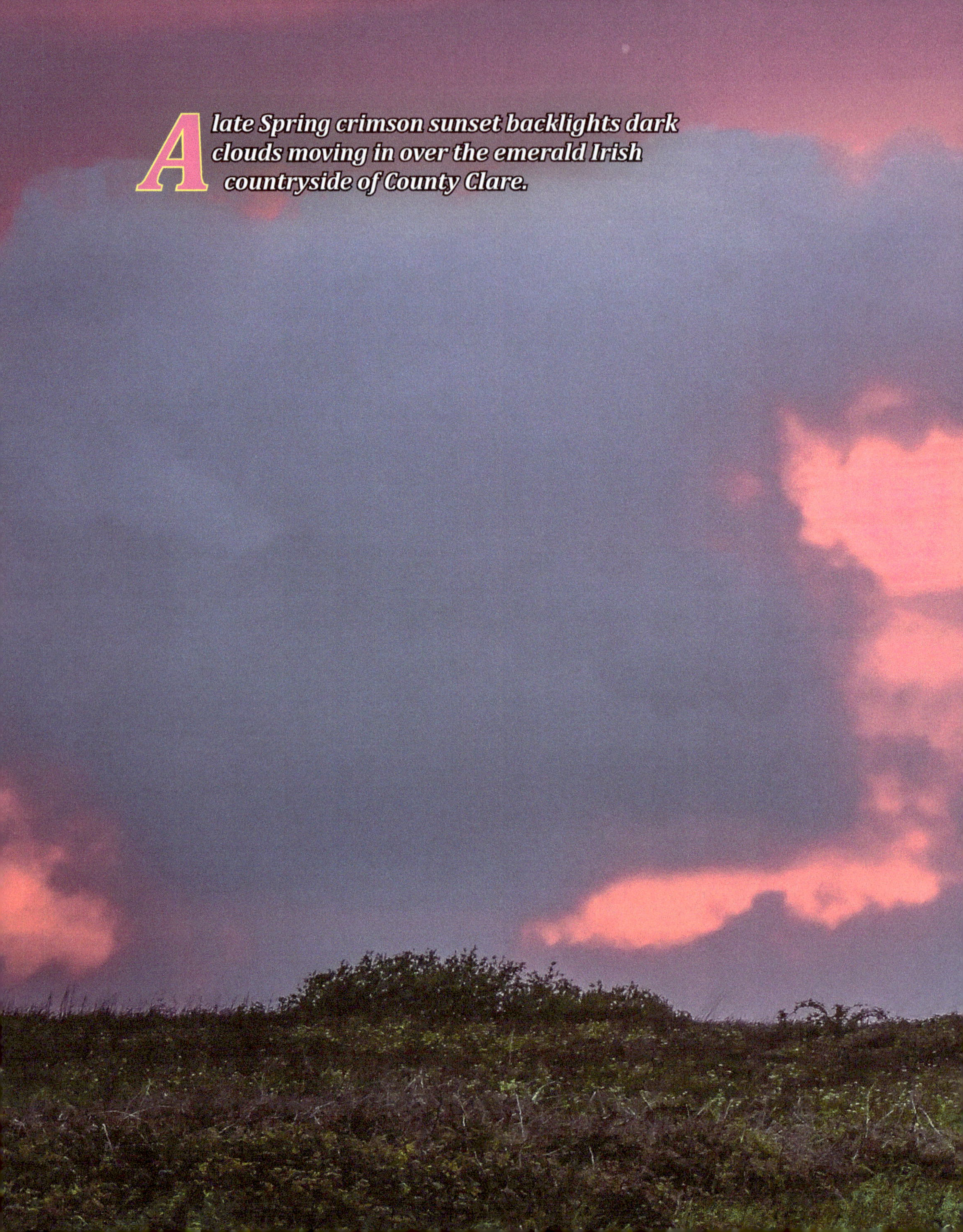

A late Spring crimson sunset backlights dark clouds moving in over the emerald Irish countryside of County Clare.

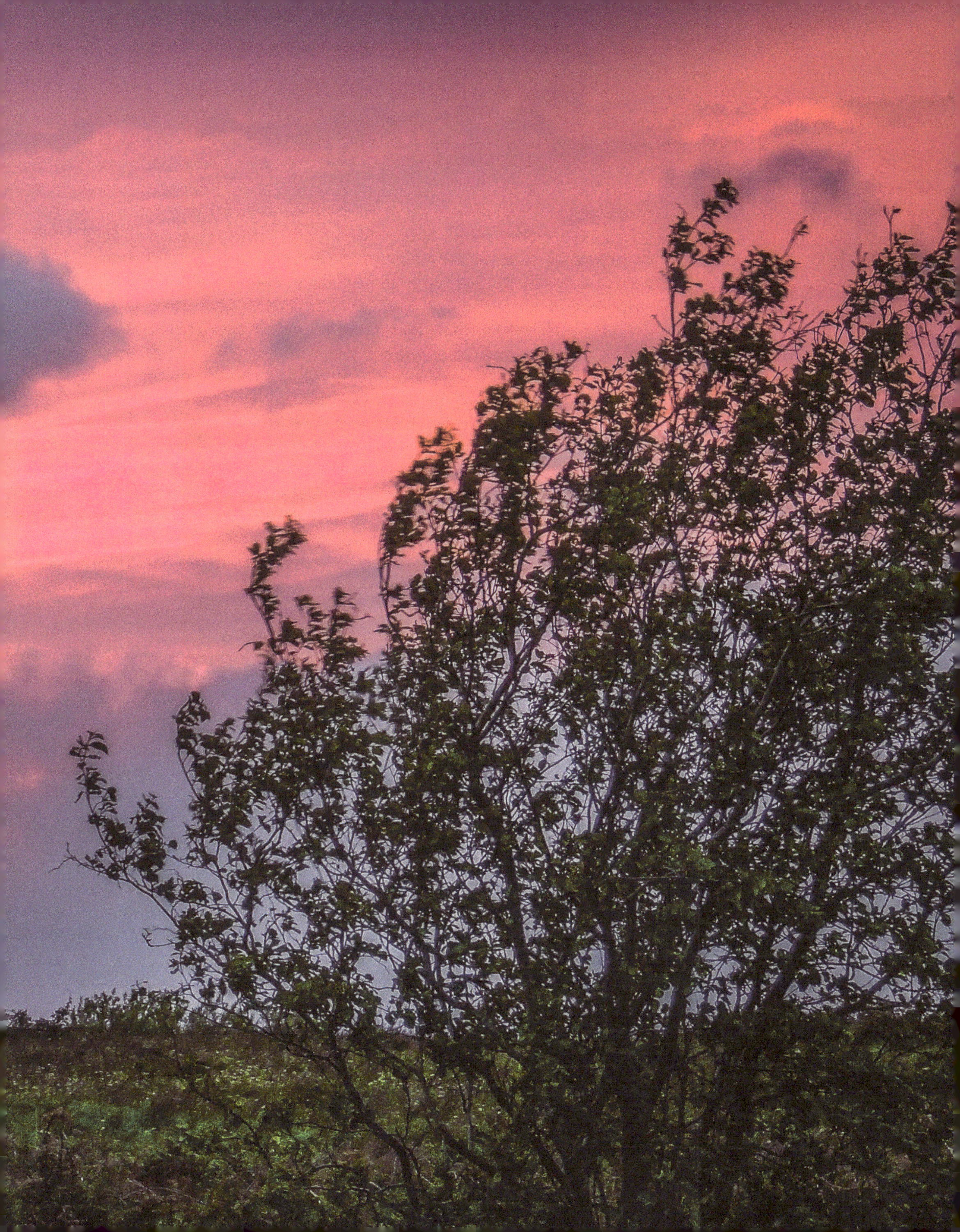

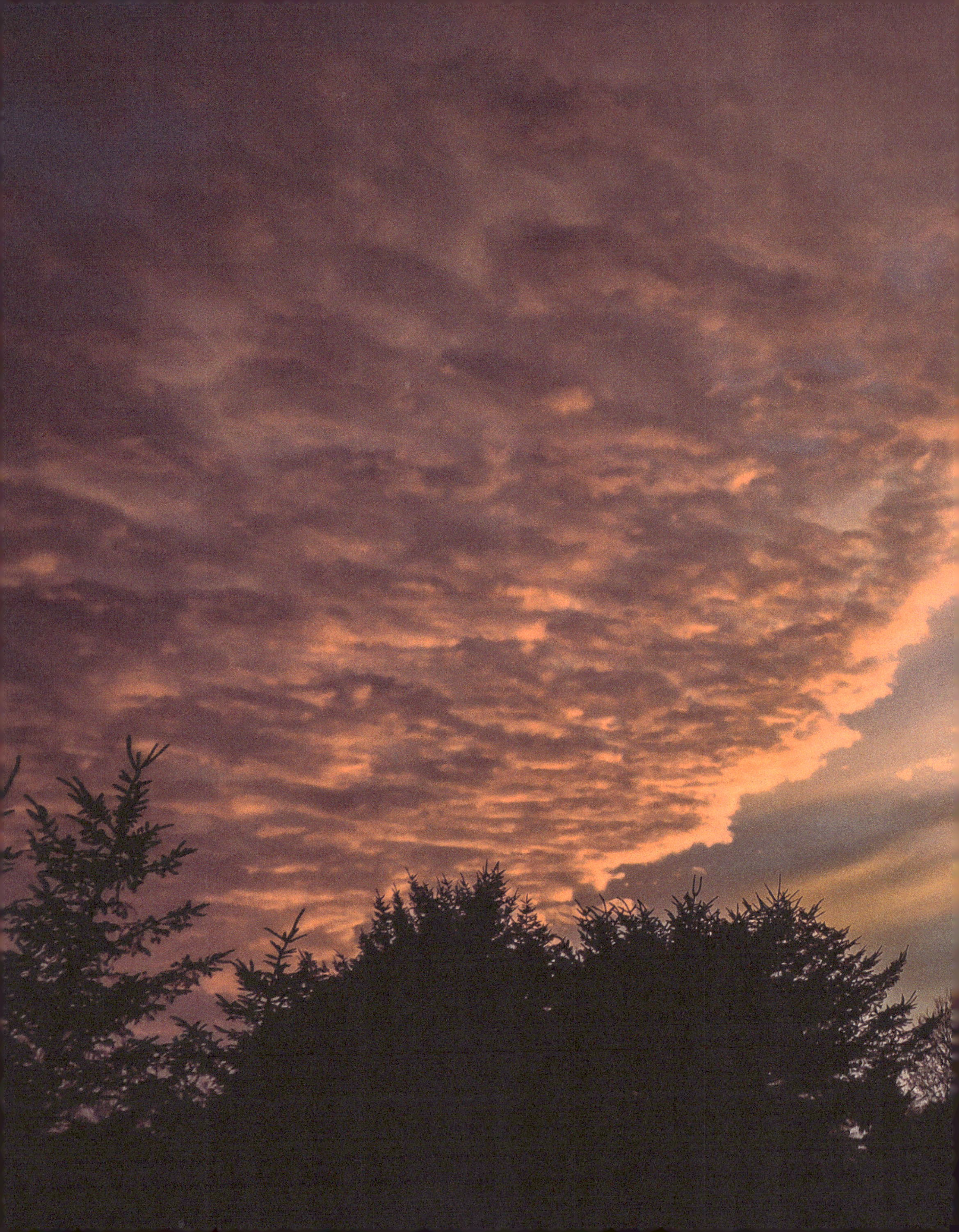

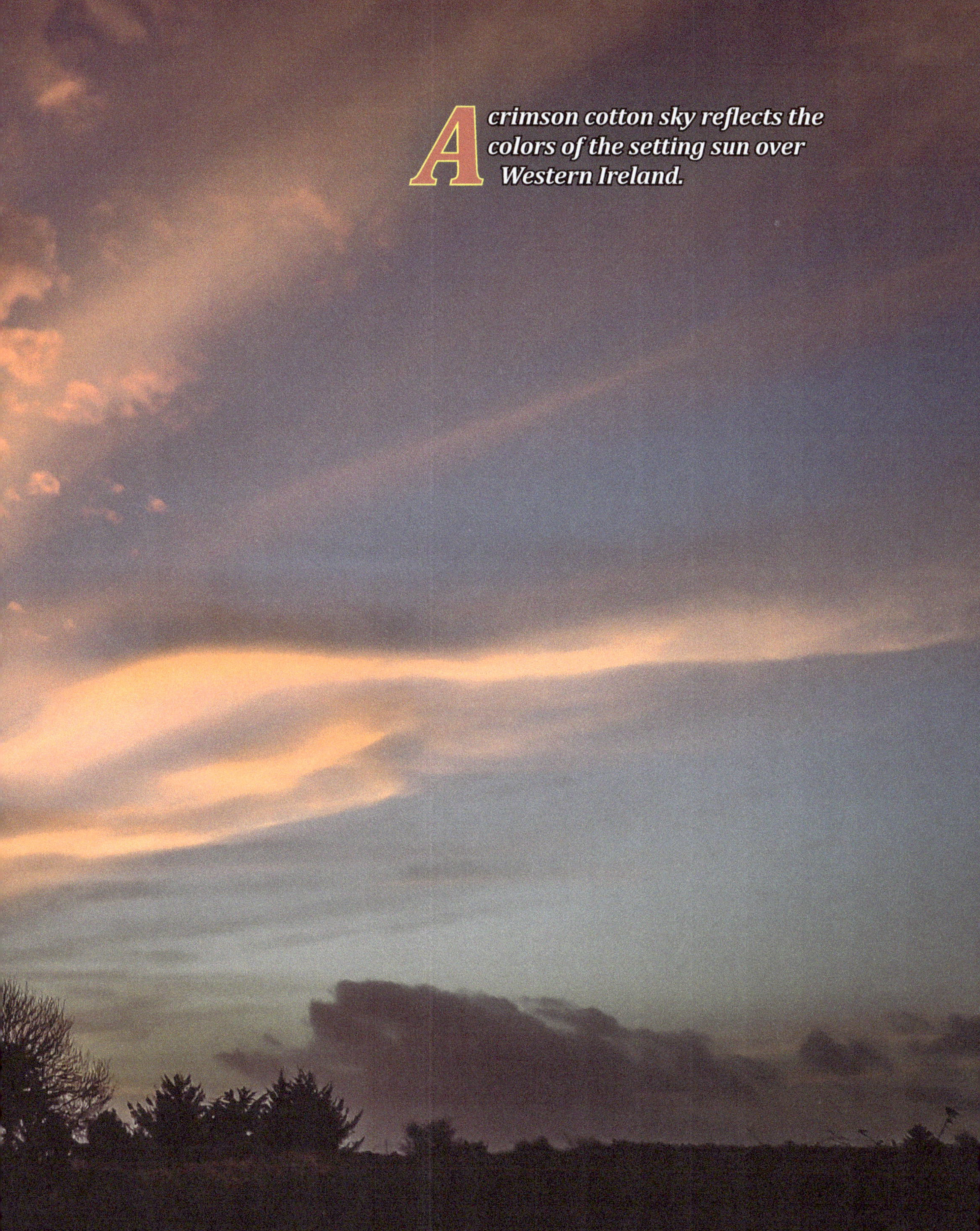
A crimson cotton sky reflects the colors of the setting sun over Western Ireland.

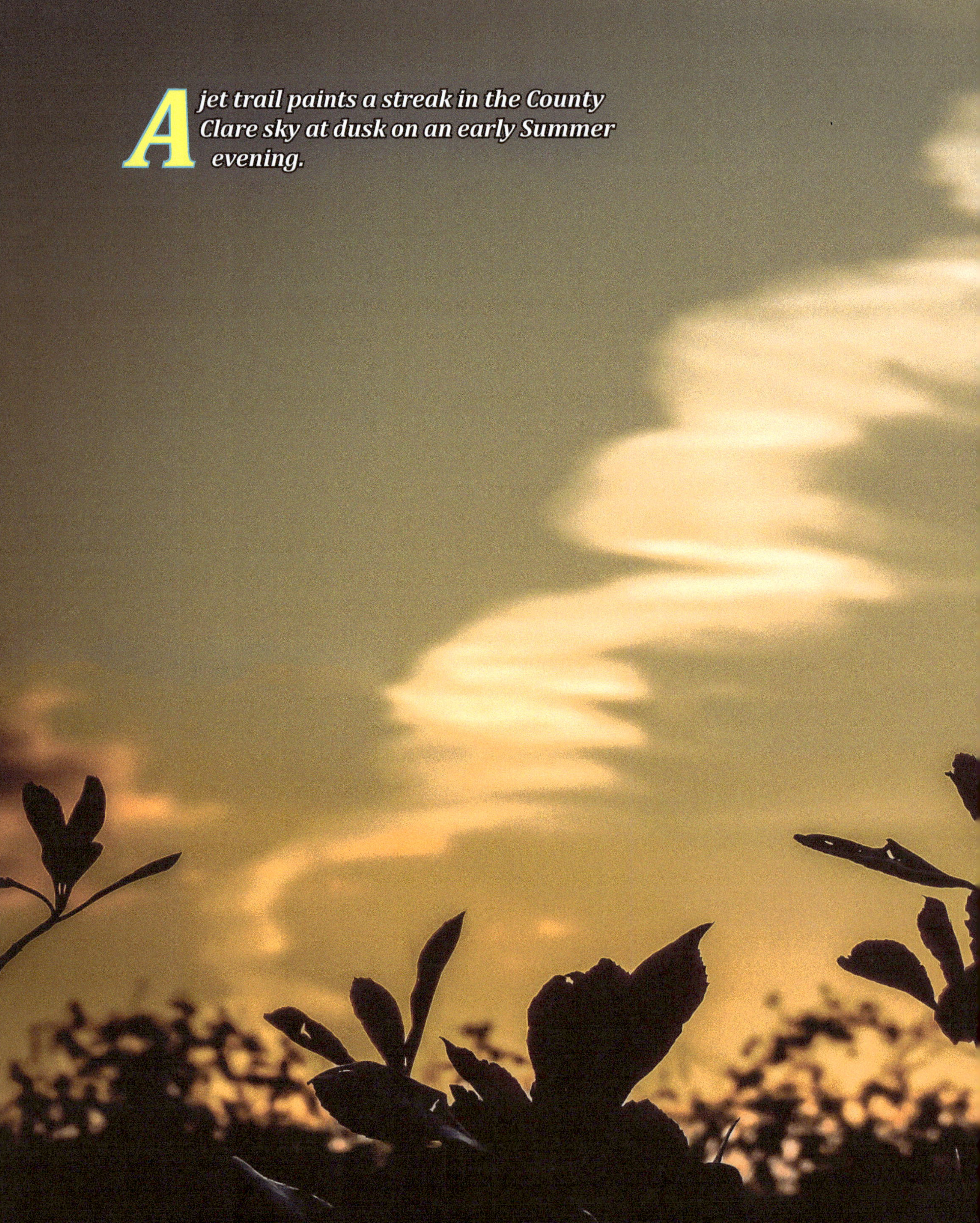
A jet trail paints a streak in the County Clare sky at dusk on an early Summer evening.

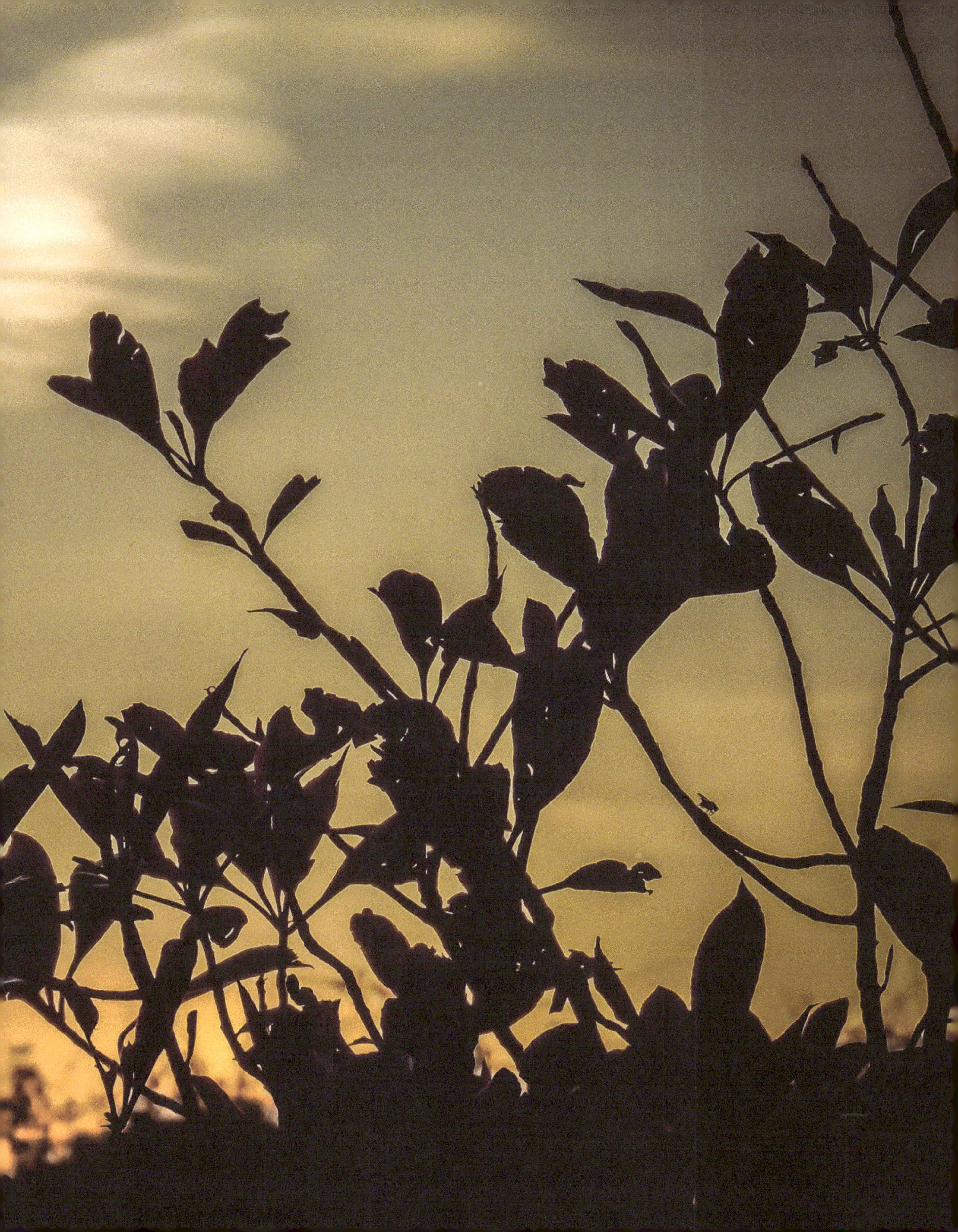

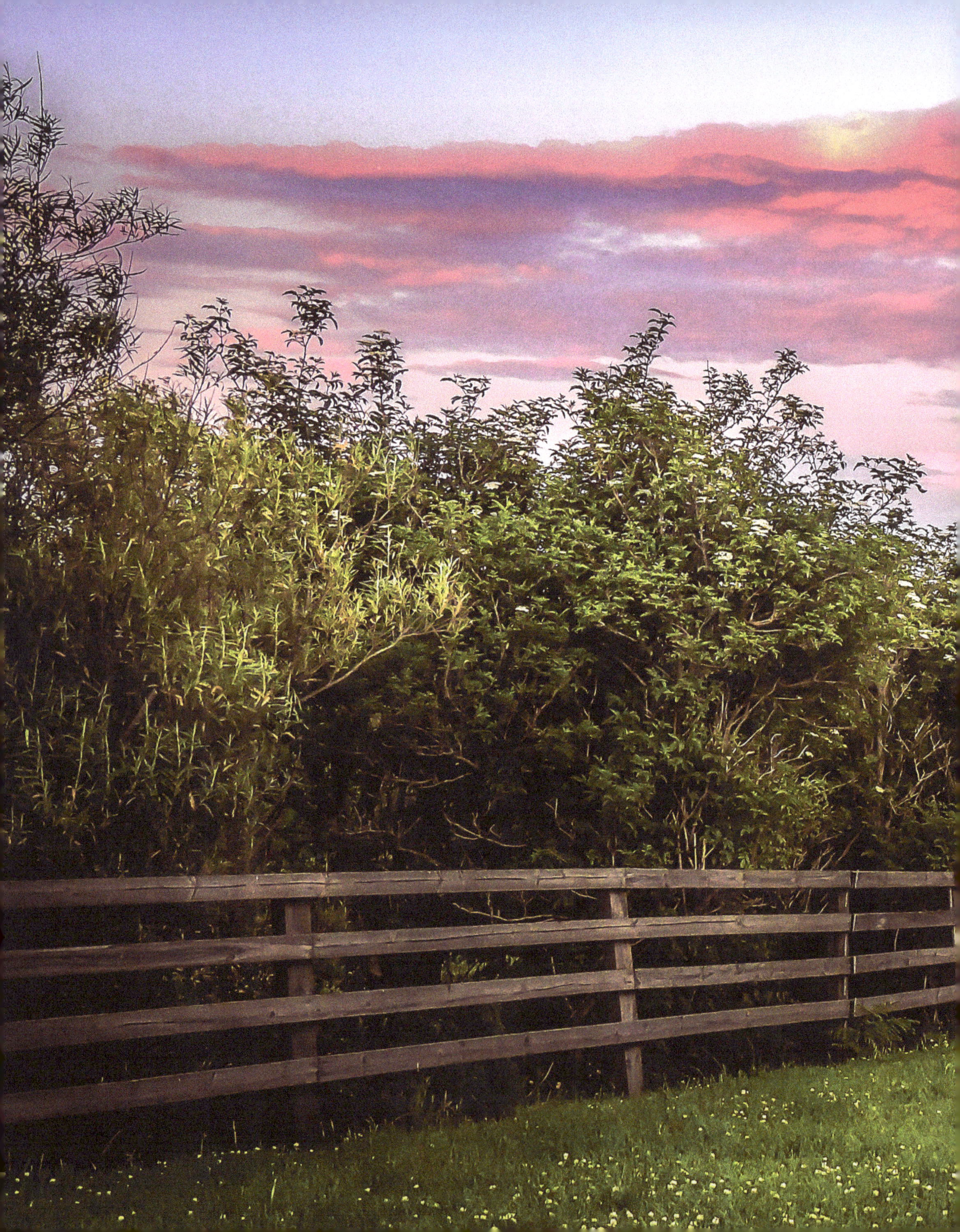

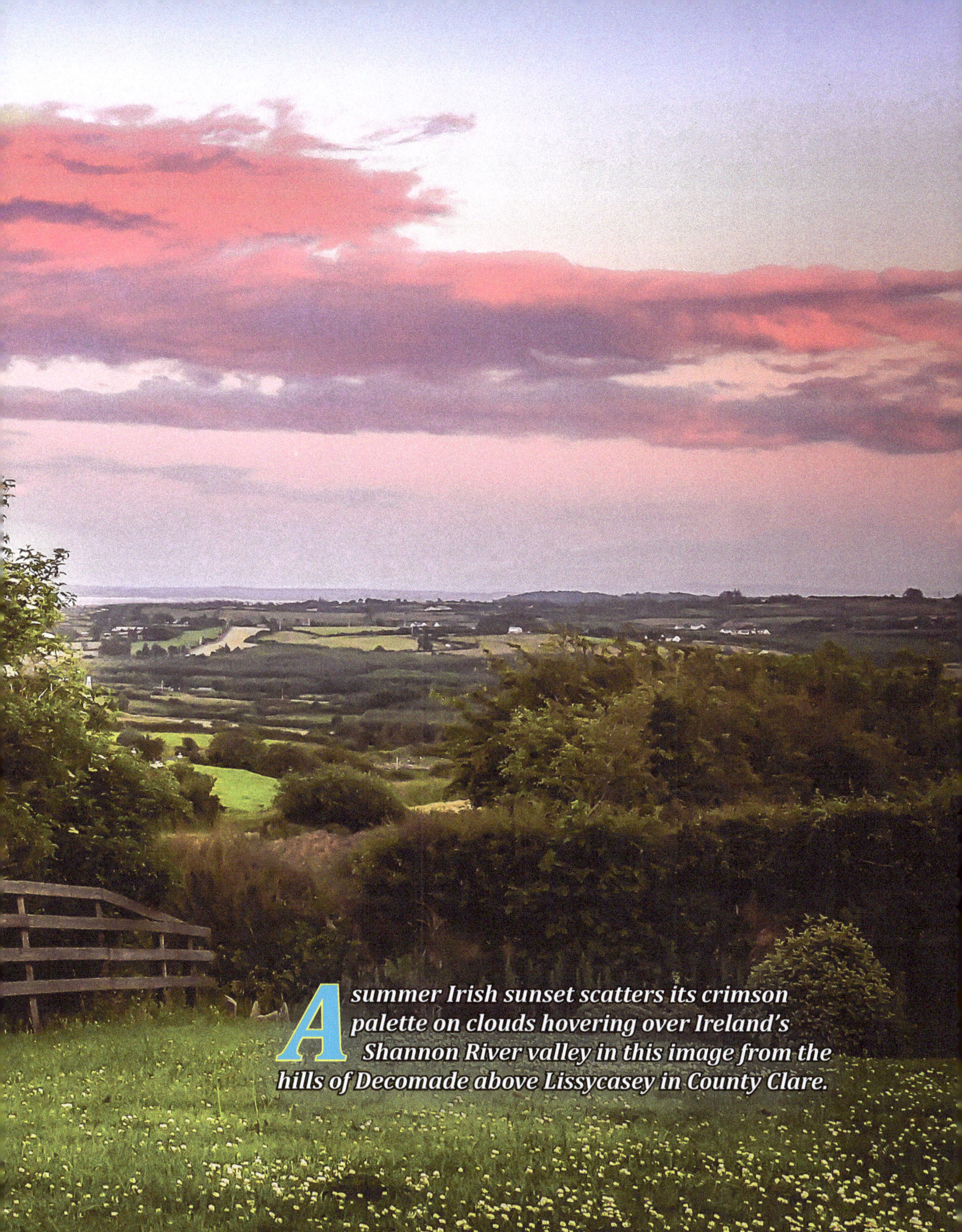

A summer Irish sunset scatters its crimson palette on clouds hovering over Ireland's Shannon River valley in this image from the hills of Decomade above Lissycasey in County Clare.

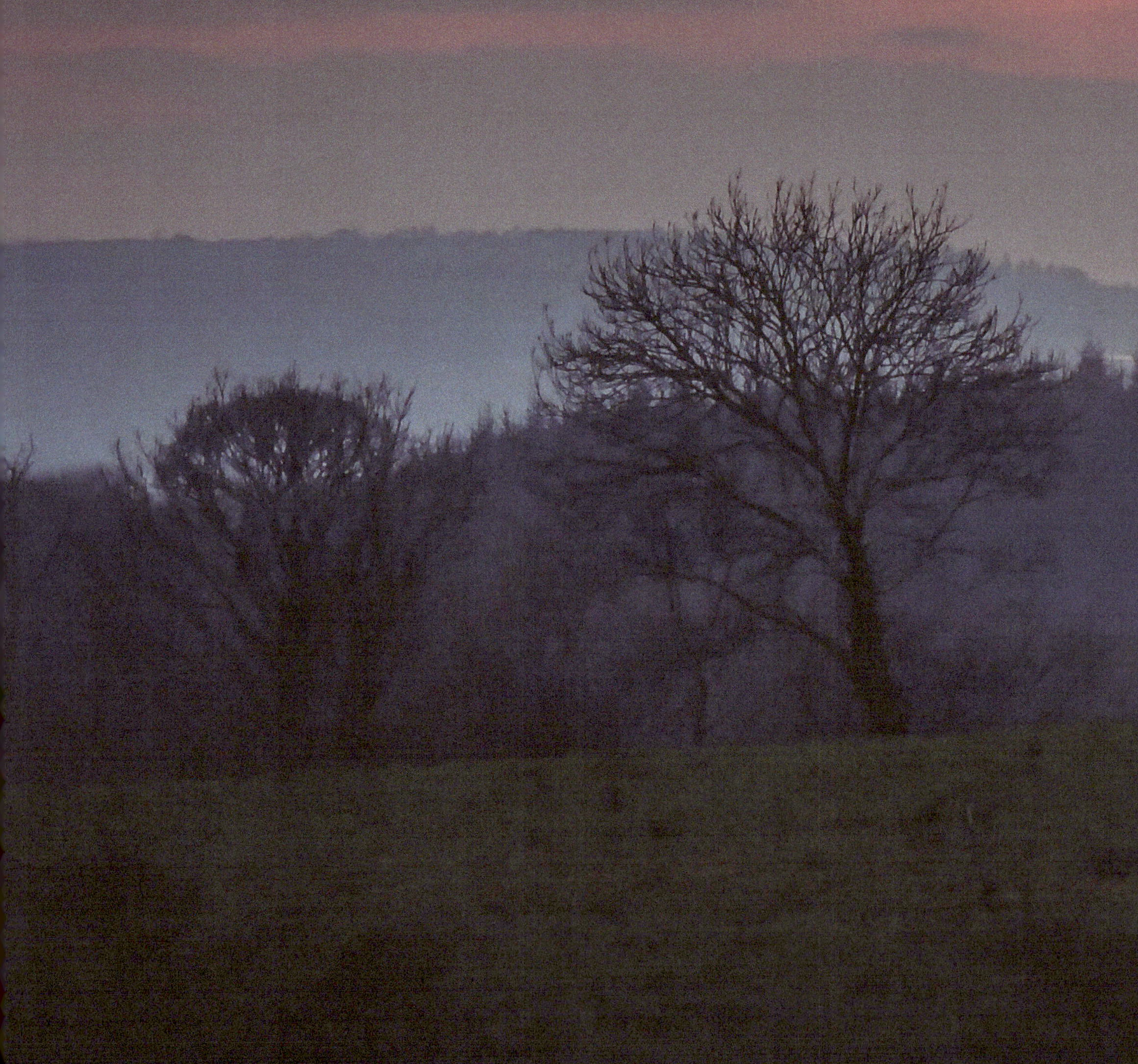
A light Winter Irish mist forms at sunset in the hills near Kildysart in County Clare.

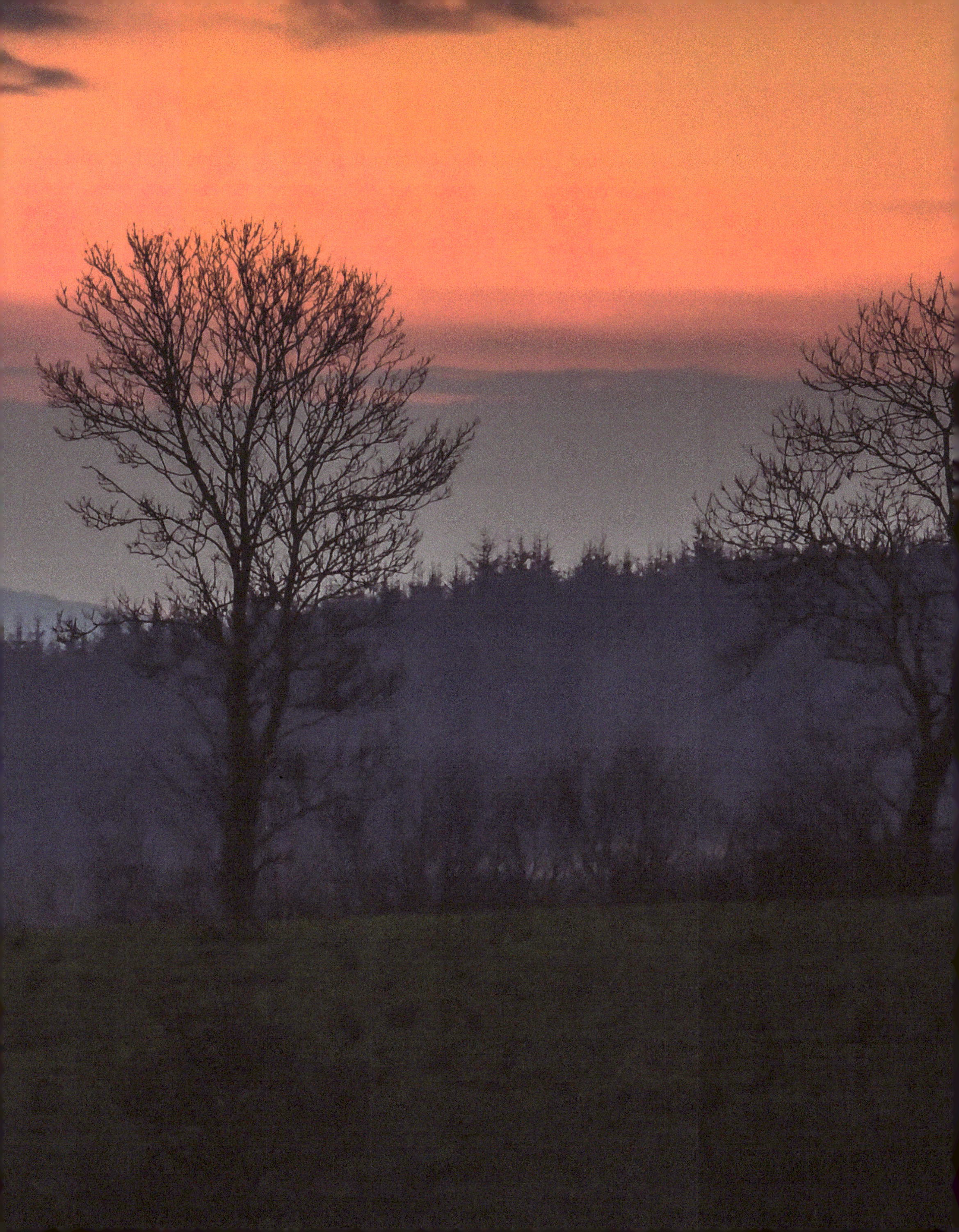

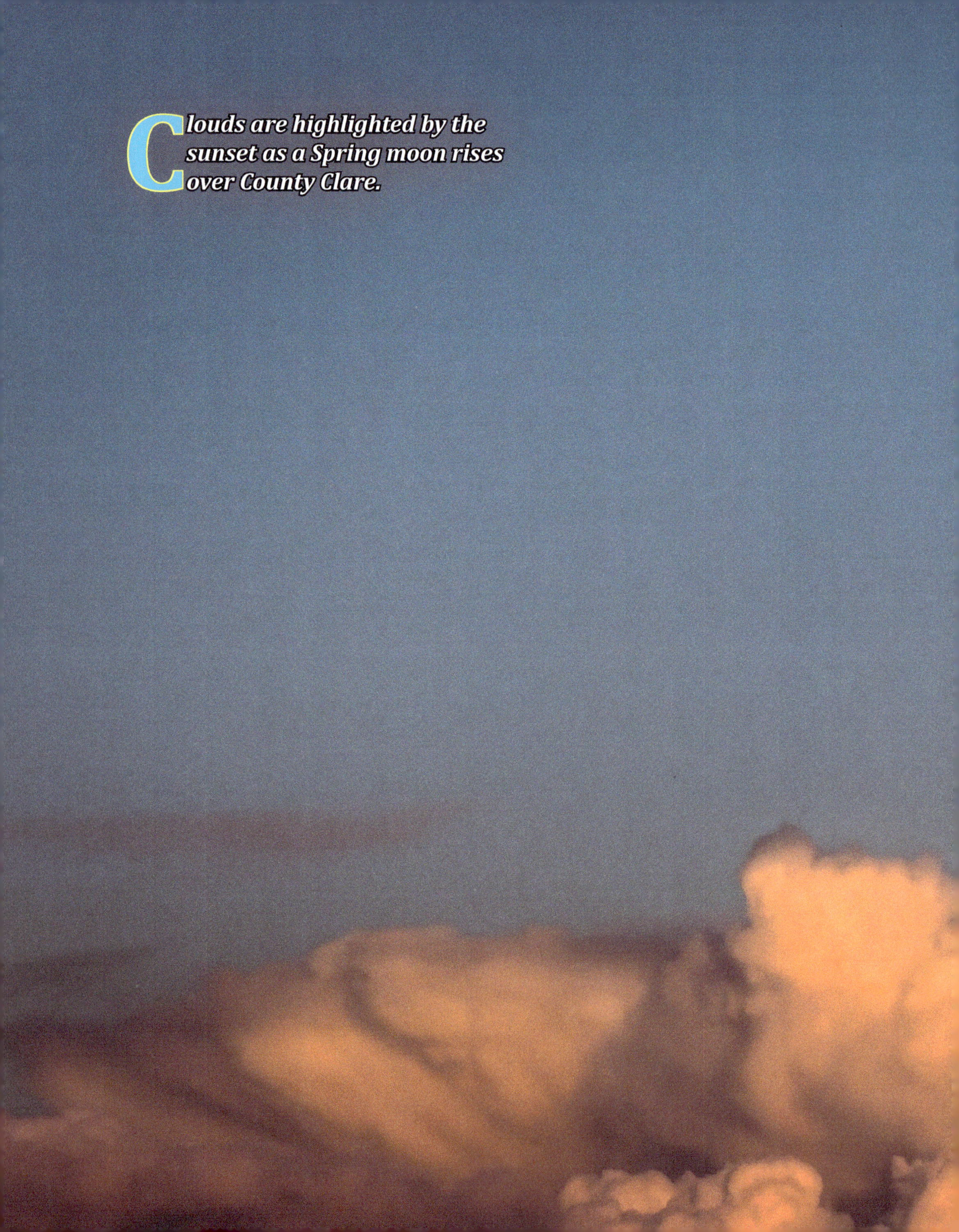

Clouds are highlighted by the sunset as a Spring moon rises over County Clare.

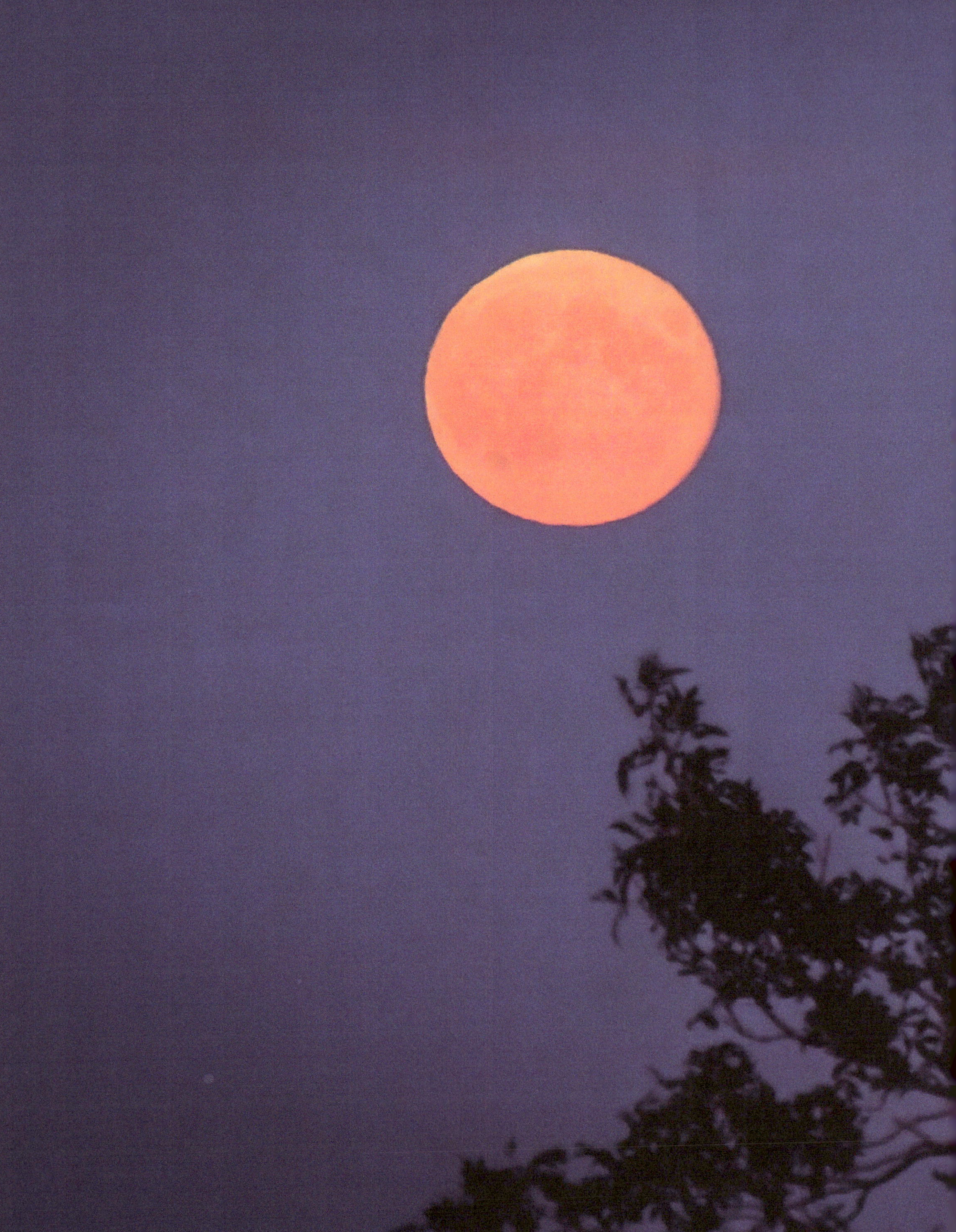

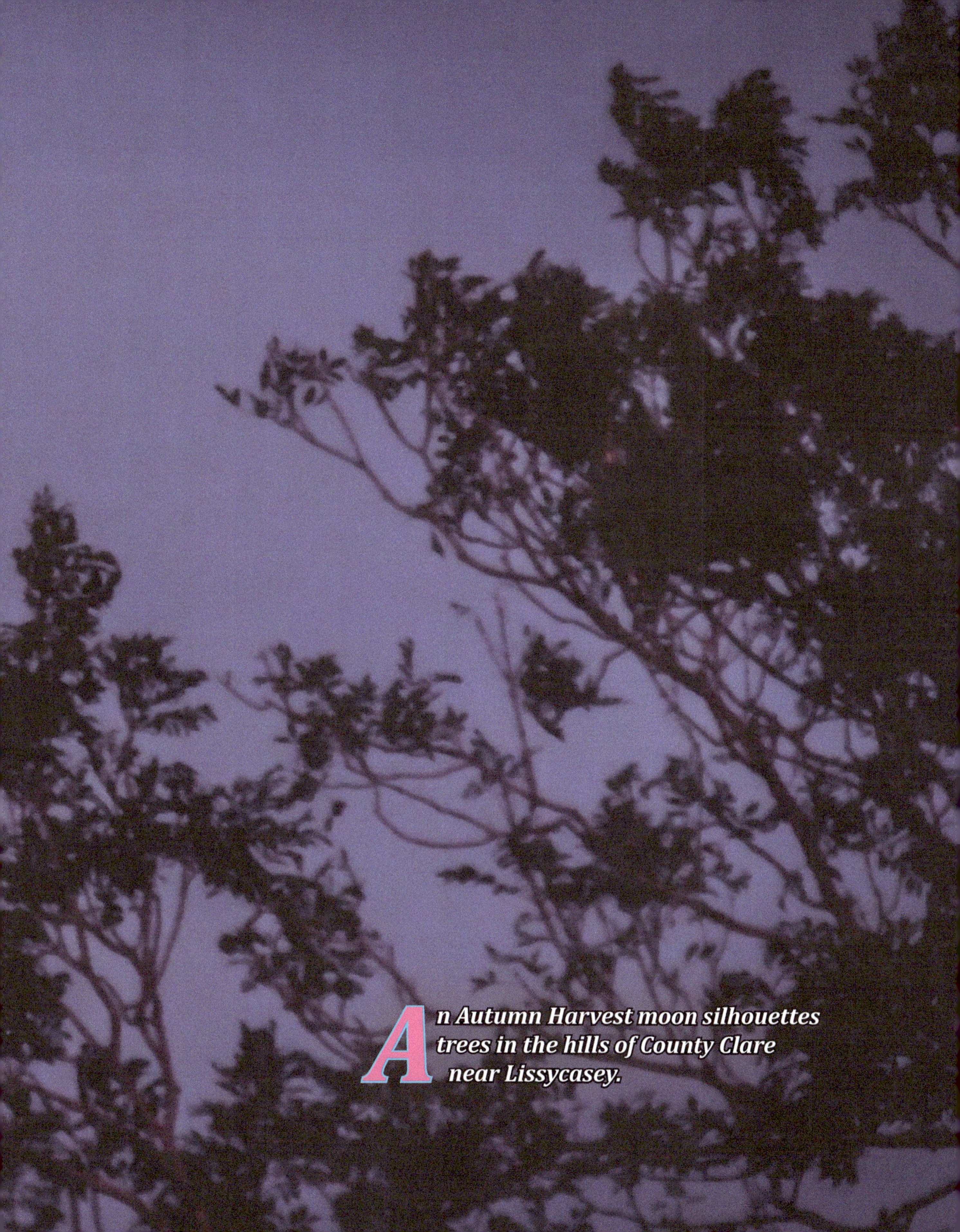

An Autumn Harvest moon silhouettes trees in the hills of County Clare near Lissycasey.

A sunset and a full moon join forces to backlight this cloud over the County Clare countryside.

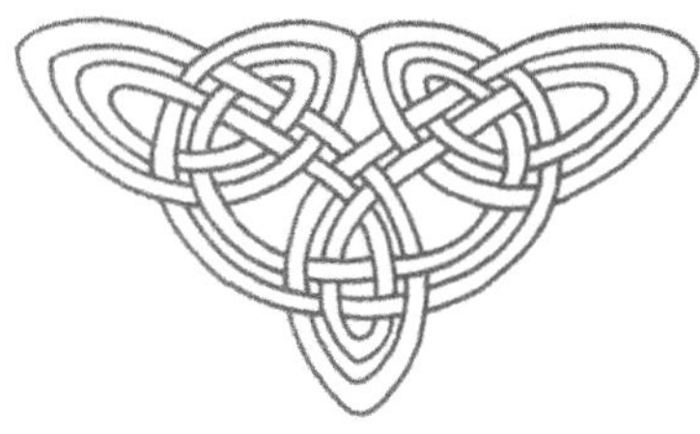

Acknowledgements

A special thank you to those who have provided encouragement and support:

Alberto Truett

Francis and Helen Murphy

John and Maureen Ginnane

Anthony Murphy

Elizabeth & David Odell

Patty Rosnel

Vivienne Nichols

Pauline McDermott-Smith

Pat and Michelle McMahon

Michael McMahon

Robert McMahon

Bridget O'Sullivan

Michael McNamara

Anthony Cavanagh

Marie Kelleher

Dr. Finbar Fitzpatrick

Other Books by James A. Truett

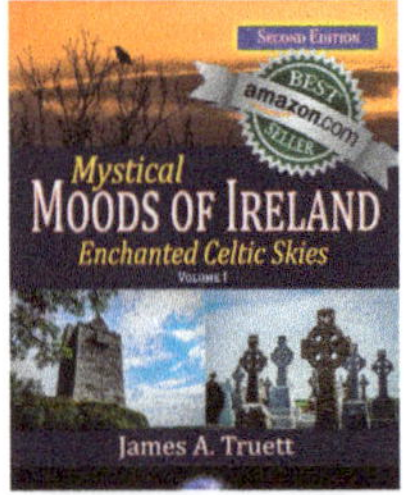

Mystical Moods of Ireland - Vol. I:
Enchanted Celtic Skies

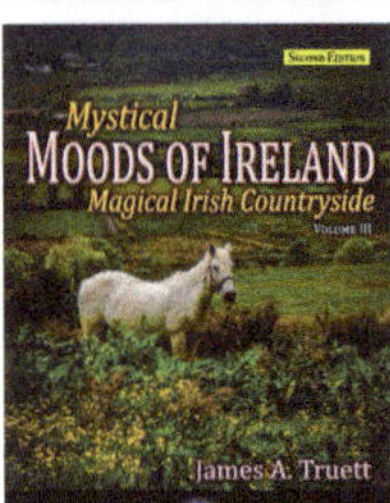

Mystical Moods of Ireland - Vol. III:
Magical Irish Countryside

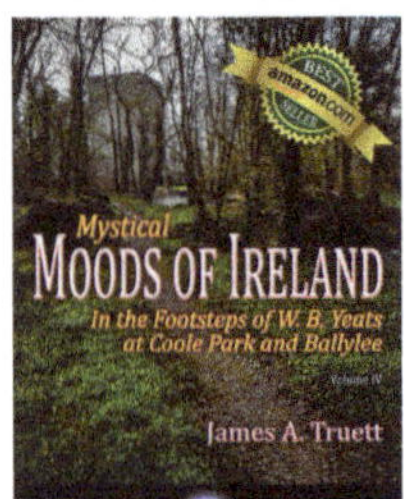

Mystical Moods of Ireland - Vol. IV:
In the Footsteps of W. B. Yeats at Coole Park and Ballylee

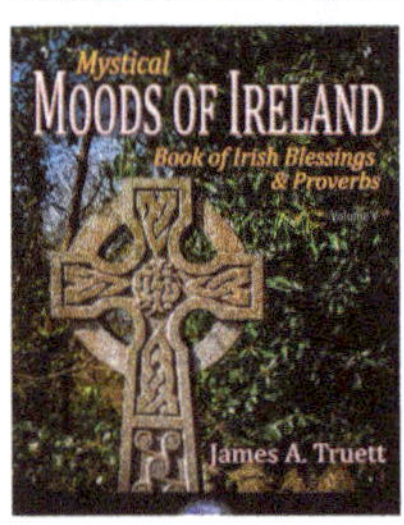

Mystical Moods of Ireland - Vol. V:
Book of Irish Blessings & Proverbs

Available through Amazon.Com and major booksellers:
www.JamesTruettBooks.Com

*Follow James A. Truett's adventures
and get free previews of his books here:*
www.JamesATruett.Com/subscribe

About James A. Truett

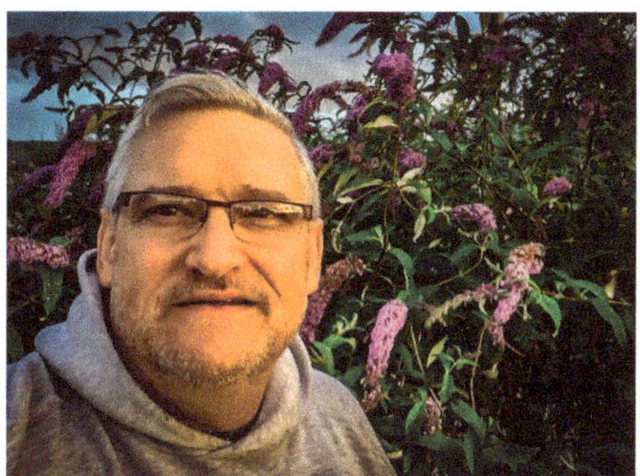

Growing up in Alaska, near the quaint hamlet of Ester, near Fairbanks, James A. Truett developed an appreciation for nature as a child, exploring the majestic wilderness of his home state both on the ground and in the air.

He began his career as a journalist and photographer for the local newspaper at the age of 14, picked up his private pilot's license at the age of 17, and by the age of 19, he had moved to Seattle and joined The Associated Press, eventually becoming one of the youngest journalists in the world to be published in every major newspaper in the world.

Over the years, he developed an avid interest in sailing and traveled extensively by boat, auto and air in the U.S., Canada, Mexico, Central America, Ireland and the UK.

After tracing his ancestral roots back to Ireland and falling in love with the beauty of the Irish countryside, he settled in County Clare from where he manages his portfolio of art, photography and publishing projects.

Connect with James A. Truett on Social Media:
www.JamesATruett.Com/social

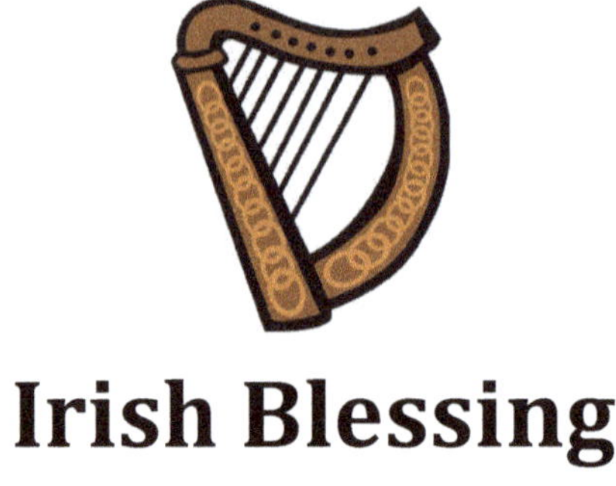

Irish Blessing

"May you always have walls for the winds,
a roof for the rain,
tea beside the fire,
laughter to cheer you,
those you love near you,
and all your heart might desire."

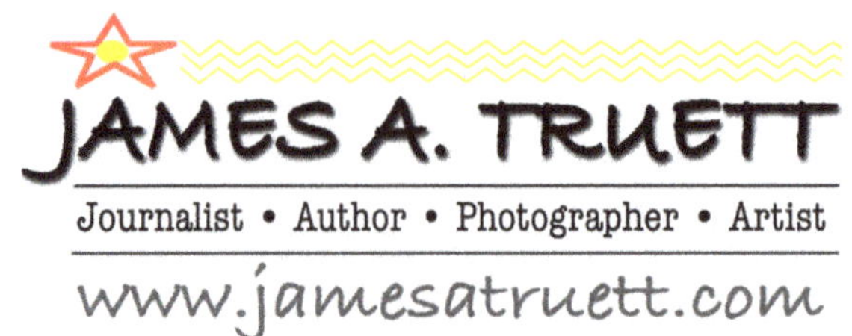

www.ingramcontent.com/pod-product-compliance
Lightning Source LLC
Chambersburg PA
CBHW041030050726
47599CB00018B/1920